PETER KENNEDY is a world authority ... system. He trained as a medical docto., ... institutions in London, and holds MD, PhD, and DSC degrees and two masters degrees in Philosophy (M.Phil, M.Litt). One of the youngest doctors ever appointed to lead a neurology department in the UK, he held the Burton Chair of Neurology at Glasgow University, Scotland for 29 years (1987–2016), where he is currently an honorary senior research fellow carrying out mainly research and teaching. He is a fellow of the Royal Society of Edinburgh and the Academy of Medical Sciences. He is the co-editor of two textbooks on neurological infections and has published more than 200 scientific papers in learned journals. He has also written five novels. He has received several awards for his scientific work including recently the Sir James Black Medal of the Royal Society of Edinburgh (its senior prize in the life sciences), and the Pioneer in Neurovirology Award of the International Society for Neurovirology of which he was President for six years. He received the CBE in the 2010 New Year Honour's List for services to clinical science.

He became enamoured with Africa as a medical student on an elective in Zambia in the 1970s, and had visited Africa 28 times since. Now part of major international efforts to increase awareness of and funding for research into sleeping sickness, he is one of only a handful of medical doctors specialising in the disease and is dedicated to finding a cure.

The Fatal Sleep received a 'Highly Commended' award in the Popular Medicine category of the 2008 British Medical Association (BMA) Medical Book Competition.

This book is very readable and entertaining at the same time and sheds some light into how fate sometimes determines the outcome of a medical career. Professor Peter Kennedy has immersed himself totally in this commitment to the eradication of trypanosomiasis and his book is a testament to that
SCOTTISH MEDICAL JOURNAL

This is not a dry academic book, rather it reveals a clinical scientist who delights in his work and who shares his enthusiasm with his readers... If Kennedy's book not only awakens readers to the problems of sleeping sickness but is the catalyst for new partnerships between North and South, it will have succeeded far beyond its original, and in this wider sphere, more limited aim
BRAIN

His book, as a memoir of a life in trypanosomiasis research, calls much-needed attention to a widespread disease of poor and isolated Africans, for whom pharmaceutical companies should spend more time developing therapeutic drugs
JOURNAL OF CLINICAL INVESTIGATION

Kennedy has provided a comprehensive account of the history of sleeping sickness, the biology of the trypanosome and of its tsetse fly vector, and how the disease affects humans and animals. These accounts are clear, comprehensive, and free of jargon and should be easily understood by the interested general reader with little scientific background... Kennedy is to be congratulated on writing a book for a general audience about an important but neglected tropical disease, and he has generously offered half his royalties to charities working to alleviate its results
BRITISH MEDICAL JOURNAL

The book has broad appeal, containing science, medicine, politics, economics, and geography. It closes with challenges and a call for organizational support to eradicate this disease. The reader would do well to allot a block of uninterrupted time for this relatively short book (just over 200 pages), because once started, it is hard to put down. It is a book you will want to share with family, friends, and colleagues
NEUROLOGY

The Fatal Sleep has a little bit of everything, and as such it is a great read... In this book Kennedy draws us into his passion for this disease, and indeed for all of Africa itself... As for medical readers I think they will be delighted, charmed, horrified and fascinated in equal measure. And even if the book does nothing more than raise awareness among medics of this terrible problem, it will have achieved a great deal.
ADVANCES IN CLINICAL NEUROSCIENCE AND REHABILITATION

The Fatal Sleep

Africa's killer disease that went undiscovered for centuries

PETER KENNEDY

Luath Press Limited

EDINBURGH

www.luath.co.uk

First published 2007
Second edition 2010
This edition 2019

ISBN: 978-1-910745-34-2

The paper used in this book is recyclable. It is made from
low chlorine pulps produced in a low energy, low emissions manner
from renewable forests.

Printed and bound by
Ashford Colour Press, Gosport

Typeset in 10.5 point Sabon by
3btype.com

Fifty per cent of the author's royalties generated from sales
of this book will be donated to Médecins Sans Frontières (MSF)
to promote human health in Africa.

This book is dedicated to all the sufferers from sleeping sickness in Africa.

Acknowledgements

Many people have assisted me in the writing of this book, and each person has contributed in their own particular way. First and foremost, I must thank Max Murray who first introduced me to the problem of African trypanosomiasis, and has been a superb colleague, friend and mentor for the last 18 years. He read all the chapters in detail, and made a large number of suggestions and corrections, all of which have improved the original manuscript. Without Max, this book would never have been written. I also want to thank Joseph Ndung'u, who has played such a major part in my work and experience in Africa. Joseph has also been a great friend and colleague, and has taught me a great deal about sleeping sickness, Kenya in general, and the nature of leadership. He also read all the chapters and expertly advised on details of the text. Peter Holmes has also helped me considerably, especially in explaining so clearly the problems of tsetse fly control and drug treatment in animal trypanosomiasis. He also checked most of the chapters and made valuable suggestions. The fourth key person I wish to thank is Jane Nevins, a highly experienced American editor, who has given so generously of her masterly advice in the art of book writing. Her constant encouragement has been crucial, and she taught me a great deal about popular science writing, and, above all, the absolute necessity to make such writing both accessible and interesting to the reader. I have done my best to aspire to her high standards, and readers will have to judge for themselves whether I have succeeded.

I want to thank all of my past and present colleagues in the trypanosomiasis research group in Glasgow for their expert and inspirational collaboration. These include: Jean Rodgers, who also read some of the chapters; Frank Jennings; Barbara Bradley; Chris Hunter; Charity Gichuki; David Eckersall; Joanne Burke; and John Gow. Our other fine research collaborators outside Glasgow whom I wish to thank are Jeremy Sternberg, Jorge Atouguia, Susan Leeman, Krister Kristensson and Dennis Grab.

Several colleagues provided valuable assistance to me by reading individual chapters, or parts of chapters, or by giving advice on specific topics. These colleagues include the following: Serap Askoy, Christian Burri, Mike Turner, Hugh Willison, Mike Barrett, Malla Rao, Keith Vickerman, Martin Odiit, and Ian Maudlin. Of course none of these are responsible for any errors that I may have made, although I have gone to considerable lengths to avoid these. I am particularly grateful to Tom Dent for his reading of Chapter Two and sharing with me his recollections of life as a mine doctor in Zambia. I have changed the names of some individuals in the early chapters, usually because I have been unable to contact them after so many years.

I am most grateful to James Beaton of the library at the Royal College of Physicians and Surgeons of Glasgow for providing me with interesting information on the life of David Livingstone, and Karen Carruthers of the David Livingstone Centre in Blantyre for providing useful information about, and providing the photograph of, Livingstone. I am grateful to Anna Smith of the Wellcome Trust for providing some of the historical photographs. I owe a particular debt of gratitude to Colin Burns of the Clinical Physics department at the Southern General Hospital for his expert and generous help in producing all the photographs in the book, a task that was quite formidable. I also thank Marian Martin of our Medical Illustration department for her assistance with the figures. I was also most fortunate that Mike Shand, an expert cartographer in the Geography Department in the University of Glasgow, produced the map of Kenya in the beginning of the book. I am also grateful to the BMJ Publishing Group, the Gyldendal Denmark (Karen Blixen's Danish publishing house) and the Rungstedlund Foundation for giving me permission to reproduce copyright material.

Three friends also gave me a great deal of encouragement for the book in its early stages of gestation, and for this I would like to thank Elaine Snell, Douglas Hutchison and Heather Armstrong. One should never underestimate the power of encouragement. I am also very grateful to Gavin MacDougall, Director of Luath Press, for his great interest in the subject of sleeping sickness and his welcome decision to publish the book. He and his staff, especially Catriona Vernal, in their Edinburgh office have been a pleasure to work with. Finally, but of course not least, I want to thank my wife Catherine for her constant encouragement between the many solitary hours of writing, and for helping so much with the meticulous research involved in describing the historical and geographical aspects of the places in Africa that I have worked in.

Contents

Foreword

THIS IS A REMARKABLE BOOK. It is filled in equal measure with passion for science and compassion for the people afflicted with this cruel disease. Yet it ends with hope.

The trypanosome, the organism causing the disease, plays 'hide and seek' and is difficult to find in the body. It is difficult to eliminate its vectors, and the disease is difficult to treat and cure. Yet sleeping sickness is an orphan disease, massively and sadly neglected by drug companies. They cannot recoup the billions they might have to spend on research to find a cure, when the only countries affected are amongst the poorest in the world, so that they cannot recover their costs from sales.

This book describes clearly all the difficulties. Suppression of the organism in vectors has not been successful so far. The current best available drug for the brain disease is so unpleasant that one patient described it as 'like having chilli peppers injected into your heart'. Untreated, the disease is 100 per cent fatal but this drug kills one in 20 of those who take it. The final irony lies in the agonising decision of doctors who have to make the diagnosis before deciding where to treat, on the basis of unreliable or inconclusive tests.

Dr Kennedy is passionate about his scientific research. He describes the body's immunological defences that can be overcome by the wily trypanosome. There is now a mouse model that should accelerate the search for better drugs. His compassion lies in his feelings for Africans, often surprisingly cheerful though surrounded by death and disease, including AIDS and malaria as well as sleeping sickness. He also writes lyrically about the beauty of Africa.

Yet finally I find two distinct strands of hope. The first is that there is still a generation of European doctors who are prepared to follow in the footsteps of Livingstone and Schweitzer, the missionaries who went to this troubled continent. Dr Kennedy went out 18 times in 31 years.

The second line of hope is that much of the pioneering scientific research has now been done and collaborative research is now successful between the African governments, world health agencies and private donors like the Gates Foundation. It is difficult not to feel some shame at the way European countries have exploited Africa in the past, but now a more respectable story is unfolding. I believe diseases like sleeping sickness can be controlled, if not eliminated. This excellent book is an inspiring tribute to the ways in which that happy day may be accelerated.

Sir Roger Bannister
March 2007

Preface to the First Edition

I HAVE WRITTEN THIS book for one main reason: to tell the non-scientist about the history and profound importance of human African trypanosomiasis, also known as sleeping sickness. The history of African trypanosomiasis in man and animals reflects the history of vast regions of the African continent itself. At the present time, one third of Africa is held captive by the tsetse fly which is so adept at transmitting the disease, and no less than 60 million people are at risk of acquiring the infection. The disease also has a profound effect on limiting the quality of life throughout sub-Saharan Africa, and both farming and livestock production have been greatly reduced by the twin scourges of the trypanosome parasite and the tsetse fly. Yet treatment of sleeping sickness has hardly progressed over the last century, and the most commonly used drug for treating late stage disease where the nervous system has been invaded actually kills one in 20 of the people who receive it. I sometimes ponder that figure and ask myself whether it can really be true. But sadly it is so. Since the infection is always fatal if untreated, African patients are at very high risk from dying from the treatment as well as the disease. Until quite recently, Western governments have shown little interest in supporting research into new drugs for sleeping sickness or for providing major funds to improve the infrastructure to better control the disease. Until now the power of the parasite and the fly has been predominant. But that does seem to be changing, slowly.

With these grim figures in mind, I decided to undertake a medical and literary journey into Africa, and I wanted the lay reader to join me and, most important of all, to truly understand everything I had to say about the disease. This is certainly not a textbook, but a popular science book that is aimed to communicate in what is currently called a 'reader friendly' way. I thought it would be fun and interesting to trace the origins of a personal passion for Africa, so I started off with some autobiographical vignettes. Fast forwarding to a welcome return to Kenya, we then learn about the institutions that have been set up in Africa to research the disease. We then reach the true horrors of the human disease and witness its extreme cruelty at first hand. After an encounter with the animal reservoirs, we look to the future and recognise all that various organisations are now doing to control the disease and to develop better drug therapy.

Most of all, I wanted this book to be enjoyable and easy to read. This has involved a completely different writing style than scientists are used to, and therein lay the real challenge. For this reason, I have continuously pestered many friends and colleagues to read various parts to test the waters so to speak, and I hope I have succeeded, at least in part, in explaining quite difficult scientific concepts while transmitting the wonders and extreme beauty of Africa. The various geographical and historical details that have been interspersed in the text have been included not only for their contextual relevance, but also to make the book easier to read. I believe that only chapter six might prove slightly challenging for the non-scientist. But I do urge the reader to persist even if it is a little tricky – just remember that it was even worse for me writing it! If that proves impossible, then the reader would not come to any harm by perusing just the opening and closing paragraphs of that chapter.

If I manage to make more people aware than before of the curse of sleeping sickness in sub-Saharan Africa, then this book will have succeeded in its most important aim. In that endeavour, let me now be your guide.

Peter Kennedy
March 2007

Preface to the Current Edition

SINCE THE SECOND EDITION of this book was published as a paper-back in 2010 there have been several developments in our knowledge and understanding of sleeping sickness. It therefore seemed appropriate to produce a third and updated edition that would reflect these advances. I have now written an additional chapter (11) which provides an overview of what I think are the most significant advances in the field while making very few changes to the main text which I have left largely as it is. These advances have been summarised for five different aspects and this has been supported by several additional references for those who want to read to some of the original studies. I am grateful to my colleagues Professors Max Murray and Joseph Ndung'u for casting their expert eyes over this chapter when it was at the draft stage.

I feel I must mention my deep sadness at the recent death of the eminent Sir Roger Bannister who had so kindly written the foreword to the original 2007 hardback edition which is reproduced here. I knew him personally for many years and he was an inspiring figure. In my view, and I suspect also his, his seminal contributions to medical science and clinical neurology were at least, if not more, important to mankind than were his groundbreaking achievements in athletics.

Peter Kennedy
November 2019

List of Acronyms and Abbreviations

ADB	African Development Bank
AIDS	Acquired Immunodeficiency Syndrome
AU-IBAR	African Union-International Bureau for Animal Resources
BBB	Blood-Brain Barrier
CATT	Card Agglutination Trypanosomiasis Test
CGIAR	Consultative Group on International Agricultural Research
CNS	Central Nervous System
CSF	Cerebrospinal Fluid
CTVM	Centre for Tropical Veterinary Medicine
DALY's	Disability of Adjusted Life Years Lost
DEET	diethyltoluamide
DFID	Department for International Development
DNDi	Drugs for Neglected Diseases Initiative
EAVRO	East African Veterinary Research Organisation
EATRO	East African Trypanosomiasis Research Organisation
EEG	Electroencephalogram
EMA	European Medicines Agency
ETEC	enterotoxigenic *Escherichia coli*
EU	European Union
FAO	Food and Agriculture Organisation
FDA	US Food and Drug Administration
FITCA	Farming in Tsetse Controlled Areas
GCS	Glasgow Coma Score
GIS	Geographic Information Systems
GPS	Global Positioning Systems

HAT	Human African Trypanosomiasis
HIV	Human Immunodeficiency Virus
IAEA	International Atomic Energy Agency
ICIPE	International Centre for Insect Physiology and Ecology
IFN	Interferon
IL	Interleukin
ILCA	International Livestock Centre for Africa
ILRAD	International Laboratory for Research in Animal Diseases
ILRI	International Livestock Research Institute
ISCTRC	International Scientific Council for Trypanosomiasis Research and Control
ITC	International Trypanotolerance Centre
KARI	Kenya Agricultural Research Institute
KEMRI	Kenya Medical Research Institute
KETRI	Kenya Trypanosomiasis Research Institute
LIRI	Livestock Health Research Institute
LRA	Lord's Resistant Army
MRI	Magnetic Resonance Imaging
MSF	Médecins Sans Frontières
NARO	National Agricultural Research Organisation
NIAID	National Institute of Allergy and Infectious Disease
NIH	National Institutes of Health
OAU	Organisation of African Unity
ODA	Overseas Development Administration
PAAT	Programme Against African Trypanosomiasis
PATTEC	Pan-African Tsetse and Trypanosomiasis Eradication Campaign
PTRE	Post-Treatment Reactive Encephalopathy
RDTS	Rapid Diagnostic Tests

REM	Rapid Eye Movement
RTTCP	Regional Tsetse and Trypanosomiasis Control Programme
SAT	Sequential Aerosol Drift technique
SIT	Sterile Insect Technique
SP	Substance P
TDR	Special Programme for Research and Training in Tropical Diseases
TRC	Trypanosomiasis Research Centre
UTRO	Uganda Trypanosomiasis Research Organisation
VSG	Variable Surface Glycoprotein
WHO	World Health Organisation

PART ONE

Kindling the Flame

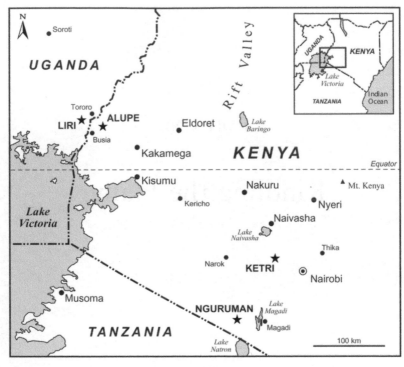

FIGURE I
Map of Kenya showing key locations described in the book (Mike Shand)

CHAPTER ONE

An Opportunity Arises

APRIL 2001: the rainy season in Kenya and five months before the fall of the twin towers. The world was still sleeping and so was I. But that delicious twilight state between dreaming and awareness that was broken now and then by the jolting of our vehicle was just an illusion. How was I to know that my own nemesis was approaching just a few miles away? Ominous storm clouds were rising like grey mountains on the horizon soon after our departure from Busia in Western Kenya, only four miles from the Ugandan border. This meant a dangerous drive back to our regional base in Kisumu, 120 km away. But we had not imagined just how hazardous this passage home would be. One thing we knew for sure – it was critical to return to Kisumu before nightfall because of the extreme danger of night time driving on those hideously damaged roads. Craters of death do not respect good intentions in this part of the world.

So my long time friend and colleague Joseph Ndung'u, our driver Moses and I set out, maybe a little foolishly, in our lightly loaded Land Rover knowing full well that our route was taking us through the centre of a developing tropical storm. In Africa anxiety often trumps good judgement. Anything to get away from these roads. Anything to get home in one piece. The main danger came from the murderously heavy rain, monsoon quality, which soon came thundering down all around us. We gripped the seats and the window straps tightly as the vehicle swayed in surprising silence, and I watched the heaving of Moses' broad shoulders as he wrenched the wheel first left, then right, and then left again, while all the time heavy goods lorries bound for Uganda were hurtling towards us. Every time we swerved my arms felt sickened with the strain.

The lorries seemed strangely ruthless in their apparent disregard for all other vehicles on the road while they advanced towards us, long dusty monsters with a continuous snake-like sideways motion as if they were trying to intimidate us into submission. Add to this the constant need to negotiate the widest and deepest potholes that I have ever seen in any road in the world, almost magnificent in their appalling size, and then maybe you will understand the tense and rather chilly atmosphere that the sudden, nauseating jolt of our Land Rover so forcefully punctured. I silently but violently cursed, not for the first or last time, the local political rivalries that had led to such a sorry state of neglect of the country's roads. 'Opposition stronghold here,' Joseph knowingly told me over his shoulder. This made me curse again, not so silently this time, and for a moment I experienced a surge of cold rage that made me feel even worse. This was a worrying and also deeply disappointing way to finish a very successful field trip which had left both Joseph and I feeling particularly gratified. Our visit to the sleeping sickness treatment hospital in Alupe had been one of the most productive so far, and had provided the seeds for several new ideas about this terrible disease we were fighting. Just for a while we had bordered on elation.

Looking back now at this incident it is evident that there was not one but four different problems – the driving rain, the monstrous lorries, the crater-like potholes and the lack of rear seatbelts. But it was this last factor that was the most significant for our safety. A speeding Uganda-bound lorry, skidding slightly because of the wet road, careered towards us leaving almost no clear road between itself and our Land Rover. Moses was left with no option but to swerve rapidly to avoid a collision, likely to be fatal for us, but in doing so our vehicle plunged at high speed into a particularly deep pothole. The Land Rover hurtled sharply downwards. Unrestrained by seatbelts, I sailed suddenly upwards, ramming the top of my head sharply, but not deeply, into the roof of the vehicle. I was stunned but not really hurt. Had I been any taller or the pothole any deeper then the damage would have been much greater. This event had three consequences, two definite and one suspected: both Joseph and Moses were, quite reasonably, horrified that I might have been injured: all my neck movements were extremely sore for weeks, if not months, afterwards; and I think I probably gained about half an inch in height as the stretching force of my sudden flight upward seemed greater than the compression when I hit.

Anyone who ever worked in Africa has a story like this to tell. My own time in the 'Dark Continent' has now spanned 18 individual visits over 31 years since medical student days, but the last 16 of these have mainly been spent in Kenya studying sleeping sickness. However much the perils come to mind – and there have been many like our dangerous drive that April evening, some worse and far more life-threatening – one simple question always arises: why do my colleagues and I keep going back? Why do these people risk serious and potentially chronic illness, the often very unpleasant side effects of anti-malarial drugs such as nausea, abdominal pain and psychiatric symptoms, the chance of physical injury from road traffic accidents, and sometimes isolation and fear, when they could be cocooned in relative safety back home in Europe or America? It's really strange because when I'm in Africa some of me wants to be back in Scotland, and when I'm nice and safe back home in friendly Glasgow then most of me wants to be back in Africa. The grass is always greener, especially on the other side of the world.

While the answers to these questions are not immediately apparent, I'll try hard in this book to provide some kind of an explanation, and one that really does ring true. Several of my medical colleagues who share a passion for Africa have often asked themselves the same question and also seem surprisingly unsure of the reasons for their repeated visits to and their enduring fascination with Africa, its people and its diseases. Mental as well as medical notes are often compared, and it is probably the dark continent itself, with its rich fabric of physical beauty, people, spirit and mystery, which is almost as much a magnet in this as the intrinsic interest of the diseases which we all study and the commitment – or even obsession – which many of us have to discovering more about the causes and cures of such dreadful killers as sleeping sickness and malaria. And one shouldn't forget that these two diseases can frequently occur together in the same person.

My colleagues and I – and that includes medical doctors and scientists – work on these diseases mostly in Africa, but the implications are global. Not only do malaria and sleeping sickness help deprive the worldwide economy of Africa's all but untouched potential, but, like Severe Acute Respiratory Syndrome (SARS) and West Nile infection of the nervous system, these diseases can travel. Malaria, of course, is familiar to people in North America and Europe, not only because of its reputation for killing millions of people worldwide, but also because some Western tourists to the African continent, distressed at the side effects or unaware of the great dangers of stopping, unwisely discontinue their anti-malarial tablets, and develop the disease weeks after their return. And a few die of its complications. Malaria is also an important occupational hazard for soldiers who are deployed in the tropics. A stunning example of this hazard occurred in 2003. Two hundred American marines who returned from service in Liberia in West Africa developed malaria, and 43 of them were ill enough to be hospitalised. Although none of the soldiers died, two of them developed cerebral malaria, the most dangerous form of the disease and one that has a 20 per cent mortality rate. Why so many soldiers developed the disease despite taking appropriate preventive anti-malarial tablets is not known for certain, but it seems likely that their blood levels of these preventive drugs were not adequate. A constant threat to travellers to Africa is that malaria parasites will develop resistance to these drugs, but no convincing evidence of resistance was apparent in the case of these unfortunate soldiers.

Sleeping sickness is the common name for human African trypanosomiasis, to give it its full medical title. For many people the words conjure up images of a mysterious and terrifying disease of the jungle and veldt, afflicting intrepid Western explorers and rural native Africans with scant access to medical care. That image is not entirely inaccurate, but this disease is staggeringly widespread and its potential for harm is no longer limited to Africa. Sleeping sickness is more exotic to us, but that could very well change. Global business and increasing tourism to Africa, together with easier and more accessible air travel between America, Europe and Africa, carries a real risk of Western travellers returning home with sleeping sickness. Several cases of Europeans developing this disease have appeared in medical literature, and travellers from America and other Western countries, as well as Asia, are vulnerable too, as their increasing numbers and time in Africa raise the odds of contact with the tsetse fly, the principal transmitter of the human form of the disease.

Sleeping sickness is often referred to as one of the 'neglected diseases'. Others are Chagas disease in South America, and visceral leishmaniasis, a widespread disease found in regions of the Middle East, Asia, South America, the Mediterranean and Africa. These diseases affect very large numbers of people in the underdeveloped world, are always serious, and often fatal. Moreover, current therapies for them are frequently out of date, not very effective and sometimes toxic. In the case of sleeping sickness, the most frequently used drug for nervous system disease actually kills five per cent of those who receive it, which is a figure almost beyond comprehension. When I mention this figure to friends and medical colleagues they sometimes suspect I am exaggerating, yet this is indeed the case. But the numerous people affected by these diseases are very poor, and the populations they represent are unable to pay for suitable health care. As a result, the Western pharmaceutical companies who have the potential to develop more effective medicines for these diseases have so far shown little interest in doing so. With very little prospect of either short or long term financial return it is hardly surprising that the drug companies have had little or no incentive to invest in the therapeutics of these diseases. Market forces do not favour such investment despite the terrible price in morbidity and mortality that has to be paid by the millions of poor people who suffer from these ghastly conditions which have such magnitude and severity. This is a global public health need that both the private and public sectors in the world have so far consistently failed to address. With less than 10 per cent of the global health research spending being directed towards the health needs of 90 per cent of the world's population, there is indeed a 'fatal imbalance' between the severity and scale of these diseases and the relatively meagre resources that are being devoted to them.

Despite considerable publicity in the medical press in 2000 when no treatment could be immediately found in London for two travellers who had recently returned from Africa with sleeping sickness – eventually medical authorities obtained and administered the drug (suramin) – Western health care systems are ill prepared for this kind of eventuality. However, some good signs are appearing. In 2000 the Bill and Melinda Gates Foundation awarded US$15 million to a multidisciplinary research programme involving teams in America, Africa and Europe to develop more effective drug therapies for sleeping sickness and leishmaniasis in Africa. The US National Institutes of Health also provides funding for research into this disease, as does the UK's Wellcome Trust research charity and other agencies. So, clearly the message is getting through to some of those who are in positions to help the situation. For now it may be enough for people to be aware of the potential problem for Western civilisation and the existing problem in Africa where 60 million people are at risk from developing the disease.

That is the background to our story and a theme that will recur as we explore the nature and implications of sleeping sickness. Yet despite the scale of this health problem, there is so much that is wonderful and magical about working in Africa, which we shall also visit. For myself, like so many visitors, perhaps the most enduring and evocative visual image of Africa is the remarkable quality of the light, both mystical and clear, especially in the early evening when it gently illuminates and seems to bathe the countryside, whether it be in the majestic regions of the savannahs or the peaceful green hills closer to the cities. African light has a quality of serenity and stillness that is almost magical. Some visitors to Greece have said similar things about the light found there. While I have certainly seen the exquisite nature of that light too, especially in the mountainous and mystical regions near Delphi, somehow it is distinctly different from that which is uniquely of Africa.

So how did all this happen? To explain that I first have to take you back to the late 1960s.

Some people fall in love with Africa as children, from storybooks or movies, or the influence of a charismatic teacher, but that wasn't the case for me. Instead I had a keen interest in biology fieldwork in the sixth form (which is more or less equivalent to the 12th grade in the US). I became progressively enamoured of the study of animal habitats in the countryside, largely due to the efforts of a young and extraordinarily enthusiastic biology teacher. Typically, Mr J would decide to discontinue or cancel a conventional school lesson and cart us all away to a pool near the school, which, until that moment, had seemed to be only that. By the time he had finished describing and demonstrating the myriad of interdependent microscopic animal and plant life contained within such a modest pool, indeed in a single drop of water, we would appreciate our previous blindness and marvel at the ecological wonders that had been there all the time had we only possessed the knowledge and insight to look for them.

Thus prepared, I decided to be a doctor and entered the 18-month 'pre-clinical' medicine course at University College London (UCL), leading to the academically demanding examination (called the 'second MB') a prerequisite to the three year clinical course at what was then University College Hospital (UCH) Medical School, which is now part of a much larger amalgamated medical school comprising several former medical schools). The University's impressive classical main building had been used some years before as the fictional hospital for the first *Doctor in the House* film starring Dirk Bogarde as the young Simon Sparrow. One sometimes half expected to see a Sir Lancelot Spratt lookalike emerge briskly from his Rolls Royce and bound up the building's steps to meet an admiring and obsequious medical and nursing entourage. As it happens, despite this character's flamboyant and bullying personality, wonderfully immortalised by the actor James Robertson Justice, he was actually rather benign compared with some of the real medical bullies who unfortunately appear here and there on the landscape of our profession. Such behaviour on the hospital wards was just about tolerated up to about 10 years ago but is now largely regarded as anathema and seldom occurs to any degree. Besides, there is a very useful golden rule: one should always be nice to juniors on their way up the career ladder because you want them to be kind to you when you are on the way down. I have endeavoured to observe this rule.

The college and the hospital were located on opposite sides of Gower Street in London, a street steeped in a rich medical and intellectual history. While the concept of a teaching hospital is now extremely familiar to people in both North America and Europe, UCH was the first British hospital that was built, in 1833, specifically for teaching purposes as well as service delivery to patients. The great UCH surgeon Robert Liston (1794–1847) was the first British surgeon to operate on a patient under ether anaesthesia, and his original operating table was still displayed in the library there. Sir William Gowers (1845–1915) one of the pioneers of Clinical Neurology, also practised at UCH, a man of great intellectual brilliance. His name also continues in the 'Gowers' ward at the renowned National Hospital for Neurology and Neurosurgery, Queen Square in London, where he also worked during his career. On the other side of Gower Street at UCL, Jeremy Bentham (1748–1832), the legendary philosopher and pioneer of the doctrine of Utilitarianism, was memorialised for many years by a remarkably lifelike model which actually contained his bones! In a tremendous act consistent with his creed, Bentham had left his body for the purpose of anatomical dissection. Also, one of the four junior student 'houses' at University College School was named after Bentham (I know because I went there). But as students we were never fully aware of the intellectual heritage of Gower Street, as we were too wrapped up in our own medical student microcosm. We were oblivious to the rich tapestry of the outside world in what was, as it is now, one of the most exciting cities to live in. But that was typical of student life for many young people at the time.

I started the pre-clinical course in October 1969, a time that seems conformist in retrospect. The evolutionary biologist Julian Huxley, the philosopher Bertrand Russell and the author J.R.R. Tolkien were still alive, decimalisation was not yet implemented, the Beatles were still playing together (just about), Rod Laver had just won the Wimbledon singles title for the second year running, George Best was still in his football heyday, a Labour government was still in power (but that would change the following year) and racial prejudice was still widespread with nothing like the social integration of different cultures that one now takes for granted.

The typical annual student grant for those living at home was comparatively low at about £330. While this sum seems ludicrously paltry now, in fact it was very useful then, though a significant part of it was used to buy medical books. Fortunately I did not need to buy a skeleton for anatomical study as I inherited 'Napoleon' from my older brother Roger who had started the same medicine course there two years ahead of me. This diminutive skeleton was real, unlike most of those used by medical students today, and I believe had once been a man living somewhere in Asia. He still lives with me in a large cardboard box in my house in Glasgow where he is much respected and well looked after, and I have never ceased to remember that he was once a human being just like me.

On the very first day at UCL, two fellow students befriended me, and we would become a triumvirate throughout our college years. Oliver, whom I met on the first day on a creaking but elegant wooden staircase en route to the anatomy department, would become a lifelong friend and play a key role in my forming a bond with Africa. Oliver and I were aware of each other's existence from the outset, as one of his close relatives was a very good friend of my parents. Oliver was extremely intelligent – he could dispose of *The Times* crossword puzzle in minimum time – and also very original in his way of thinking and in his general perception of the world. He saw people and things clearly for what they really were, devoid of any falseness, and this unusual quality is just as evident today. He was also very cultured compared with most of his peers, with a remarkable knowledge of musical history, and an extraordinary thirst for acquiring new knowledge and novel ideas. Such admirable qualities as these were not necessarily useful in studying medicine as it was systematically taught at that time; the necessary acquisition of vast numbers of facts, learned almost by rote, does not always come easily to people with highly intelligent and original minds. I was fortunate in having a good memory for factual information, so this was less of a problem for me. (Today the pendulum has swung in the opposite direction with an emphasis on understanding principles rather than facts, to the extent that it is quite possible for medical students in their third year to be unsure of the course of the three main nerves supplying the hand.) We also shared a very youthful appearance, and looked somewhat similar (as we still do), so that we were mistaken at least once for cousins. Both Oliver and our other friend Douglas went on to become successful general practitioners specialising in family medicine, while I took a longer path to become a hospital consultant in neurology. In a way I found the clinical course rather dull and I emerged from it worldly wiser but less analytical.

Oliver, myself, and Douglas became almost inseparable and studied together throughout the entire four-and-a-half year medical course. One of our particular habits was to have lunch virtually every day in the general refectory at the nearby Birkbeck College, where we mingled with older students, and, surprisingly, nobody ever asked us what we were doing there. They probably would now. Maybe some of them were also visitors like us. We liked the fact that these other students were studying non-medical subjects such as physics and chemistry as it made us feel more like 'real' university students, not 'medics'. (In the UK, of course, this denotes a doctor and not a paramedic as it does in the US.) We both still have very fond memories of that friendly institution.

Douglas was more than a dozen years older than Oliver and me and so he had a great deal more life experience; he acted rather like a benign and wise older brother to us. He was also married with several children and, together with his good judgement and rather avuncular nature, added a valuable stabilising and balancing influence to our comparative immaturity and inexperience. The three of us spent many hours at lunch dissecting the merits and deficiencies of our various lecturers, and trying to work out exactly what they were trying so hard to teach us. This happy camaraderie proves the merit of UCL's innovative policy of admitting students from widely differing social backgrounds and with quite large age variations. There were many 'mature' students of around 25–30 years, who to us teenagers seemed as old as Methuselah. Our year also included an older student from South Africa. While we got on well with him, he had a certain air of mystery and, while friendly, very much kept himself to himself, perhaps from a perceived fear of racial prejudice from some unexpected quarter.

The word 'dissection' immediately conjures up very specific memories, especially those of an olfactory nature, as many of us were never quite able to get used to the characteristic foul reek of dead bodies and formaldehyde emanating from the dissecting room where part of our anatomy studies were carried out (although it was nothing compared to the gut-wrenching smell of the post-mortem room which, as with many people, I found, and continue to find, almost intolerable). Real bodies were dissected at that time and it was obvious at the outset that a few students were deeply upset by the contact with dead people. For some reason I used to get particularly nauseated at the sight of thick layers of fat overlying the muscles. Why this was so I have no idea. We took some comfort from the knowledge that our own subject for dissection had reached the ripe old age of 100 years – we felt that he had had a good innings so to speak. I took care not to think of him as he might have been during life. To do this somehow seemed ghoulish and invited distress.

Usually six students worked on each of the approximately 20 cadavers. My group was reasonably assiduous in turning up for dissection sessions, and we would be tested orally on our knowledge of specific regions every few weeks by the anatomy demonstrators. Anatomy demonstrators were either senior academics, or more frequently, younger tutors who were either aspiring surgeons studying for their qualifying 'fellowship' examinations or doctoral students who had taken the pre-clinical course and were engaged in research rather than clinical medicine. A few of the doctoral students would eventually take the clinical course themselves; they were a very mixed bunch of people, some benign, some severe, some brilliant, and some disinterested – and some blended a few or all of these qualities. As a group we both respected and feared them.

Some of the demonstrators were far too kind and generous for our own good, having a very low threshold for giving 'A' grades during these tests. (The most generous and also stimulating of these tutors is now one of the world's most distinguished neuroscientists whom I still see from time to time when I visit London.) On the other hand, a few of them were pretty mean with their grades and would reward really competent performances with 'B minus' or even 'C' grades. That really used to upset us. Somewhere in the middle was Dr M, a young general surgeon from Ceylon (as it was called at that time before it became Sri Lanka in 1972) in his late twenties. He was rather tall, somewhat stern and extremely fair in his mark allocation, and had an amusing dislike of people 'inventing names' of body parts. For example, he would get really irritated if students mixed up the names of major arteries and veins and then mistakenly identify some non-existent blood vessel with a hybrid name. 'Don't invent names!' he would shout at the offender. He was a no-nonsense individual whom I liked immediately, and I think this feeling was mutual. It was he who three years later was to give Oliver and I the chance of a lifetime to experience life and work in Africa. If it were not for Dr M then I wouldn't be writing this book.

Undergraduate life at UCL was pretty hard work but very stimulating. A number of the lecturers and staff were world-renowned scientists including Sir Andrew Huxley (whom we all found to be a profoundly modest man) and the late Sir Bernard Katz, both Nobel prize-winning physiologists. The teachers also included the remarkable Professor J.Z. Young who had been head of the anatomy department for many years. We students, like others, referred to this great man affectionately as 'JZ' and he had the unusual ability to communicate the excitement of science and medicine to his audience while ensuring that they were also competent in their basic knowledge. He had the ability to make everything he said clear, interesting and accessible. In a masterly and at times truly riveting series of lectures, he instructed us in a wide range of anatomical and general biological subjects, including the somewhat esoteric topic of the origin of life.

We also had the pleasure of meeting Dr Alex Comfort, the erudite scientist and expert on ageing who later won worldwide fame for his book *The Joy of Sex*. I remember most his seriousness in conversation, his obvious popularity with his students in the zoology department and his telling me, as if repeating a mantra, that 'it is much easier to postpone a rate than to rewrite a programme' when devising methods to overcome the process of ageing.

Another scientist who made a very strong impression was the late and greatly missed Professor Patrick Wall, the eminent expert on pain whose theories have been very influential in the clinical management of chronic pain, in particular through the development of a treatment called transcutaneous electrical nerve stimulation (commonly abbreviated to TENS) which was based on the 'gate' theory of pain. He once expressed to us during an anatomy lecture the remarkable notion that a doctor treating a patient with a bullet wound has a duty to *understand* why that bullet came to be fired in the first place. Following on from this he thought that the doctor should pursue this line of enquiry and find out exactly how the patient came to be shot. Some of us thought that this introduced an inappropriate political dimension to patient management but it certainly made us think hard about the issue. He also used to roll his own cigarettes and I used to be mesmerised during his lectures by the deft way he would do this using a compact little oblong container that looked to me like one of my father's oriental antiques. He would calmly lick the sticky end of the paper at some point during his lecture and seemingly out of nowhere a thin cigarette would emerge. I met him on many subsequent occasions, and it was he who first steered me towards my future PhD supervisor, the eminent Martin Raff in the zoology department at UCL several years later, so I owe him a debt of gratitude for his good judgement and sound career advice. He also demonstrated well how it is possible to be both a brilliant and innovative scientist and also a profoundly decent and kind human being. I miss him a lot.

From time to time we would have a foretaste of the lecturing styles and personalities of the clinically active university staff of UCH, the teaching hospital right beside us. Exposure to these 'real doctors' could be inspiring, amusing and daunting at the same time, and students were usually impressed by the calm and authoritative demeanour of these suave medical doctors. And they all wore smart suits. A senior neurosurgeon who exuded gravitas managed to terrify many of us with his 'in your face' brain operation slides with bloody tissues and swabs everywhere, and an unsuspecting physician failed to notice the silver fairy wand that a mischievous student had secretly stuck on to the tip of his wooden pointer. The unfortunate man completely misinterpreted the audience's laughter as a reaction to his own sparkling wit as he leaped around the lecture podium.

I particularly remember the stern warning given to us all by Professor Charles Dent, an extremely eminent expert in metabolic medicine and one of only a few clinicians to be elected a fellow of the Royal Society (the direct equivalent of the US National Academy of Sciences). He transfixed us with his penetrating gaze and told us that there were two rules that we were always to observe during our medical careers. The first was to have clean fingernails and hands, and the second was to never get emotionally involved with a patient under our care, a crime punishable by possibly being struck off the medical register. Thinking about it now this was actually pretty sound advice, especially at that early impressionable stage. The next time you are in the presence of a group of medical doctors I suggest you try the following experiment. Try counting how many of them have clean fingernails. I guarantee that most, if not all, will! Through an odd twist of fate Professor Dent had a lasting influence on our later African experience.

Each department at UCL also seemed to have its own distinctive physical environment. For example, the anatomy department had a distinctive 'academic' smell, not at all unpleasant, and its floors and walls, and each small laboratory or office, seemed wrapped in an individual mystique that we hoped we would experience one day. Many of us deeply envied the cool PhD students who worked in those romantic corridors. The Cerebral Functions Research Group, headed by Patrick Wall, glowed as the epitome of scientific achievement. The physiology department, full of current and future scientific stars, had a more spacious architectural style compared with the intimate dwellings of anatomy, while the biochemistry department was a vast series of modern laboratories with wooden brown sliding doors and rows of laboratory glassware and chemicals, and housed ultra bright people, not all of whom seemed to enjoy teaching medical students. The well-stocked library was nearby and for many months I was unable to identify a rhythmic hooting noise that seemed to emanate from there. Eventually I realised that it was merely the cries of the local pigeons which were clearly of an academic bent.

Oliver, Douglas and I passed the second MB examinations without much trouble and skipped the opportunity of spending another

18 months' studying for an additional Bachelor of Science degree. I came to later regret that decision. We shared an overwhelming desire to get onto the wards and become 'real' doctors, and therefore started the three year clinical course at UCH in April 1971.

UCH was profoundly different from UCL, because it involved seeing live patients. Our contact with the hospital, which had an interesting physical structure resembling a Maltese cross, had been virtually non-existent during the previous 18 months. Apart from exposure to the few visiting lecturers, it had been limited to a brief obligatory visit to the operating theatre – where the green-gowned surgeon uttered a kind of low growl as a form of greeting on being alerted to our presence – and also the radiology department which appeared less forbidding despite x-ray machines that would not have been out of place in the recent *War of the Worlds* movie. Now that we were at the hospital to study sick people and healing, it was necessary to rapidly alter one's whole perception of life and to adopt a more mature attitude. In these initial few months we had our first contact with the processes of dying, both quick and slow, and we were impressed by the extent to which some people are so incredibly unlucky with their health. How unwittingly fortunate the rest of us were!

During the introductory week many of us were inspired by the encouraging words of the UCH Professor of Medicine, Lord Rosenheim, who sadly died shortly afterwards. He assured us that many chronic untreatable diseases that we were currently seeing would be cured in our lifetimes, and that some of us would almost certainly play a role in making that happen. We kind of believed him, and in fact he was partly right. Perhaps the most inspirational teacher we met during that week, and indeed in the entire course, was the neurologist Gerald Stern, who remains to this day a good friend and mentor. Immediately after his three hour session with us on neurological disorders I had made my mind up to be a neurologist, and never wavered from this course such was the strength of the impression that he made.

UCH had an outstanding reputation in both clinical medicine and scientific achievement. A number of physicians working at UCH at that time possessed exceptional clinical acumen and judgement. Some of the younger of these went on to occupy major Chairs and other high positions in London and elsewhere in the United Kingdom as well as North America, and the clinical skills of many of the physicians and surgeons at UCH were legendary.

During the first year we were divided into small groups of about six students, and rotated on medical and surgical 'firms' which were clinical units consisting of two or more consultants both at UCH and the affiliated Whittington Hospital in Archway, London. Our small London group was a friendly and motley crew that, in typical UCL style, was drawn from many different walks of life and age ranges.

The clinical course at that time was essentially a series of attachments to the various medical and surgical specialities, some of which, such as sexually transmitted diseases and general practice, were very brief although enjoyable. There was also a strong pathology component to our studies. Ironically, I narrowly failed to win a pathology prize mainly because of my total failure to recognise a blood slide under the microscope of human African trypanosomiasis – the medical name for sleeping sickness, my future life's work. I then made things even worse by saying that the evolutionary pioneer Charles Darwin had suffered from trypanosomiasis (meaning the South American form of the disease), which was also untrue. Not an impressive performance.

Some attachments were to units at other hospitals that often provided a refreshing break from the somewhat rarefied teaching hospital atmosphere as well as our first contact with medicine without the halo of academia. We spent an unusual and interesting week studying infectious diseases at the South Middlesex Hospital where our rather severe consultant teacher would encourage us to think for ourselves now that we were no longer in the 'marble halls' of UCH. 'Let's have some cerebration!' he would proclaim after one of us had given a particularly incompetent analysis of a patient's condition. Some of us also spent a senior medical attachment at the North Middlesex Hospital in London, while others went to the West Middlesex Hospital. (As far as I know there is no 'East Middlesex' hospital!)

Oliver and I generally attended the same courses, and we spent a particularly insightful fortnight in a large old style psychiatric hospital outside London, where we formed the friendliest relationships with the psychiatrists. On our first day there, we were warmly greeted by a rather strange, jovial man in a white coat who, from his knowledgeable conversation and instructions, we took without question to be the resident psychiatric ward doctor. He showed us around, explained the general layout of the hospital wards and the daily routine, and talked sympathetically and insightfully about some of the patients. We soon learned that he was a long stay psychiatric patient who liked to think of himself as a doctor. He certainly fooled us!

Two senior psychiatrists at UCH, Roger Tredgold and Heinz Wolff (sadly now both passed away), were the most kindly, sympathetic and stimulating teachers who seemed like an oasis in a sometimes severe hospital environment. They treated the medical students as both professional and human colleagues, and practised psychiatry in an analytical, humane and totally non-judgemental way. Unquestionably the outstanding quality of the psychiatric teaching at UCH was a factor in my older brother Roger's decision to become a psychiatrist, and I was very attracted to that specialty for many months. Some of the students, including myself, were allowed to follow up a psychiatric patient over many weeks or months, and this innovative approach was extremely effective in helping the students to develop and sustain a good doctor-patient relationship.

Relationships with other staff varied a lot. A few people seemed to regard hostility to medical students as their birthright, or at least part of their job description. Some of these included a few of the senior ward sisters and consultant surgeons whose power on the wards was absolute, but many were kind and delightful so I make no generalisations. But this was the era before true social integration and racial equality and some of the things I heard from some quite senior people, which I will not repeat here, should be consigned to the gutter of history. I sometimes see my generation as being the one linking two great medical eras – the previous era of learning by rote and osmosis, overwork and total consultant autonomy and the later era of very much greater respect for patients and colleagues but increasingly constrained by over-regulation of doctors and political correctness.

Throughout these three years we were frequently assessed by end of specialty examinations as well as optional prize examinations. The essence of these examinations was to quickly work out the 'differential diagnosis', that is, all the possible conditions the patient might be suffering from- and then present the case to the examiners in the light of those possibilities. For example, if you were examining a patient with a goitre (a visible and palpable swelling of the thyroid gland in the neck) you would make a point of showing the examiner that you had also tested muscle strength in the shoulders since sometimes over-activity of the thyroid gland can be associated with muscle weakness, especially in the shoulders and hips. Essentially, success was a question of demonstrating medical knowledge in the specific context of the particular patient in a very relevant and focused way. I did well in these exams – in part, I have to admit, because the patients had a tendency to tell me their diagnoses as soon as we started talking. It was never clear whether they did this because they felt sorry for me, or they perceived somehow that I felt compassionate about them. Perhaps a bit of both. Not all of my fellow students were so fortunate – one of my friends had a patient in her surgical final exams who would not even say what her symptoms were as she had clearly misinterpreted the examiner's request that she not reveal her diagnosis. Her response to every single question asked by the bewildered examinee was 'Wouldn't you like to know?' My greatest luck in this regard was in the medical finals where the kindly patient handed me a pen, told me to sit down, relax and take detailed notes. There was nothing that he did not know about his blood condition and I was a most eager and attentive pupil. A good moment to become lucky.

In our final year of medical school, the door to Africa swung open. Then, as now, it was customary for all medical students in their final year to spend an 'elective period' of two to three months where they could do their own thing so to speak. In general, we could choose one of three types of elective, one spent in a third world country, usually Africa, a period spent in North America, usually the USA, or an elective spent in a UK institution, often a leading academic hospital such as the Hammersmith in London. Oliver and I were very keen to do an African elective and told the Undergraduate Dean's office so, in the hope and expectation that they would recommend us to potential sponsors. Shortly afterwards, around early 1973, the Dean's secretary told us the exciting news that a certain Dr M, whom we immediately recognised as our old anatomy demonstrator, was working as a surgeon in a mine hospital in Zambia and was willing to take on one or two medical students for an elective period. Our eagerness to join him was quickly transmitted to him, and within a couple of weeks he had accepted us for November and December 1973. Later that year Dr M himself was in London for another reason, and met us both at the stylish medical school refectory to brief us on the upcoming adventure. It was good to see him again and he seemed much more relaxed and friendly than we had remembered, but perhaps our increasing maturity made the relationship more collegial than when we were younger students. He also advised us about the immunisations we needed for the trip. Within a few weeks we felt like human pincushions after being vaccinated against smallpox, yellow fever, tetanus, typhoid and cholera.

Money for the trip was a potential problem, especially for me, as I was not really in a position to borrow from my parents, who were not at all well off. However, I had won many examination prizes, a fortunate number of which were quite lucrative and together accounted for more than half of the £400 this trip would cost each of us. The rest of the money I had saved from my grant so the trip was on. Off we went to a rather seedy shop in the city to purchase our air tickets. Some things about the fares struck us as odd: the return airfare to Nairobi in Kenya was only £90 with East African Airways, but the other part of the trip from Nairobi to Lusaka in Zambia with the onward connection to our final destination with Zambian Airways cost twice as much. We had no idea this foreshadowed a serious problem with the return journey from Nairobi to London. Our minds at that time were totally focused on the African adventure ahead.

CHAPTER TWO

Copper Mines and Spitting Cobras

OUR VERY FIRST JOURNEY to Africa began just as it was to end – in total chaos. The plan was to get to Chililabombwe, our final destination on the Zambian copper belt, in three stages. We would fly from London to Nairobi, and then on to Lusaka in Zambia. After an overnight stay in Lusaka, we would take a short flight north to Kitwe, where Dr M would be waiting. He would then drive us to his home near the mine hospital.

The outbound East African Airways flight from London was scheduled for a late evening at the end of October 1973. As Oliver and I were driven along the motorway to the airport, a cold dense fog suddenly engulfed the city and clung damply to the fabric of the land. I knew immediately that this spelled trouble, as there was absolutely no way that any flights would leave a heavily fogbound airport. I can still recall the chill in my bones from the dank weather and the visceral fear of flying. So off we went back to my home in the north of the city to try again the following morning. When we awoke the next day the fog had almost cleared as if by a miraculous ordinance. We set out a second time and soon found ourselves cocooned together in a remarkably cramped but rather impressive Super VC10 aircraft. It had been pointed out to me that none other than the Queen herself often travelled on these planes so I should have no fears about safety. This was nonsense – at that time I was terrified of flying, as I had only flown once before. That was on a rather decrepit DC6 plane 10 years previously on a family holiday to Italy so I was anything but relaxed. But as so often happens to adventurous spirits, excitement trumped anxiety – a recurring theme for African travellers.

The take-off was rapid and exhilarating and vivid images of

imagined Africa soon appeared in my mind as I periodically nodded off to sleep during the eight hour flight. I ate virtually nothing as my throat was closed, and Oliver was given a tour of the flight cockpit, a courtesy that is sadly now relegated to the past in these troubled times. At last we approached Nairobi when an amazing sight appeared on our right. Three evenly separated giant triangles of white cloud, each miles in length, and with irregular edges, straddled our flight path, and like ancient gods or mighty guardians of the heavens, seemed to point out the way and beckon us to Africa. Precisely what type of cloud formation they were I am still not sure, but ever since I have not seen such an overwhelming and uncanny sight during any of my air travels. Like celestial beacons, it seemed rather unwise for our plane to fly through them.

Two things struck us as unusual on arrival at four in the morning at Nairobi. The airport was named after Jomo Kenyatta, Kenya's first President whose portraits were displayed all around the airport buildings. While this is common in the US and many other countries, this was a new experience for us. Second, there was a large sign near the entrance saying that it was a criminal offence to destroy Kenyan bank notes. Now why on earth, we thought, would anyone in their right mind want to do that? Anyway, when I bought a 20 shilling Kenyan note I took great care of it. Indeed I still have it to this day. We waited patiently in the airport lounge for a few hours until daybreak came. But as the day went on sleep deprivation was to slowly take its toll on our good judgement.

The bright Nairobi morning slowly coming to life was a revelation. An exquisite blue sky that appeared somehow higher than that of our native London framed the top of a bustling city teeming with people strolling to work, chaotic traffic and tropical trees and plants of alluring beauty. Luscious trees including the striking jacaranda, flame trees, pine trees and eucalyptus could be seen lining the streets. The ever-present bougainvillea, purple and pink in particular, seemed to capture the spirit of the city that was, almost paradoxically, both relaxed and forbidding. Ever since that first delicious glimpse of Kenya those colourful plants have epitomised for me the very spirit of the country. Whenever I now see bougainvillea in Africa or elsewhere, my mind always returns to Kenya.

Our first expedition to the city took place in a ludicrously over-crowded matatu. These still exist of course but were then small vans stuffed with as many people as is humanly possible without impairing their breathing. They were clearly death traps on the road and recent laws in Kenya have, fortunately, restricted their activities, but at that time we were blissfully unaware of the considerable danger to which we were exposing ourselves. And we did indeed have an accident, albeit a minor fender bender producing a dull but sickening thud that made everyone inside laugh. People often behave like that when they have had a bit of a fright. After a minor altercation with the other driver we carried on and made a quick reconnaissance of the city in the few short hours that were still available before our onward flight to Lusaka.

Although time was in very short supply the city was so vibrant and picturesque that even a few hours were sufficient to burn colourful images into our minds. We also had to run the gauntlet of impoverished 'students' who slowly and politely asked us for large amounts of money to sponsor them for their university stud-ies. How many of them were genuine students we just couldn't tell but sadly they were barking up the wrong tree. We felt deeply for them but were clearly unable to give them what they wanted. Our courteous refusals sometimes revealed pent up dismay or even aggression, reactions which hinted at true depths of despondency that we could only guess at. Thus impressed with a sense of the exotic we made mental notes of the best places to revisit on the return leg two months later. So ended our first brief taste of Africa, dominated by rich foliage, an inner darkness, organised chaos, and many friendly faces.

On the plane to Lusaka we were delighted to find ourselves sitting next to the referee for the upcoming World Cup qualifying football match between Zambia and Zaire (as it was then known).

He was a charming man but during our conversation we became suddenly united in terror as the plane banked steeply, horrifyingly, to the right as it ascended and flew out of Nairobi. Maybe it was a routine procedure to avoid mountains but for about 30 seconds we genuinely thought we were going to crash. The plane soon levelled, because, or in spite of, our silent prayers, and within a few hours we emerged sleepy-eyed into the spacious arrival hall of Lusaka airport. By now it was late evening and dark and, somewhat unwisely, we had not pre-booked a hotel. Remember that this was decades before the Internet, and international telephone calls were prohibitively expensive for most people.

Our next moves were reckless but perhaps understandable in view of our youthful inexperience and exhaustion. We took a taxi into the downtown area of the city and spent a few hours trying, unsuccessfully as it turned out, to get a suitable room for the night. The hotels were just too expensive for us. We then made a terrible error of judgement. We took a taxi back to the airport in the hope that we might get help from the authorities there to find accommodation. If the worst came to the worst, we reckoned, we might be able to sleep on chairs in the airport. We reckoned wrongly.

While trying to decide what to do for the best at the airport we at last succumbed to prolonged sleep deprivation and quickly fell asleep on a hard bench in one of the waiting areas. But the dangers of inappropriate sleep can sometimes be underestimated. The next thing I remember in a foggy haze of awareness was the spectre of a large rifle barrel aimed straight at my chest, and the quiet but firm words of a patrolling soldier who politely told us to accompany him to his chief. What then followed was surreal. We were told to sit on a long wooden bench in a security office at one end of the airport. On my left, a thin and frightened young man wearing what seemed like nothing more than green rags, asked me what we had done wrong.

'No idea,' I told him. 'We're just medical students. We came here to help.'

'So what are you here for?' I asked him.

He looked at me with rather doleful eyes and said, 'Loitering with intent.' I guessed that was likely to be our offence too.

At that point an extremely tall and lean police officer wearing blue dungarees walked briskly into the office, fixed his penetrating eyes in our direction, strode towards us and suddenly started to shout.

'What are you doing here? How do I know you aren't spies?' he bellowed at us.

While no physical contact with us was ever made, or even threatened, this shouting was terrifying. We kept our cool, rather to my surprise, and explained politely but clearly exactly what had happened. Meanwhile, about 15 regular police officers had gathered around us and gave us sympathetic looks.

'We know you are innocent,' they seemed to be saying, or so we thought. Their obvious compassion gave us heart and after a few minutes our interrogator left, saying that he would be back shortly. He was laughing to his colleagues as he went out and something told me that, despite his impressive display of power and intimidation, he probably thought we were harmless. But Oliver and I realised well enough that we were in a 'situation' that could possibly spark off a diplomatic incident.

By this time it was three in the morning. Soon afterwards a rather younger and clearly more sophisticated officer in a khaki uniform entered the office, talked with the others for a minute or two, and then looked our way and quietly spoke to us. He was clearly a very different kettle of fish than his predecessor, and had a distinct air of calm but real authority. I suspected he was from intelligence rather than being just the 'good cop' so to speak.

'Well boys,' he said pleasantly, 'What's going on?'

I briefly told him our sorry story again, after which he smiled and said that he totally believed us but that we had put ourselves in considerable danger. The man in the blue dungarees was apparently a member of the mobile paramilitary force which had a formidable reputation in the country for their toughness and also, so I was told later, a degree of brutality. I detected in his words an element of tension between the two forces.

'So what are we going to do with you two for the night?' he asked us, smiling benignly.

'Please get us a hotel, whatever the cost,' I said.

He agreed to this, but said he needed some kind of objective proof that we were who we said we were. Our luggage was parked in the 'left luggage' area and his police officers managed to retrieve our suitcases using their batons in unison as levers. When I opened my cheap case the items visible on the very top were my stethoscope and a copy of *Clinical Pharmacology* by D.R. Laurence, our standard text on the subject by one of UCH's most eminent professors. This immediately satisfied the friendly officer who then spent an hour trying to get us fixed up in a city hotel. Thank you Professor Laurence!

'We must get you two out of here,' he said, clearly concerned.

But there were no vacancies anywhere in the city so he eventually allowed us, very reluctantly, to sleep on the hideously uncomfortable benches in the main airport lounge, guarded by armed officers.

'Whatever you do, don't run away,' he warned us. 'If you need to go to the toilet then ask and someone will accompany you. When it gets to about seven in the morning the guards will go and you will disappear into the restaurant and stay there until your plane leaves. Do you understand?'

We understood and our guardian angel then wished us good fortune and left, but not before telling us not to repeat this folly on the return journey. Three utterly sleepless hours later we escaped, thankful to be free. While in the bright and pleasant restaurant at eight in the morning I became aware of a painful irritating rash on the insides of my legs, not unlike an early sort of 'prickly heat', presumably from the extreme stress, oppressive heat, and chaffing from the dark woollen suit that I was travelling in. I also had a deep unpleasant aching in my teeth and gums that must have been due in part to not being able to brush them for so long. We all maintain a state of homeostasis – an internal regulation of bodily functions that is automatic to us – but faced with major external stress the whole mechanism starts to break down. It took us several days to fully recover, both physically and mentally, from this episode.

Later on we discovered why the authorities were so tense and suspicious. In fact the reasons were obvious. While Zambia, previously called Northern Rhodesia, had gained independence from British rule in 1964, the situation in neighbouring Rhodesia under Ian Smith, which had declared its own independence with the Unilateral Declaration of Independence (UDI) in 1965, was very different, the independent Zimbabwe only being formalised later in 1980. There had been longstanding tension between Zambia and Rhodesia, especially from 1965 to 1980, and the fear of attacks was very real. Of course the internal war within Rhodesia from UDI to independence made this area very unstable during this time. So naturally the security officers were going to view two stray young Europeans found sleeping in their main airport with great suspicion. The fact that we had lily-white complexions, and that we were clearly as naive as one could be, counted for very little under these circumstances. One could certainly understand their heightened suspicion.

Dr M was waiting for us, as planned, at Kitwe airport where we made our landfall on the Zambian copper belt. Naturally, we were relieved to see him after our little misadventure.

'But why didn't you phone me from the airport?' he asked us when we had told him the full story.

Why not indeed? But somehow I doubt it would have made much difference. His reaction was a curious combination of great amusement at our predicament and a recognition that we really had been in significant danger. After all, there had been fatalities due to misunderstandings before in Western tourists visiting Africa, and one tragically in Zambia itself shortly before we arrived. As you can imagine, we dined out on that airport adventure for many weeks and beyond.

Before independence, Chililabombwe was called Bancroft, after one of its colonial founders, and as we drove the 60 km to the town, Dr M briefed us on the dos and don'ts of social life in our temporary home. For example, one should never use the words 'silly' or 'stupid' when referring or talking to a Zambian as it was considered highly insulting – presumably a throwback to abuse towards them in colonial days. (Why would we use those terms to anyone, we thought.) Also, we were exhorted not to speak in a negative way about the then President, Kenneth Kaunda, usually referred to as 'KK', and take particular care not to step on a newspaper or magazine that had his picture on it. It was also essential to be punctual at work and for social occasions. As we sped through the rather flat and pleasant Zambian countryside, we absorbed all these injunctions.

The history of Zambian copper mining is very interesting, and is inextricably linked to the country's political, economic and social development, and to the discovery of other more precious metals (gold) and stones (diamonds) in South Africa. These in turn are closely associated with Cecil Rhodes, the British entrepreneur who arrived in Kimberley in 1871 aged 18 to join his brother. By 1880, Rhodes was a major partner in De Beers Consolidated Diamond Mining Company which had a monopoly of the diamond trade in Kimberley by 1891. In 1899, when he took over the British South Africa Company, Rhodes was able to fulfil his ambition of mining other metals in other areas, including Northern Rhodesia.

Although there is evidence of the use of copper from around the Iron Age, when it seems to have been used mainly for bangles, its discovery on a larger scale came much later. Most copper in areas other than Zambia had been discovered earlier by the recognition of various identifying factors such as traces of oxidised ores. Even when such indicators were present it was difficult to date any findings. In the case of Zambia, in 1902, William Collier found large deposits while hunting roan antelope. Collier was in fact part of a team hired by the Rhodesia Copper Company to search for copper. Around 1920, the work of engineers such as Bancroft was important. New mines were discovered, and copper was often referred to as 'red gold' as it became more lucrative. However, this prosperity was not reflected in the rest of the country, and poverty persisted, particularly in more rural areas.

Within the context of this book it is impossible to do justice to the intricate mesh of political, economic and social factors involved in the evolution of the copper industry and of Zambia itself. However, it is possible to identify briefly a number of factors that serve to highlight the changing course of what remains a hugely important element in Zambia's history. It is complex in that several elements were at play at any given time with political factors influencing every stage.

An early significant event was the strike in 1935 by African miners. Although the industry began to thrive from around 1930, there was general dissatisfaction among the African miners, mainly concerning low wages and the dangers within the mines. This strike, which affected three mines, raised awareness of the plight of African mine workers. In 1952 the African Mine Workers' Union procured better wages for the workers.

Another important milestone was the nationalisation of the copper mines in 1969 under the first President of Zambia, Kenneth Kaunda. He had become President in October 1964 and his term of office lasted 27 years. Under Kaunda, the mines were managed by the government, and money generated from the industry was directed towards education and health. For some time the copper trade flourished, but by the early seventies, around the time we visited Zambia, it began to plummet. Political factors, particularly UDI by Rhodesia, also influenced the situation in Zambia. The National debt was high and there was growing opposition to the government, and in 1991 Frederick Chiluba replaced Kenneth Kaunda as President.

The Chiluba Presidency (1991–2001) constitutes a further major development in the history of the copper mining industry.

This time the 'free market' approach was introduced, with privatisation of major industries including copper. This appears to have mixed effects, leading to greater efficiency on the one hand, but also job losses and a reduction of major outputs on the other. By late 2002, most of the major companies, including most of ZCCM (Zambian Consolidated Copper Mines), had been privatised under organisations such as Anglo American. However, Anglo American, which had been the main investor in the Konkola Mine, pulled out of the deal in 2002. Then, in 2004, a London FTSE 250 listed mining company called Vedanta became a major investor in the Konkola Mines (one of the largest mines). Recent reports indicate that copper prices are now rising and output is increasing. However, it may take several years for the country to recover its previous losses. We will return to the copper mines later.

Our arrival at Dr M's house at Chililabombwe was like stepping into a tropical paradise. Our two day journey and our interrogation in Lusaka had been traumatic to be sure and we were badly in need of a shower and more. As we emerged bleary-eyed from her husband's Toyota, Mrs M and her two lively young children came out into the garden and warmly greeted us. She was a woman of exceptional kindness and sensitivity and immediately recognised that we were both in a bit of a state. After she quickly showed us the bedroom that we were to share for the duration, Oliver and I literally dived into the house's two bathrooms and let the elegant metal showers gently sprinkle us with healing water droplets that soothed our discomfort and seemed to literally wash away the painful memories of our recent journey.

Biologically, water is essential to life, and for us water also became a rejuvenator of life. Skin rashes, headaches and gum pain all disappeared within a few hours of drinking the atmosphere of this lovely family. Our immediate sense of well being was undoubtedly heightened by the agreeable climate with an average temperature at that time of around 70–75° F. It was the very low humidity that meant that while we would lose a good deal of salt through perspiration, we never really felt uncomfortable from the heat itself. But it also increased the chances of getting salt depleted, as I would later find out. Though refreshed, Oliver and I also felt exceptionally sleepy those first few days, due, I am pretty sure, to a mixture of mental and physical exhaustion, a touch of jetlag, and the high altitude of the town which was 4,435 ft above sea level. Eventually our bodies acclimatised through a physiological response to the lower amounts of oxygen in the atmosphere, and after that happened we stopped feeling like zombies and became more alert.

Their house was a spacious and luxurious bungalow. Long and rather rambling, it contained three large bedrooms, two bathrooms, three elegant living rooms leading into a narrow hall, a well-equipped kitchen, a pleasant balcony and some outbuildings. The beautiful one acre garden displayed an impressive array of flowers and trees bearing tropical fruits. Passion fruit, mango, banana and avocado pear trees stood alongside the less familiar gardenias, oleander and jasmine. There was also a flower that was said to bloom for only a few days every year. A few hundred yards along the road outside there were impressive purple and red bougainvillea. The house was a natural home to numerous geckos, swift little lizards that would promptly auto-amputate their tails, leaving them behind when we came too close and startled them. We soon came to see them as our companions. Other animal delights which we beheld in the vicinity included flying ants, enormous croaking frogs, giant snails, and the occasional snake which had been tempted to travel down the high ground opposite us. In the nearby 'hippo pool' resided a hippopotamus and two crocodiles.

We were also warned about the ever-present danger of the dreaded spitting cobra which, we were told, could spit venom directly into your eyes from a distance of up to 15 feet. We were never quite sure if our hosts were having us on when we were told to always wear sunglasses at night to protect our eyes from this beast. The facts are slightly different. The discharge range of a large snake is three metres, and the cobras actually spray rather than spit. The venom seems to be pushed into the fangs by the action of muscle contraction and it is then sprayed out. The Ringhals and certain African species of Naja are the most effective 'spitters'. Corneal damage, which can lead to blindness, can result from an attack. If actually bitten, the main evidence of envenomation is necrosis, that is, death of the affected tissues, which may be followed by neurological dysfunction and paralysis due to the neurotoxins in the venom. So we were right to be cautious! Even more dangerous were the puff adder and black mamba that were to be found in other regions of the country. We wondered whether we would ever come face to face with the famous spitting cobra.

The quality of housing enjoyed by a mine employee was directly dependent on the seniority and importance of the post he or she held. This socio-economic stratification operated throughout the entire mining organisation. Medical officers such as Dr M were pretty high up in the system and were directly comparable in status with the mine captains, both of whom had considerable 'hands on' responsibilities in either medical care or mine operations. This equivalence of status was reflected by identical housing – the spacious bungalow in our case. The side of the road one lived on could also be significant, one side being more prestigious than the other. While such officers with families were given the bungalows, single medical officers and their equivalents had the choice of well appointed two-bedroom apartments which were actually small houses with two floors and could have easily housed four people.

The perks of the jobs were considerable, and there was no doubt that the medical officers enjoyed a high standard of living that they could only have dreamed about back home. It was also a good way to save money that could be taken back home in the future. It was quite difficult and very expensive to recruit and retain medical staff so the authorities ensured that their employees were given excellent living conditions. For example, a house, a car with unlimited petrol, telephone bills, water and electricity, cablegrams and photographic film were all supplied free of charge. Salaries were also very high for the period with a minimum annual salary paid to a newly registered doctor of £5,200. (By contrast, I was paid about £960 six months later as a recently qualified doctor in England.) Below the mine captains was a level of employee known as shift bosses who occupied pleasant but more modest houses. Some way below them in the expatriate society hierarchy were the so-called 'artisans', mainly from the UK, who occupied more physical, but equally valuable, work such as carpentry. The term 'artisan' always rankled when we heard it as it seemed inappropriate. At the very top of the mining organisation were the three top managers of the mine who lived in a quasi-royal enclave some distance away from us. We could only imagine the luxury they must have enjoyed. Near the end of the stay we met the second in command whom we found approachable and affable.

On the very first evening of our arrival we began to appreciate the rather complex and hierarchical social structure of this somewhat rigid but outwardly friendly expatriate community. The town's total population at that time was about 56,000, similar to the present. Of these only a few hundred were non-Zambian expatriates. They were mainly White or Asian, many were from the UK or Afrikaners from South Africa, and of the latter, all I personally met were anti-apartheid in their home country, so we were at particular ease with them. Indeed we found that the South Africans in Zambia were an extremely open and friendly group of people. While individuals from different social levels generally had a tendency to socialise apart, Dr and Mrs M had a wide variety of friends, irrespective of which part of the social ladder they occupied. We had indeed chosen our hosts well. Many of the local Zambian residents lived in a 'compound' where many of the mine workers and, therefore, hospital patients lived. The expatriates seldom entered that enclave, and it was out of bounds to us other than for medical reasons. The higher echelons of the mine community, including of course a number of highly placed Zambians, frequently had house servants who did the washing, routine shopping, cooking and cleaning. A quiet, pleasant young man of about 20 years called Ronald was our 'houseboy' and while appreciating his worth and his happiness at actually having a job, we never ceased to feel rather uncomfortable about his official title and made a point of treating him with perhaps what might have been seen by others as exaggerated respect. Notwithstanding that, our hosts treated him exceptionally well and he showed no outward signs of latent discontent so far as we were aware.

The morning after we arrived in Chililabombwe Dr M drove us the few miles to the Mine Hospital where we were to learn, observe and work. After a courteous mine policeman ushered our car through the main iron gates that protected the buildings, we beheld for the first time our new workplace. The hospital was modern and very well equipped and staffed compared with the typical government hospitals. It was also run with great efficiency. There were several large wards containing medical and surgical patients, a paediatric ward, a neonatal ward, an obstetric unit, extensive outpatient facilities, operating theatres, a radiology suite and a diagnostic pathology laboratory equipped for carrying out haematology, biochemistry and microbiological tests. There were also comfortable staff offices and a doctors' sitting room where we all met at break times to share meals, coffee, shoptalk and any amount of gossip. All of the senior staff, including the medical doctors, had an 'AA' number, which meant that Anglo American employed them. The number of working hours they performed was strictly laid out and ran from 7.30am to 12 midday and then after lunch from 2pm to 4pm. There were two breaks of 30 minutes in the morning and afternoon so the jobs were certainly not physically onerous – far from it. But woe betides any employee who was late for work as this was an absolute 'No No'. Being late for work on more than a few occasions would not have been tolerated. Doctors were on call for emergencies one night per week and one weekend in three.

There were seven medical officers altogether, six of whom had trained in the UK. The chief, or superintendent, doctor was a distinguished general surgeon in his sixties from England who could carry out an extraordinary variety of surgical operations ranging from orthopaedics and paediatric surgery to bowel operations and plastic surgery. I think he must have been one of the last great all-encompassing general surgeons working in Africa, or anywhere for that matter. He was a quiet, modest and extremely courteous man who literally radiated formidable personal authority and integrity and because of this was greatly revered by everyone in the hospital. He was particularly pleasant and welcoming to us and treated us like members of his team. So many times have I observed this quality of quiet humility in the truly gifted. There was also a senior medical officer, an anaesthetist as I recall, who deputised for the chief in his administrative role.

Our own Dr M was primarily a general surgeon and there was another doctor from Asia, trained in Germany, who was a highly skilled obstetrician and gynaecologist. There were also three younger doctors, two males and a female, who had all recently qualified from the UK. While they were all relatively inexperienced on arrival, they rapidly became very competent generalists although they were primarily physicians rather than surgeons. Despite this, the doctors frequently had to deal with some exceptionally challenging and complex cases, sometimes in the middle of the night, which were very near the limits of their experience and competence. The fact that they managed to survive so well in this environment testifies to their ability to rise to the occasion when necessary and somehow to find the required strength and reserves from within themselves. And they always did their best. To our amazement and delight one of the 'youngsters' was Tom Dent who had trained at our own medical school, UCH, and was none other than the son of Professor Charles Dent, whom you will recall was the man who warned us to have clean hands. Tom was highly competent and quietly confident, and the most laidback of the medical officers. We both felt very at ease with him. After 30 years I recently re-established contact with him in the UK, where he is now a part-time general practitioner in the Midlands of England. He was able to corroborate most of my observations and notes of these times and also to add some of his own.

All the doctors cross-covered for each other in the different specialties, including anaesthetics and paediatrics, but only three of the doctors were designated surgeons. Some of them, in addition, conducted weekly clinics in health centres within the town. Two outside medical and surgical consultants with special expertise from nearby towns on the copper belt visited the hospital on a weekly and monthly basis to help out with the most difficult and challenging patients. We learned a lot from them too. On rare occasions it might be necessary to fly in special medical supplies from elsewhere, or for patients to be transferred to a hospital with more advanced facilities and expertise, possibly outside the country. This happened once during our stay when one of the visiting British physicians had to take his own very seriously ill child back to England for intensive therapy. Fortunately the child fully recovered.

In practice, most of a doctor's time was spent in long outpatient clinics that were run very much like busy family doctors' surgeries in England. There were several clinics per day usually with two doctors working together who would each see a vast number of patients in each session. Outpatients 1 predominantly provided for the expatriates and the Zambian managers whilst Outpatients 2 was for the mine workers. We saw both common and rare conditions in these clinics, indeed everything you can imagine, ranging from venereal diseases which were very common in the general community, to mild chest and viral infections; injured and strained joints and ligaments; gastric ulcers; psychiatric problems, including so-called cases of malingering; malnutrition; a range of skin conditions; more serious infections such as tuberculosis and malaria, and many others. Because of time constraints – for a massive number needed to be seen each half day – patients were dealt with politely but occasionally brusquely. Seriously ill patients were given much longer. It was an intensive experience but could be punctuated by lighter moments such as the sudden appearance out of nowhere of a large foot on our consulting table from an elderly man who was sidling up behind us. He said nothing but pointed nonchalantly to his big toe that had the largest 'ram's horn' deformity that we had ever seen, technically known as an 'onychogryphosis'. It looked as if a giant seashell had been grafted onto his toe.

'OK, we'll fix it,' said the bemused doctor. And off the patient went, apparently satisfied.

Tom particularly remembers the exceptional efficiency of the clinics. Within about 30 minutes of ordering a blood count and an x-ray on a patient, one of the two outpatient sisters would walk in with the blood test and waive a fresh wet chest x-ray film. One would seldom see or expect such efficiency in any hospital back home. I recall another interesting variation from UK medicine where patients tended to view different symptoms as requiring separate medicines. For example, if a patient had a sore throat and a bad cough from what we thought was a viral infection, they would often be pre-scribed two lots of medicine, one for each symptom. The notion of one root cause of several symptoms was not widely held. I learned a few phrases of Bemba, the main local dialect (one of no less than 70 local languages in Zambia), and well remember Dr M saying something resembling *'Muti par window three'*, meaning 'collect your tablets at window three'. It was seldom just one drug that was prescribed. Another common phrase which has stuck in my mind was *'Fimbrini shirt maqui'* (or at least that was what it sounded like), meaning 'lift up your shirt, sir'. Because of the practical dif-ficulties of following patients up in the hospital or local health clinics, large single doses of some drugs were sometimes given on a one-off basis. A hefty single dose of penicillin for gonorrhoea would cure about 90 per cent of cases there and then. The expatriates also needed medical care from time to time with the same kinds of ill-nesses seen back home. But this was medicine in the early 1970s. For example, gastric ulcers, which were not that uncommon there, were treated with many weeks' enforced bed rest. Today, thanks to the discoveries of James Black and Barry Marshall (both Nobel Laureates in Medicine), they would be given a specific course of a gastric acid antagonist and antibiotics and sent on their way.

The illnesses we saw in the hospital wards were more serious. As with the outpatients, the variety of medical conditions was very extensive. Some conditions, such as pneumonia and tuberculosis, were already familiar to us but here they became more real, somehow tangible and understandable. By becoming physically closer to and more engaged with the patients we became more familiar with their illnesses. I examined patients, encountering physical signs such as 'bronchial breathing' that denoted a patch of pneumonia. I had never clearly heard this in London, where all too often the most I could hear through my stethoscope was the noise of the radio of the patient in the next bed. Not that I would ever have admitted such a failing back home. Here there was no room nor need for pretence. Dr M taught us very efficiently and effectively, without fuss or the showmanship that characterised a small number of our teaching hospital consultants. Here there was no humility in ignorance. There was only a steep personal learning curve.

We both became depressingly adept at recognising the tell tale signs of that severe malnutrition known as Kwashiorkor which was due to severe protein deficiency. The hair of the unfortunate child was invariably affected and was often soft, fine and straw coloured. Alteration of skin pigmentation and changes in the mouth and tongue were also frequent, as was an enlarged liver and swollen abdomen. Advanced cases had a high mortality. Once we saw a doomed three month old infant brought in weighing just a few pounds. The mother was surprisingly well nourished in comparison. Trachoma-induced blindness was not uncommon. Tropical ulcers, usually on patients' legs, were particularly troublesome. These were usually long-standing and very resistant to treatment. Several different causes for these ulcers had been identified, notably chronic malnutrition and multiple infections. Bacteria that were said to be associated with these ulcers included a type of 'fusiform' bacteria and also a kind of spirochaetal bacteria related to but not the same as the type causing syphilis, so correct antibiotic treatment played a crucial role in the patient's recovery. Tuberculosis was common but I had never been in such close contact with patients with such florid forms of disease. When I examined these patients on the ward rounds, which Dr M always allowed us to do, I was struck if not amazed by the severity of the physical signs and I could instinctively sense the cavitating lung lesions produced by this disease. My humble stethoscope, purchased from John Bell and Croyden in London, had never before been put to such good use.

Many types of trauma were treated in the hospital and not all of them were due to accidents occurring in the copper mines. The latter included head, limb and chest injuries from machinery accidents or falling rocks. Road traffic accidents also took a heavy toll on people in the town and throughout the country, many cases being alcohol-related. Burns, especially in children, were also seen quite often. The most dramatic trauma case we saw occurred in the early hours of one morning when Dr M had to deal with an unfortunate young lady who had been attacked by a crocodile in a nearby river. She had suffered horrifying leg fractures as well as damaged muscles and tendons. She required long and extensive reconstructive surgery to her leg, which Dr M managed to save. The savage damage that had been inflicted on her with just one bite was incredible and she was fortunate to escape with her life. Before the operation I remember looking at the dramatic leg x-ray in the small radiology suite, where, hanging prominently on the wall, was a striking photograph of Winston Churchill. The elderly Zambian radiographer in charge, whom I established had served in the forces, had placed it there himself and clearly revered the great man.

Snake bites also had to be dealt with from time to time but I am pleased to say I never saw a fatal one. The efficient pharmacy was well stocked with a range of anti-venom drugs. As one may expect, we also saw a wide variety of infectious diseases. There were some tragic cases of polio producing permanent limb paralysis that would almost certainly have been prevented by an efficient immunisation programme. Measles may have been familiar to those in highly developed countries as an unpleasant childhood infection experienced personally by those of us above a certain age, but not by those younger people whose parents have had their children immunised against measles. But here measles was a killer. The characteristic red blotchy rash was less obvious in the darker pig-mented skin of the children compared with Caucasian children so one always needed to be on guard for this disease in case the early stages might be missed. The main problem was the high incidence of a severe pneumonia complicating the infection that could quick-ly claim the life of the child or leave it permanently disabled. Measles can also lead to severe encephalitis, an infection of the brain, which was another constant concern. When we saw measles we were always worried.

Naturally, we also saw cases of malaria, although many people in Africa have an innate degree of immunity to the infection that can be chronic, low grade and only flare up occasionally. Despite the enormous interest in sleeping sickness that I was to develop later, I never actually saw a case during this period, presumably because we were in a small area of a country that is officially classified as at 'low risk' from the disease. Tom tells me, however, that he remem-bers being stopped by a tsetse fly check-point staffed by an officer with a pump spray clearly concerned that the flies may have been hitching a ride! One infection that we never saw of course was AIDS (acquired immunodeficiency syndrome) as this was the end of 1973, almost a decade before this disaster burst with such vengeance onto humanity. Thirty years after this time the figure for HIV (human immunodeficiency virus) infection, the cause of AIDS, was a staggering 89,000 deaths recorded in Zambia in 2003, and 16.5 per cent of the entire adult population were HIV-infected.

There was a very good obstetric unit at the hospital with expe-rienced medical and nursing staff. They had to be very competent to deal with the sheer range and severity of the cases that presented, which included all kinds of acute obstetric emergency. Working closely and efficiently with this unit was the small but effective neonatal unit located nearby. It was challenged unremittingly on a daily basis. As well as the usual childhood illnesses that one would expect to see anywhere, we saw two cases of Burkitt's lymphoma. This is a rare tumour of the immune system where cells known as B cells, which make antibodies, multiply out of control to produce tumours of the lymph nodes, usually in the neck and jaw. The children we saw had enormous compressing tumours that disfigured and distorted the lower parts of their faces. First described by the English physician Dennis Burkitt in the 1950s, the lymphoma is prevalent in equatorial regions of Africa, mainly East Africa and also New Guinea. The geographical distribution of this condition is remarkable. It occurs in regions of low altitude where malaria is common but not at those high altitudes where malaria parasites are unable to survive. It has been suggested that in some way an early infection with the malaria parasite interferes with the child's immune system making it more susceptible to undergo malignant change and result in this condition. In the 1960s, a particular virus known as the Epstein Barr Virus (EBV, named after its two discoverers) was isolated from Burkitt's lymphoma tissues and is thought to play a key role in producing the condition although we still don't fully understand the mechanism. EBV, a member of the herpes virus group, is also the virus which produces glandular fever, known medically as infectious mononucleosis, which, as some people may know, can spread by intimate kissing (hence the name 'kissing disease'). In Africa it may do far more than that.

Although most of our time was spent on the wards and at the outpatient clinics, we also spent a week in the pathology laboratory and another week in the public health department. In the former, we saw an array of 'tropical nasties' on microscope slides. Also, for the first and I think only time, we saw exactly how one determines routine biochemical values in blood samples such as sodium and potassium. It was odd that we had to travel over 5,000 miles to see how that was done! Our time with the local public health officer, who was also attached to the hospital with a staff grade equivalent to a shift boss (as reflected by the size of his house), was a real highlight of the trip. We went on exciting expeditions to nearby villages, as well as those much further into the bush area, coming into much closer contact with the local population in their homes than before. We were surprised to learn that having twins was considered unlucky while the rare arrival of triplets was a source of joy. I recall the exquisitely embroidered multicoloured shawls worn by many of the women in the villages and our own status as objects of friendly curiosity. All kinds of rather shaggy and malnourished dogs barked and jumped up here and there while roaming around the villages. I wondered just how healthy they were and feared being bitten by one as they licked our legs with canine relish. Our Land Rover was a top of the range model and cut across swathes of dense bush country. Short tree stumps and jagged stones jutted from the uneven ground and offered no impediment to our progress and were effortlessly trampled beneath us. It seemed that nothing could interfere with our sense of motion and freedom.

During this public health attachment I spent a few days with a Zambian official. He was about the same age as I was. We spent many hours talking about our respective lives in England and Zambia. Whilst doing this we also sprayed insecticide from special hand pumps into every stagnant pool that we came across as part of a wider malaria control programme. Before 1980, malaria was kept under effective control in Chililabombwe by annual residual spraying programmes, but I recently came across a report saying that the annual incidence of malaria in the town jumped from about 20 per 1,000 people in the 1970s to 158 per 1,000 people in 2000. This high incidence was brought down again over the next two years by a single annual round of house spraying with insecticide.

This was the first time during the trip that I was able to really get to know a Zambian personally for, until then, there had been little opportunity to socialise with anyone other than a local white expatriate. Besides, time was in relatively short supply. We travelled everywhere by bicycle, which was slow but efficient, and at times dangerous. I recall the two of us shooting the breeze and leisurely cycling along a narrow road under the brilliant afternoon sunshine when out of nowhere two massive lorries sped towards us completely occupying both sides of the road at 70 mph. To avoid a collision we had no choice but to swerve off the road. It was so sudden we fell off our bicycles onto the verge ignominiously. I was pretty shaken but my friend was unfazed, saying that the general rule of the road was that the larger vehicle has complete right of way. His equanimity was impressive.

We ended our attachment to the public health department with an upsetting episode in which at least 30 stray town dogs were captured and summarily shot with a gun resembled a starting pistol with a retractable bolt called a 'humane killer'. I had never witnessed any deliberate act of killing in my life before and was nauseated and shocked by the efficient way in which the dogs were despatched by our officer. I realise it was a very necessary measure to prevent the possible spread of rabies, which was endemic, as well as other diseases, but it was difficult for me to witness and I have never forgotten it. The whole township seemed to be on the side of the dogs and cheered when one of them escaped through a gap in the cage. Oliver, perhaps unwisely, took a few photographs of the process for the record. It was not a complete surprise to me when the pictures came back from the local photographic shop with all of these images mysteriously erased while the rest of his photographs came out perfectly.

During our stay we also went on a number of visits to the countryside and other towns on weekends, always accompanied by colleagues and friends. Dr M, Oliver and I drove 200 km east to the town of Solwezi along a series of hot and dusty roads. Solwezi is the administrative capital of Zambia's North Western Province. On the outskirts of the town we explored a disused copper mine where my latent interest in geology became rejuvenated. We collected a number of unusually shaped stones, some of them iron pyrites – also known as 'fool's gold' because of its deceptive yellow lustre – and, in particular, malachite which was dull green in its natural state.

I realised during this trip that I had become salt depleted. The low humidity and high temperature had facilitated the loss of salt and water through 'insensible loss' through the skin. I suddenly began to feel very dizzy, faint and nauseated, symptoms that were made even worse by foolishly drinking large amounts of tap water that I had bottled. You can't cure salt depletion just by drinking water. Dr M soon recognised the problem and gave me salt to eat which rapidly got rid of the symptoms. It was another example to us of how easy it was to forget that we were in the middle of the African bush. We soon came across a beautiful river which we carefully crossed on foot using conveniently placed grey rocks as stepping stones, and visited a temporarily deserted bush village nearby where we saw what was almost certainly an enclosure where initiation rites were performed. We felt that we were intruding and, feeling an odd sense of acute unease, left quickly. On the journey home we saw for the first and only time a real spitting cobra moving at great speed across the road in front of us. Against a beautiful early evening Zambian sky with gently interlacing grey and white cloud formations, we saw a group of eagles forming a visual backdrop which added a new dimension to our memories of Africa.

Another trip was taken with two nursing colleagues into the northern bush near the Congolese border (known as Zaire at that time). It was quite picturesque, but we must have inadvertently (and I think illegally) crossed the border with Zambia for all the people around us were suddenly speaking French. The posters on the trees were now in French. On another occasion we joined a convoy of Toyotas with reinforced bodywork appropriate for hazardous driving deep into the bush territory. We travelled many miles, and negotiated dreadful red dirt roads with frequent potholes and fallen tree branches blocking our progress. At one stage the convoy became split, but after passing a few more friendly villages, and what we thought were non-poisonous snakes, we eventually found each other again.

A constant feature of all car journeys at that time were the police check-points stationed every 30 km. I am sure these were set up for all sorts of good reasons but we always found them a complete nightmare. Usually we were just simply waved through the barrier, but now and then we had to stop and answer questions. Occasionally the car would be briefly searched. The police were reasonably courteous, although we felt an underlying anxiety, as they could sometimes appear intimidating. I recall Dr M once being berated by a plain clothed police officer because one of his tyres was unacceptably worn, though I doubt that was the real reason for our being stopped.

Without doubt the most exciting and memorable trip of all was to the town's copper mine. Dr M strongly encouraged this visit and we were also keen to see exactly where and how most of our patients worked. Our guide and teacher, P, was one of the most senior and capable of the mine captains, a cultured and friendly South African man who was also a very good friend of our hosts, and certainly no friend of apartheid which he detested. A quietly spoken and courteous Afrikaner, P also had an impressive physical presence, being powerfully built and well over six feet tall. He was also a keen sportsman and had an individual golf handicap of just two. He was also the leader of the local mine 'proto-team', an elite multi-disciplinary band of highly trained mine personnel who were prepared at all times to mount an instant rescue in the case of a mine accident. In fact the mine in Chililabombwe had an excellent safety record so there was little in reality to worry about. We were aware, however, of the potential dangers as evidenced by the disaster that had occurred in the Mufulira mine in September 1970, when 89 workers lost their lives.

Before our visit 'below ground', P used diagrams and three dimensional models to explain the structure of the mine. My anxiety prevented me from taking in more than a few technical terms such as 'ore body' and 'fault'. He instructed us to keep close to him at all times during the tour, which would last about three hours. I must explain here that I suffer from a real fear of heights and I have a low threshold for claustrophobia, both contributing to my apprehension about letting down my colleagues. But I have found that a fear of humiliation often ignites a new courage and determination to overcome fear.

We donned special overalls and hard hats equipped with powerful lights. The lift descended to the main pit 2,000 ft below in just one minute which was extremely fast and made me glad that I had no breakfast that morning. My stomach was left on the surface and my head was already spinning. We then walked down the longest and steepest stairway that I had ever used. It seemed as if it would never end and our steady motion and the steep gradient created an odd illusion of moving forwards as well as downwards. But end it did, and once we were at the bottom, the real tour started. We walked and climbed and walked and descended and crawled and scrambled along countless ladders, shafts, passages, tracks, holes and pathways for about three hours. It was both terrifying and exhilarating. Most of the time it was very dark and we had to rely on the sound of P's voice as well as his large shadowy form. The worst part was negotiating the rope and steel ladders, especially when descending, as the orientation of the ladders, which fortunately ran close to the mine walls, frequently terminated abruptly without warning so that your foot would suddenly tread on nothing but air. You had to find a neighbouring ladder below, and then swing right round to get a foothold onto the continuation ladder which was 90 degrees in relation to the top one to which it was securely bound by ropes. I would hate to think what would happen to a person here if they froze in fear for there was nothing to protect you from falling hundreds of feet into the black nothingness below. Because P was so fit and accustomed to the rigours of the mineshafts he moved extremely fast and it was a real struggle to keep up with him. I thought I had lost contact with him on several occasions but he always had his eye on us. The hard hat was essential in the dark as I kept hitting the uncompromising and brutally hard rock around my head continuously. Without the protection of the hat, any knock would have rendered me instantly unconscious.

The conditions for the working miners in the pit seemed pretty grim to me but I had no previous experience of any mine so I couldn't really judge. It was very hot at 80° F, oppressive, dark, smelly, choking because of the dust, and incredibly loud due to the drills. I saw one monster drill about 10 ft long and four ft wide that looked like the anti-aircraft gun on a battleship. Apparently, workers operating the drills at the mine face were very well paid. This didn't stop the normally quiet P bellowing at them for encouragement, or occasionally in concealed anger, at the very top of his voice that sounded like a loud foghorn. The transformation in him was uncanny. I also made the common error of sticking my fingers in my ears to keep the deafening noises at bay. P promptly dislodged my fingers as the pain of exposure to the noise of the drills would seem much less when it was continuous than when it was intermittent.

Eventually we came to the end of the tour, by which time every muscle in my body was aching. The finale was quite magical as we passed through a massive structure that looked like a giant circular magnet. On either side of us as we walked down a narrow pathway were neat square compartments containing strange dark water courses which had an unusual blueish black tinge and a choppy forwards and backwards motion. We almost felt like swimming in them and I couldn't fathom at that point whether this was real or an illusion.

During the tour we met several miners, both of low and high ranking, and were struck by the strange 'language' they spoke, which was very different from that above ground. This language seemed to me an odd mixture of English, Bemba, French and swear words with, often, at least one 'f' word per sentence. To give you some examples which I wrote down at the time (those of a nervous disposition should skip this next paragraph):

'There's a f—-g fault here.'

'Here they learn beaucoup de Medicine and soon they'll be full doctors.'

And to us: 'You must be f—-g good if you can afford to f around the world just before your final exams.'

What was so remarkable is that the moment the miners, including the mine captains, returned to the surface they spoke with their customary civility. The utterer of that last mentioned example would have said to us something like:

'Well it's been a great pleasure meeting you and I wish you all the very best in your future careers.'

So there were two languages, one for the world above and one for the world below.

On a later occasion we were given a tour of the ground level operations and machinery and saw at first hand what happens to the copper after it has been mined and brought up to the surface from underground. The copper would be purified and then concentrated, after which it would have to be transferred to Kitwe, 50 miles away, where it would be smelted. As I now think about this at my desk I can almost smell the sharp sickly odour of the copper mounds. Why is this? Probably because both the sensation of smell and memory are processed in the temporal lobes of the brain so that the nervous impulses signalling both types of experience connect with each other when one remembers something vivid like this.

Almost as awe-inspiring as this experience was a visit to the 'Open Pit' copper mine, officially an opencast mine, in nearby Chingola 20 km away which was one of the largest of its kind in the world and certainly the largest in Africa. It was a massive man-made hole hewn out of the ground, one km deep and one by three km wide. It looked rather like a giant footprint. The dramatic view of the pit from the edge of the rim provided a magnificent panorama equal to virtually any sight that could be imagined. The sights were no less impressive from the bottom of the pit. Most memorable at this level were the massive trucks, each as tall as a house and capable of carrying a single load of 200 tons of copper ore. The hugely expensive tyres alone stood about 11 ft high and the highly skilled drivers had a 12 ft blindspot which made a confrontation with these giant monsters potentially hazardous. As previously mentioned, the Rule of the Road was that a smaller vehicle always gives way to a larger one. Despite such dangers this opencast mine had a particularly impressive safety record.

In between work at the hospital and the trips above and below ground, we were also caught up in the town's social environment. Although we appreciated the general approachability and the friendliness of the expatriates, we found it occasionally claustrophobic and stifling. We attended, rather grudgingly I have to admit, coffee mornings, and some, perhaps a little pretentious, musical evenings where 20 people or so would sit in a circle listening appreciatively to a record of Handel's *Messiah*. More welcome were the tasty barbecues conducted under the midday sun or in the early evening shadows. A constant irritation for us was the presence of large guard dogs which many expatriates kept to maintain security. We were frequently terrorised by these large beasts, indoors and outdoors, and the three owned by our next door neighbour were the most fearsome of all. Dr M had a smaller, friendlier dog called Buster but we could contend with him fairly easily. Unfortunately the poor animal suddenly became ill one day, probably from pneumonia, and despite my injection of an antibiotic into his leg, he died the next day. We buried him solemnly in a peaceful corner of the garden.

Being both transient and rather young looking, I think we held little real attraction for the unattached female expatriates who were much older than we were. Although irritating for us at the time, this was probably quite a good thing in retrospect, since in that close-knit society any liaison might easily have proved somewhat disruptive. We also saw and learned things that we would never have even contemplated back home. The best example of this was the visit of the community's main butcher who spent half a day cutting up an entire cow. I soon learnt from direct observation where, in precise anatomical terms, rump steak, porterhouse, sirloin and silverside cuts come from. I also recall seeing a junior helper being fiercely criticised by the butcher for placing a sharp knife below a piece of meat. The sharp object must always be exposed to avoid nasty accidents. This is something I always advise others to do.

But while we learned medicine and a host of other practical things such as butchery, flower arranging and elements of basic ballroom dancing, life in England had turned distinctly miserable. Although we had no access to UK newspapers or TV news (CNN and BBC News 24 were of course not around at that time), I received a constant succession of letters from my parents giving me graphic and depressing descriptions of the breakdown of government and public services in England. That period was one of considerable national and global instability. The 1973 Yom Kippur war in the Middle East had lasted 18 days from 6 October so had only just officially ended as we left England. Industrial unrest was taking effect on various public services and on the general mood of the country. The Conservative government under Edward Heath was under pressure to deal with a mounting crisis within the electrical and coal industries. An overtime ban by these two groups of workers led to a state of emergency on 12 November. The overtime ban plus the diminished oil supply by Arab states led to the enforcement of a serious of restrictions. These restrictions amounted to a reduction in petrol and fuel deliveries, a 50 mph speed limit, and limited use of lighting in offices and shops. By the end of December 1973 the decision to impose a three-day week had been taken and this became a reality in early January 1974. So while all this turmoil was happening in Britain, we were engrossed in a time and place that seemed to have no relation to the life that we had temporarily left behind. We could have been living on a different planet.

For the first six weeks of the trip we enjoyed very good health, had a great sense of well being, and took frequent walks along the attractive roads near our bungalow. We also played squash (badly in my case). Sport, especially golf, was very popular and well played in Chililabombwe. But then our luck ran out. Oliver was the first to succumb to a sudden gastro-enteritis that struck him out of the blue. About two days later when he was already recovering, I was poleaxed by severe nausea and vomiting that was so persistent that it could only be stopped by an injection of a drug called Stemetil, which sent me to sleep for a day. I am sure it was an enterovirus infection that we had both caught rather than food poisoning because we ate the same food and the time delay between our two illnesses was very suggestive of an infection. Poisoning would have struck us down simultaneously. Although I recovered after a few days, I lost seven pounds in weight in two days and never felt quite right again for the rest of the trip.

But the most dramatic episode was experienced by Oliver. After a swim one day he dried himself with a towel that had been lying on the grass. Two days afterwards he noticed what he thought were mosquito bites on his back although they looked more like boils to me. They got progressively worse and inflamed, and Dr M carefully inspected them every day for a week, saying nothing at all to us. I suspected something was wrong and after seven days at the height of Oliver's discomfort, Dr M firmly squeezed the rim of one of the 'bites' and to my horror a wriggling white maggot emerged from the centre of the boil. This caused Oliver severe pain and the process was successfully repeated eight times until nine wriggling, thankfully intact, maggots were extracted and placed into a little glass jar. At that point his pain ceased abruptly to everyone's relief. Oliver had been invaded by the dreaded putzi fly, known also as the African tumbu fly, and technically called myiasis. What happened is either that the fly had laid its eggs on the towel, or the towel may have been contaminated by egg-infested grass or soil. When Oliver dried himself with the towel the eggs were transferred to his skin where they hatched and the emerging larvae had burrowed deep into his skin. There they had grown progressively larger and, had they not been removed when they had, would have eventually emerged as adult flies after two weeks and left behind ghastly abscesses. Not very nice. In practice, the problem is avoided by thoroughly cleaning and ironing all clothes which kills off the eggs. The natural hosts for these ghastly parasites are dogs and rats but many other types of animal can be invaded including, clearly, man. We never told our folks back home what had really happened to him.

Sadly, our time in Zambia drew to a close and we had the unusual experience of spending Christmas in the tropics. Emerging into the bright afternoon sunshine eating extraordinarily delicious mince pies was almost surreal. Many of the older children of the expatriates had recently returned from their respective boarding schools spread throughout the world and their presence added to the festive atmosphere. A few still attended schools in South Africa which meant they had to stop over in Malawi first before being allowed to enter Zambia as it was not politically possible for them to fly here directly. They always had 'short back and sides' haircuts as anyone with much longer hair (such as myself) would probably have had problems entering Malawi at that time.

Oliver and I showed off our collection of African 'curios' which we had bought from the Congolese vendors who had crossed over the northern border a few miles away. The 'semi-precious' stones we had accumulated included tiger's eye, polished malachite ashtrays, sculptures and eggs, black and ordinary amethyst, agate, rose quartz, and jasper. Most of these cost about one Zambian kwatcha, which at that time was equivalent to 65 pence or one US dollar. (I was amazed to learn recently that following devaluation, one kwacha is now worth £0.0001748 which means that 1GBP is worth 5,719.72 Zambian kwacha!) I was very proud of this supposedly precious jewellery collection but was disappointed when an amused customs officer at Heathrow airport later declined to charge me any duty on them as they were worth so little! We also bought a motley array of clay figurines, woodcarvings, banana leaf paintings and drums. The one item that we didn't buy was copperware as, paradoxically, it was extremely expensive. My star purchase that I was thrilled to own was a Congolese mahogany chair with a flame of Zaire carving on the back. I had bought it for just 11 Kwacha which was a remarkable bargain. Far too heavy to carry back home, I paid the nine Kwacha for it to be sent to London by sea. Thirty years later I am still waiting for it to arrive.

After bidding an exceptionally painful farewell to our hosts, whom we were never to see again, we took a flight to Livingstone where we spent a day admiring the spectacular Victoria Falls. This magnificent waterfall, with water falling down a 100m deep chasm, had been discovered and named in 1855 by the missionary and explorer David Livingstone during his pioneering West to East traversal of Africa. The local population had called it 'the smoke that thunders', and I can certainly see why. You just don't expect to see such an awesome sight so suddenly as you walk through a neat garden full of jumpy and rather aggressive baboons and then through a narrow pathway between the trees. All one can do at that point is stare and let the beauty and spray literally wash through your body. Sixteen years later I saw the Falls from the Zimbabwean side which was equally if not more beautiful to my eyes. Profoundly impressed, later that day we flew on to Lusaka where we quickly found a reasonably priced hotel and spent the next day exploring that pleasant and bright city, including its impressive cathedral, in some detail. While we would have loved to have visited the country's fine game parks, this was not possible as they were closed at that time of the year.

When we arrived back in Nairobi the following morning the full force of Kenya's beauty really hit us. However fair the city had seemed on our first visit, this time round it looked like a kind of colourful urban paradise. Particularly impressive was the elegant Nairobi mosque, the stately Parliament buildings, the trees and flowers adorning the Uhuru highway, the university campus with its colourful bougainvillea and the National Museum. Our pleasure was quashed, however, for a few hours by the unwelcome news that our return East African Airways flight to London had been cancelled. We had always felt that there was something a bit fishy about our tickets. Oliver and I together expressed our outrage and commanded the travel agent to rebook us on another flight at no extra charge, which he did. Soon afterwards we hired a taxi to spend an afternoon at the relatively small, but still impressive, Nairobi game park where I first became aware of what I most loved about the African countryside – the light. As I saw the early evening sunlight and shadows so gently bathe the birds and flowers that thrived in the midst of a large pool I knew that I must and that I really would return to this wonderful continent. What still amazes me is that it took another 15 years for that to happen.

PART TWO

The Fly and the Mouse

CHAPTER THREE

The Problem of Sleeping Sickness

TO ENTER GLASGOW UNIVERSITY'S spacious Veterinary School campus on the Garscube Estate you have to keep a close eye on the traffic lights and turn off carefully from the main Bearsden Road. You then pass through a security checkpoint with a barrier and a narrow winding road that passes though rolling green fields and a network of old and new buildings. If you look a little further still as you continue, the playing fields appear on your left bounded by numerous trees and rich foliage. Just 30 minutes away from the campus is Loch Lomond, leading to the magnificent Trossachs. Two features that often impress the new visitor are the sheer size of the campus and the frequent sights and smells of domestic animals such as dogs, cows and horses; some of them on their way to or emerging from the animal hospital clinics, while others are there to play an important role in the world class research that is carried out here by academic staff. I would also add a third feature – the unfailing courtesy that one encounters from just about everyone connected with the institution.

One of my first contacts with the School was in 1988 when I was asked to give a lecture on a 'slow virus' infection of sheep called *visna-maedi*, first described in Iceland, and a disease that causes the afflicted animals to waste away with pneumonia and a brain infection (*visna* is Icelandic for 'wasting'). No-one there thought it odd or inappropriate that a Professor of Neurology and clinical neurologist like myself should be encroaching upon their own territory to lecture to a group of vets on a natural animal disease. I had been studying *visna* at Johns Hopkins University in Baltimore in the US before returning to Glasgow two years before in 1986. This particular audience contained some of the School's leading lights in science so I was even more nervous than usual when presenting seminars.

Sitting near the back of the small but rather cosy lecture theatre was a man of about medium height in his late forties with a very friendly open face and manner and also a remarkably intelligent and penetrating gaze. He seemed to be listening to everything I was saying with intense concentration. His questions to me at the end were as pertinent and challenging as I had expected and I gave the best answers I could think of. The man in question was Maxwell Murray who was Professor and Head of the Department of Veterinary Medicine and known to be one of the most scientifically accomplished and charismatic professors in the university. He was a home grown Glaswegian academic who had first trained as a veterinary surgeon and scientist and then spent 10 years as head of a pathology and immunology unit at a renowned scientific institution in Kenya called the International Laboratory for Research on Animal Diseases (ILRAD). I shall say more about this centre at a later stage. He had then returned to Glasgow University in 1985 to take up the Chair of Veterinary Medicine, two years before I took up my current position.

Max had a long held belief that human and veterinary scientists can learn a great deal from each other and that they should collaborate much more closely than they actually do, a view also held fervently by myself based on my own experience in America working with veterinary colleagues. After I had finished talking we agreed an early date to meet up again to discuss possible research that could be of mutual interest and benefit. He had a strong feeling that my own expertise in immunology and infectious diseases (such as it was) could be brought to bear on his own specialty, African trypanosomiasis, a disease that affects both man (as sleeping sickness) and animals. At the time I had no more than a vague awareness of that disease. So in a nutshell that's how it all began – with a chance meeting.

Shortly after that first encounter we met up in his large office in the Veterinary School to discuss tactics. The office had an enormous oblong conference table that would become very familiar to me as a brainstorming site over the ensuing years and was covered with all kinds of papers, official looking files, books, letters and pictures. In fact it was a model of organised chaos. But what really caught my attention were the dramatic pictures and photographs of African landscapes hanging on the walls. The most impressive, hanging at the back of the office, was a colour image of a herd of buffalos moving forward on an African savannah. At that moment before we even spoke I felt as if I had been transported back 14 years to the Nairobi game reserve, almost a feeling of déjà vu. Max's home in Glasgow is also adorned with a wide variety of similar African pictures and objects (as is mine now, to a lesser extent).

He then launched into a one hour long slide show for my benefit that I found spellbinding. First he gave a lucid description of the history and current situation of animal trypanosomiasis in Africa. That was interesting enough, but what then followed was far more relevant to a human doctor, and that was the worsening problem of human African trypanosomiasis in sub-Saharan Africa. The sheer scale of the infection and its impact on farming and people's health was completely new to me. After he had finished his presentation I was hooked on the subject, and I think he realised that straight away. He had re-ignited a spark of interest that had been kindled many years before. I shall now take some time to tell you what I first learned about this enigmatic tropical infection.

Sleeping sickness in humans and animals has been familiar to mankind for many centuries, possibly even as long as a thousand years ago when camels and horses were inexplicably stricken in sub-Saharan Africa. There is a written record of a mysterious illness particularly affecting sleep in the inhabitants of Western Sudan including Mari Jata, the despotic Emperor of Mali. In 1721 an English naval surgeon, John Atkins, commented on what he called the 'sleepy distemper of negroes' along the coast of Guinea.

A significant milestone was reached in 1803 when a physician working in the West African colony of Sierra Leone called Thomas

Masterman Winterbottom (1766–1859) described a disease in the native population called 'negro lethargy'. Winterbottom was born in England and studied in Edinburgh and, later, Glasgow, where he graduated in 1792. A particular feature of this illness he described was the presence of 'small glandular tumours' in the neck. Slave traders in the region recognised such a neck swelling as indicating poor health in potential slaves that would severely limit their commercial value. The traders would therefore 'either never buy such slaves or get quit of them as soon as they observe any such appearances.' It is now recognised that a visible enlargement of the lymph glands in the region of the back of the neck is a very characteristic feature of sleeping sickness in West Africa and is called Winterbottom's sign after its discoverer. By current standards his descriptions of the illness makes disturbing reading as shown by the following brief extract from his book, *An Account of the Native Africans in the Neighbourhood of Sierra Leone*:

> The Africans are very subject to a species of lethargy which they are much afraid of, as it proves fatal in every instance... The disposition to sleep is so strong, as scarcely to leave a sufficient respite for the taking of food; even the repeated application of a whip, a remedy which has been frequently used, is hardly sufficient to keep the poor wretch awake... the disease, under every mode of treatment, usually proves fatal within three or four months. The natives are totally at a loss to what cause this complaint ought to be attributed...

During the 19th century various theories for what then came to be known as 'sleeping sickness' in Africa were propounded, but it was not until the 1890s that the cause of trypanosomiasis in animals was discovered by David Bruce. But before describing that it is worth noting the insightful contribution that David Livingstone made to this field. He is of course extremely well known to most people as a missionary, doctor, African explorer, scientist and anti-slavery activist, but what is not well known is that he was the first person to treat animal trypanosomiasis with arsenic, a drug that, as we shall see later, is still given to people with the disease, often with terrible side effects.

Born in Blantyre in Scotland in 1813, one would perhaps not have predicted Livingstone's subsequent greatness from his humble origins. At the age of 10, he was put out to work in the mills, but he was single-minded and determined enough to attend night school, and in 1836 he went on to study medicine at Anderson's College in Glasgow. His medical education was undertaken with the intention of becoming a medical missionary, which would require him to study medicine and to become an ordained minister. During this time he also studied Greek and Divinity at Glasgow University. In 1840 he went to London to continue his medical education, and studied at the British and Foreign Medical School, Charing Cross Hospital and Moorfields. Later that year he sat the examinations for the License of the Faculty of Physicians and Surgeons of Glasgow. He was duly admitted as a 'licentiate' meaning that he could practise as a doctor, and was also ordained as a minister the same month. In December 1840 he sailed for Africa, and his subsequent life and career has been recounted in numerous biographies. But a few milestones are worth noting.

In 1841 he joined Robert Moffat's Kuruman mission in South Africa, and two years later established a new mission in Mabotsa where, in 1844, he was attacked by a lion which severely injured his left shoulder and arm which never again regained full function. (Amongst the Livingstone memorabilia currently housed in the Royal College of Physicians and Surgeons of Glasgow is a cast of his left humerus bone (in the upper arm) broken by this mauling.) He married Moffat's daughter in 1845. He crossed the Kalahari in 1849 to find Lake Ngami, and two years later he discovered the upper Zambesi. Between 1853 and 1856 he crossed the entire African interior from the west to the east coast, and was the first European to discover the Victoria Falls. (If you visit the Falls from the Zimbabwean side you will see a fine statue of David Livingstone.)

He returned to the United Kingdom in 1856, but then two years later returned to Africa to explore the Zambesi region further. In 1866 he started the fourth and final phase of his illustrious exploring career when he began to search for the source of the Nile. He reached the shore of Lake Tanganyika in 1869, arrived at Ujiji on that lake the following year, and then in 1871 had his famous meeting with the reporter Henry Stanley. In 1873 Livingstone's health failed and he died in that year. It is not generally well known that he also suffered from severe anaemia from bleeding haemorrhoids. During his lifetime of just 60 years, he discovered numerous lakes and had crossed the entire length of Lake Tanganyika, discovered the upper Zambesi, Victoria Falls and many other rivers, had covered about 29,000 miles and attempted valiantly to abolish the slave trade in Africa.

Of particular interest to our subject was his letter published in the *British Medical Journal* in May 1858 entitled 'Arsenic as a remedy for the tsetse bite'. This title is revealing as it shows that even at that stage there was some idea that a fatal wasting disease in animals occurred within certain latitudes and was related to the bite of the tsetse fly. He starts his letter by referring to his experience in 1847 or 1848 when he treated a horse with arsenic following 'the bite of the tsetse fly'. He goes on:

> A mare... was brought to Kolobeng, after prolonged exposure to the bite of the insect... I gave it two grains of arsenic in a little barley water for about a week, when an eruption resembling small-pox appeared. This induced me to discontinue the medicine; and when the eruption disappeared, the animal's coat became so smooth and glossy that I had imagined I had cured the complaint; for, after the bite is inflicted, the coat stares as if the animal were cold.

He then continues:

> The mare, though apparently cured, continued lean. This I was rather glad of, as it is well known between latitudes 20° and

27° s that, when a horse becomes fat, he is almost sure to be cut off by a species of pneumonia commonly caused the 'horse sickness'. About two months after this apparent cure, the coat began to stare again; but this time it had remarkable dryness and harshness. I tried the arsenic again; but the mare became like a skeleton, and refused to touch the barley. When I tried to coax her, she turned her mild eye so imploringly, and so evidently meaning, 'My dear fellow, I would rather die of the disease than of the doctor', that I could not force her. I got her lifted every morning to feed, and saw her at last perish through sheer exhaustion; and this was nearly *six months* after the bite was inflicted.

There are several interesting points that emerge from this brief description. Livingstone had acknowledged the relation of the animal disease to both latitude and the bite of the tsetse fly, and had observed the usual short duration and fatal outcome of the disease, the novel beneficial effect of the arsenic, the skin rash following therapy, and the severe and miserable side effects of the drug. Later we shall see that the current situation with this drug has not actually changed very much!

The cause of sleeping sickness in both animals and humans was finally discovered during the period 1894 to 1910. In fact, single celled 'protozoan' organisms called trypanosomes had been detected in the blood of animals and humans before this time but had not yet been linked to sleeping sickness. In 1894 there was a major public health problem in Zululand where a fatal wasting disease called *nagana* was wiping out entire herds of cattle threatening economic disaster to the local population. The 'fly disease' in horses, to which Livingstone had referred earlier, was later recognised to be the same as *nagana*. The governor of the area then appointed an already distinguished Scottish microbiologist called David Bruce (later to be knighted in 1909) to use his proven formidable scientific expertise to try to sort the problem out.

Bruce had already discovered the bacterial cause of 'Malta fever', which became known as *Brucella melitensis* after him, and you may well have heard of a disease called 'brucellosis' which present-day farmers are particularly at risk of catching either through exposure to infected animals or through drinking unpasteurised milk. Bruce, ably assisted by his wife Mary, carried out a brilliant and rigorous series of experiments in his first year in Zululand, and in 1895 he managed to show that trypanosomes could be identified in the blood of cattle with *nagana*. Over the next few years he performed a large number of transfer experiments in which, for example, he inoculated blood from infected animals into healthy animals. He was soon able to conclude that the trypanosome parasites were the cause of the disease in cattle, and that healthy wild animals were the host reservoirs of the disease, which was transmitted by the bite of the tsetse fly to domestic animals which then became ill with *nagana*.

The notion of an animal or human 'reservoir' of disease is an important one and is a key element of the transmission, and therefore the control of the disease, as we shall explore later. The key insight that Bruce obtained was the definitive linking of the three elements of the condition, that is, the trypanosome, the disease in animals, and the tsetse fly. In 1899 the trypanosome he had identified was called *Trypanosoma brucei* after him. Bruce initially considered that the fly transmitted the parasites through a mechanical means, but it was later shown that the parasite becomes infective only after it has been progressively altered in the fly's gut. For this and other pioneering work Bruce was elected a fellow of the Royal Society (FRS) in 1899, the UK's highest recognition of scientific achievement.

The next major milestone in this story was reported in 1903 when Aldo Castellani, a talented 24 year old Italian microbiologist from an ancient Florentine family, reported the presence of trypanosomes in the cerebrospinal fluid (CSF) and blood of patients with sleeping sickness. The CSF is the fluid that is present and circulates in the cavities called ventricles inside the brain and also between the covering layers of the spinal cord. If an organism is detected there it is unequivocal evidence that the central nervous system (known as the CNS) has been breached and invaded. The history of this discovery, however, has remained somewhat controversial since it was first reported.

The Royal Society, very concerned about a serious outbreak of sleeping sickness in people in Uganda, despatched to Entebbe in 1902 the First Sleeping Sickness Commission, consisting of Castellani and two other men, Doctors Low and Christy. Castellani had the great insight to use a piece of apparatus called a centrifuge, which spun the human CSF specimens at very high speeds, to help him isolate any microorganisms that might be lurking there in very small quantities. The spinning motion of the centrifuge causes a very small pellet to be deposited at the bottom of the test tube, and this pellet may contain disease-causing organisms. Initially he did detect these in some of the CSF specimens, both trypanosomes and also some streptococci bacteria, which are very different types of microorganisms that cause, for example, tonsillitis and many other infections that can now be treated with antibiotics (unlike trypanosome infections). The Royal Society was generally supportive but rather sceptical about the actual significance of Castellani's findings. Soon afterwards, David Bruce was sent out to Uganda to assist Castellani in his investigations, and they eventually met up in Entebbe. The work on identification of trypanosomes in patients' blood and CSF then proceeded at an accelerated pace and Castellani's findings were confirmed and extended. In March 1903, after Castellani had returned home, the second Sleeping Sickness Commission, which included Bruce, was despatched to Entebbe to continue the work. Before very long it was established beyond any reasonable doubt that the trypanosome was indeed the cause of human sleeping sickness.

Unfortunately that is not the end of the story. An unpleasant and to some extent still ongoing controversy then followed about Castellani's exact role in identifying the trypanosomes as the cause of sleeping sickness. While there has never been any doubt whatsoever that he was the first person to identify trypanosomes in the blood and CSF of individuals with sleeping sickness, it was felt by Bruce, and also some others, that Castellani had probably not completely appreciated the aetiological significance of his findings which only fully came to light after Bruce had assisted him with his investigations. This situation, of course, is not that uncommon in science, where several individuals feel that they have contributed to a discovery.

Understandably, Castellani was keen to be considered the sole discoverer of the cause of sleeping sickness. There has even been a film by the Wellcome Trust about this controversy between the two men called 'Entebbe Encounter'. Castellani went on to have a highly eventful and extremely illustrious career, and 'Professor Sir Aldo Castellani' (he received an honorary KCMG from King George V in 1927) died in 1971. During his fascinating life he was Mussolini's doctor for 20 years, and acted as Royal Physician and friend to the exiled Italian King Umberto and his family. In 1973 Sir John Boyd wrote a penetrating and meticulously researched article on the Castellani-Bruce controversy that I have read in some detail. Overall, it seems very clear to me that Castellani's first description of trypanosomes in the blood and CSF of sleeping sickness patients was a fundamental landmark discovery in the history of tropical medicine. There does also appear to be some compelling evidence that he was subsequently assisted to a greater or lesser extent by Bruce in the interpretation and further development of his findings. I have to say that if the latter interpretation is correct, then I certainly have no problem with it. It seems to me to be a real pity that this controversial situation ever arose.

Around the time that Castellani was making his observations in Uganda, another major discovery was taking place in The Gambia in West Africa. Dr Everett Dutton from the Liverpool School of Tropical Medicine examined the blood of a European man with a feverish illness and identified trypanosomes under the microscope. In 1902 Dutton named this trypanosome *Trypanosoma gambiense* after the place where the disease had occurred. This organism, which is now known officially as *Trypanosoma brucei gambiense* (usually abbreviated to *T.b.gambiense*), is the cause of what we call West African sleeping sickness. Note that the middle term is named *brucei* after David Bruce. Much work in this area was then undertaken over the next decade by various researchers and our knowledge of the infection steadily grew. Then in 1910 another breakthrough occurred. Two men, J.W.W. Stephens and H.B. Fantham, examined the blood from a patient infected with sleeping sickness in what was then known as northeast Rhodesia, and identified a new species of trypanosome which they called *Trypanosoma rhodesiense* after the location where it occurred. This organism, which is now officially known as *Trypanosoma brucei rhodesiense* (usually abbreviated to *T.b.rhodesiense*), is the cause of what we now call East African sleeping sickness.

An explanation of the current classification of the various trypanosomes is required. The *T.brucei* subgroup contains *T.b.brucei*, *T.b.gambiense* and *T.b rhodesiense*. The first of these is a cause of animal, but not human, trypanosomiasis, but only these last two trypanosomes cause human trypanosomiasis as we have seen. The two most important causes of animal trypanosomiasis are *T.vivax* and *T.congolense* but it may also be caused by *T.b.brucei* as well as *T.evansi*, *T.simiae* and *T.equiperdum*.

What about the trypanosome itself and the life cycle in both its natural host and the tsetse fly vector? The term 'vector' merely refers to the animal – in this case the blood-sucking tsetse fly – which transmits the parasite from the animal or human reservoirs of the disease to the susceptible 'host' animal or human which it bites.

When I say 'reservoirs' I am of course referring to those infected animals, which may or may not have symptoms of the disease, which act as a constant source of parasites in the population or herd which are blood-sucked by the tsetse fly vector, which may then transmit the ingested parasites to a susceptible 'host', which then comes down with the disease.

PLATE 3 shows a rather simplified view of a typical trypanosome.

As you can see it has a characteristic sort of creepy S shape together with a nucleus, a mitochondrion (which is crucial for the energy production of the cell), and a structure called a flagellum. The kinetoplast is a structure which is attached at one end to the 'basal body' of the flagellum and is located inside the mitochondrion. The kinetoplast contains a large amount of deoxyribonucleic acid (DNA) which defines the organism's genetic make-up. Most of an organism's DNA is usually found in the cell nucleus but some of it, as is the case here with trypanosomes, is also found outside the nucleus in the mitochondrion within the cytoplasm.

The flagellum looks like an elongated rod which produces an unusual sort of corkscrew motion that propels the organism along as it moves in the bloodstream and body fluids. That's how it gets around in the organism it has invaded. At the base of this structure is called the flagellar pocket. Scientists at present are very interested indeed in the flagellum because it is important for more than just movement of the parasite. The flagellum is important in determining the overall shape of the trypanosome, and the flagellar pocket, which it 'defines', allows it to interact with the myriad of different molecules that it encounters in its immediate environment. Some of these molecules could be nutrients which the parasite needs to take in to maintain itself, while others could be antibodies which it needs to destroy to ensure its survival. The flagellar pocket is very effective at taking in, surrounding and then breaking down antibodies that may come its way. The flagellum is also required for the parasite to attach itself to the tsetse fly's salivary gland once it has passed through its gut, and for the division of the kinetoplast and its DNA. Being a protozoan, the trypanosome is a single celled organism, but the apparent simplicity is somewhat deceptive as it is actually a highly complex organism which is a consummate little predator capable of wreaking havoc in vast swathes of Africa. It also has an uncanny knack of constantly evading the protective immune response of its host – but that we shall explain in another chapter when we will also talk about its genetic make-up.

How big is a trypanosome? On average it is about 20 micro-metres long. One micrometre is one millionth of a metre, or one thousandth of a millimetre. So if you drew a line just one centimetre long then, assuming you could persuade the trypanosomes to completely straighten up for you (which I am sure they wouldn't even if you asked them nicely), then you could fit about 500 of them into that little line. If you then drew a line one metre long then you could fit about 50,000 trypanosomes into it. A trypanosome is also roughly three times as long as a red blood cell which means that they are readily visible under an ordinary light microscope that is capable of visualising a regular blood smear. However, you normally need to treat the blood smear with a special stain in order to show up the parasite. PLATE 3 shows what an infected blood smear on a glass slide looks like under the microscope where the stained trypanosomes are easily identifiable. This size is actually quite big (as micro-organisms go) especially if you compare it with, say, the Herpes virus Type 1 that causes cold sores which is actually one of the larger sized viruses. You could fit about 100,000 Herpes virus particles in a one centimetre line and as many as 10 million of them in a line one metre long. So that's quite a difference.

So what do we need to know about the life cycle of the try-panosome in the tsetse fly and the human host? The vector for the disease is the tsetse fly of the genus *Glossina*, and the latest estimates are that there are at least 31 different species of tsetse fly which are restricted to Africa. However, a fossilised tsetse fly has been discovered in Colorado and has been shown to be 35 million years old! Tsetse flies are conventionally classified into three groups broadly based on the type of habitat where they are found. The *fusca* group of flies infest the forested regions of West and Central Africa. The *palpalis* group occur in the wet 'riverine' areas as well as forested regions throughout Africa. The third group are the *morsitans* flies which are distributed in the savannah regions. However, only about eight of these species are economically important, and at least six can transmit the disease to humans. In fact, all the species of tsetse fly can transmit trypanosomes but their significance as vectors for human and animal diseases varies. Strictly speaking, it is not possible to say for sure that some species can transmit only the human and some only the animal disease parasites. The species that are important as human vectors are thought to have co-evolved with human habitats. We shall find out more about the various control measures to combat the tsetse in a later chapter when we visit an animal field station. A close up view of this rather unpleasant insect can be seen in the photo section.

PLATE 4 summarises graphically the parasite's life cycle, including the technical names for the various parasite forms. Let's start at the point when the fly bites an infected host shown at the bottom and left of the diagram. Colleagues of mine who have been bitten, but fortunately not infected by, a tsetse fly tell me that the bite is extremely painful. I have, so far at least, never been bitten myself. Clearly they have no taste. The blood-sucking fly thus takes from the infected human or animal host a 'blood meal' which contains forms of the trypanosome which are called 'trypomastigotes'. After ingestion, the parasites then undergo a complex and progressive series of changes in both their shape and metabolism as they pass through the fly's gut. Initially the ingested parasites are not infective but become so as they pass through the fly's midgut where the infection is initially established. These long slender forms then leave the midgut and transform into another form which then move up to multiply in the fly's salivary gland. In turn, these forms of parasite develop into yet another short stumpy *infective* form which enter the bite wound of the host through the fly's mouth. On average, flies become capable of transmitting the infection three weeks after feeding on an infected host. This whole cycle is probably only successfully completed in about one in 10 tsetse flies, and about 2–10 per cent of all flies in an endemic area are infected with trypanosomes. Once infected, a fly remains infective for the rest of its life so that man/fly contact is a crucial component of the disease. Some species of tsetse fly, such as the *fusca* group, have a greater tendency to take 'blood meals' from humans and hence are very important vectors.

So that's what happens in the fly. What goes on in the human host after it has been bitten and infected? This is summarised at the top and right part of the diagram. The injected infected parasites enter the bloodstream and transform into the form called trypomastigotes. These forms then multiply throughout the body fluids such as the blood and lymph fluid and spread to many organs within the body such as the spleen, liver, lymph glands, endocrine system, skin, heart and eyes causing a whole host of clinical problems. After an interval of weeks to many months the trypanosomes eventually reach the central nervous system (known as the CNS, as you will recall) to cause a bewildering array of nervous system disorders.

We will discuss all the clinical features later, but it should be appreciated that without treatment the infected human patient will invariably die. This contrasts with malaria where the infection is not always fatal, although of course it often is in that condition, especially when it affects the brain. So, we have two stages of sleeping sickness, the *early stage*, also known as the first or haemolymphatic stage, and then the *late stage*, also known as the second or encephalitic stage when the infection has reached the CNS ('encephalitis' refers to an inflammation of the brain). The speed with which these processes occur differs markedly in the two forms of the human disease.

In East African sleeping sickness, which you will recall is caused by *T.b.rhodesiense*, the process is fast with the CNS invaded after three to four weeks and death occurring within three months in the untreated patient. By contrast, in West African sleeping sickness, which you will recall is caused by *T.b.gambiense*, the disease course is much slower, with the CNS being invaded after many months, and the disease may last months to even years in some cases before death. The reason for this difference in disease 'tempo' is probably related to the greater adaptation of the *gambiense* parasite to its human host. Since the trypomastigotes continue circulating in the blood throughout the host infection, a different tsetse fly can then bite the infected person or animal enabling the whole cycle to start all over again. It really is what you might call a vicious cycle.

Different species of tsetse fly transmit the two forms of sleeping sickness. The riverine tsetse flies *Glossina palpalis* (*G.palpalis*), *G.tachinoides and G.fuscipes,* are the insect vectors for transmitting *gambiense* disease. These flies live in dense vegetation along rivers and forests where warm and moist conditions prevail so their distribution tends to be localised to particular areas. Humans are the preferred hosts and are often bitten at water sites, and both humans and domestic animals such as dogs, pigs and goats are important reservoirs of the disease. The *rhodesiense* form of the disease is transmitted by *G.morsitans, G.pallidipes and G.swynnerton* flies which are widely distributed in the woodland areas of the savannahs and lakes in East Africa. The main reservoirs of this disease are wild animals such as antelope, especially bushbuck and hartebeest, although cattle are also domestic reservoirs. Animals which quickly succumb to this more aggressive form of disease are, as you would expect, not good reservoirs because they die before they can assist in transmitting the disease.

Since these tsetse flies are dependent on wild animals, it is not surprising that *rhodesiense* disease is a particular occupational hazard of hunters, fishermen and game wardens in these areas, and also of Western tourists and others who visit the East African game reserves. When one reads in newspapers and medical journals about Westerners developing sleeping sickness it is usually in people who have recently returned from African safaris in East Africa. The geographical distribution of the two types of sleeping sickness are illustrated in the map of Africa (PLATE 5) which also shows the relative incidence of the disease at the present time. As you can see, the four 'hot spots' where there are epidemics of sleeping sickness are Sudan, the Democratic Republic of Congo, Uganda and Angola. Interestingly, these are also countries where wars have waged.

The statistics and epidemiology of sleeping sickness are remarkable. In the first half of the 20th century soon after the discovery of the cause of the disease, the measures taken by colonial govern-ments in Africa to control the disease were pretty drastic, if not draconian. Mass culling of potential animal reservoirs of infection was carried out, and massive areas of land were completely cleared of any vegetation that might harbour the tsetse fly. But it should be appreciated that during this time devastating epidemics of sleeping sickness were literally wiping out entire communities in central and East Africa with hundreds of thousands of deaths in some regions. The surveillance of human cases also progressively improved so that, with all these measures, the disease was virtually brought under control during the period 1949 to 1965 when there were relatively few newly registered cases, with almost no deaths at all from sleeping sickness during 1960 to 1962.

After this relatively golden period the situation progressively deteriorated with an increase in both the incidence and death rate of the disease. There are several likely reasons for this resurgence but almost certainly one of the most important is the decreased level of surveillance of the population at risk. To control the disease it is essential to quickly identify and treat patients with the disease so they are no longer sources of infection for other individuals. The most important cause of the disruption of disease surveillance and con-trol is the socio-economic unrest caused by war. This was seen during the recent war in Angola, and also during the current war in Sudan, when the number of new cases increased markedly. But many other factors also play an important role. These include inadequate finan-cial allocation of critical resources to the disease during peacetime by successive governments, including insufficient measures to control the tsetse fly population; various changes in climate and vegetation which affect the man/tsetse fly contact; increasing parasite resistance to drugs; the emergence of new virulent parasite strains; unpredicted population movements of the animal reservoirs; and changes in host susceptibility to the disease. That's quite a list! Of course these factors don't usually act in isolation but operate simultaneously with a cumulative effect. Over the last few decades there have been several epidemics and localised resurgences of the disease in different regions of the African continent. These are still occurring at this very moment in, for example, regions of Uganda.

The World Health Organisation (WHO) has for some time kept a watching brief on the disease and most of us in this area broadly accept their epidemiological estimates. The often quoted statistics are as follows. The disease occurs in 36 of the 52 African countries, and its distribution is limited to sub-Saharan Africa between latitudes 14° North and 29° South – the so-called 'tsetse belt'. About 60 million people in Africa are at risk from developing the disease, about 300,000 cases have the disease at any one time, and up to around 50,000 people die from the disease annually. Many of those deaths are due to the toxic effects of treatment of the disease. It has been estimated that 100,000 survivors of the disease are left disabled in some way. I should mention, however, that very recent estimates by WHO have suggested that the prevalence of the disease is now coming down significantly due to better surveillance procedures. These more recent incidence figures, and the likely reasons for them, are summarised in Chapter 11.

While many cases of sleeping sickness go unreported to official sources for logistical reasons, it should be appreciated that precise figures for the incidence are difficult to ascertain and we don't actually know for certain just how widespread, or otherwise, the disease really is. Some authorities have very recently told me that the true incidence of sleeping sickness in Africa is now decreasing because of the more effective control measures that have been put in place. Time will tell just how much progress has been made, but clearly this is a promising trend. The area of Africa which is infested with the tsetse fly, or as Max Murray has graphically put it, are 'held captive by the tsetse fly', is about 10 million square km which is one third of the entire land mass of Africa – an area greater than the whole of the USA. Africa itself occupies one fifth of the land mass of the whole world. Farming is impossible or severely limited in these infested areas because of the effect on domestic cattle. This is a tragedy for the African people and also deprives the world's economy of Africa's huge and largely untapped potential.

A very interesting question is how trypanosomes evolved to become such successful predators on human and animals. Naturally, no-one knows for sure because we have only been around for a relatively short time, and the trypanosomes have clearly been around for a very long time. But some very clever scientists using highly sophisticated molecular biology and mathematical models have made some interesting suggestions. Because of the absence of a fossil record our view of the evolution of trypanosomes has to be based on inspired speculation. But it is possible to carry out detailed molecular analyses of the genetic make-up of different species of trypanosomes, and put forward hypotheses as to how and when they evolved.

This sort of 'phylogenetic analysis' has allowed their molecular evolution to be guessed. The resulting 'phylogenetic trees' (which are like family trees except that they are for trypanosomes) obtained using these methods can also be linked to known biogeographical events, thus allowing a possible sequence of evolutionary events, including species divergence, to be reconstructed. Using this ingenious approach – the so-called 'history written in the genes'– Jamie Stevens and Wendy Gibson of the University of Exeter have presented data which are consistent with *T.brucei* and *T.cruzi* (which you will remember causes Chagas disease in America) having shared a common ancestor about 100 million years ago. Furthermore, they suggest that *T.brucei* may have shared the long period of primate evolution which resulted in the eventual emergence of the genus *Homo* (that's us!) about three million years ago. It is also presumed that our *Homo* ancestors during all this time were in constant contact with the ancient versions of the tsetse fly so that the eventual fates of man, the fly and the parasite were intimately linked.

But how can we explain what we think is a much greater adaptation of the *T.b. gambiense* parasite to we humans, compared with *T.b.rhodesiense*? After all, while the former parasite can produce a protracted, even chronic, infection which eventually kills us, the latter parasite usually kills us within a few weeks or months at the most. Presumably it must again relate in some way to our physical proximity to the different parasites as we evolved over millions of years. Susan Welburn, Ian Maudlin, and their colleagues at Edinburgh University have recently suggested an elegant explanation of how this may have occurred. If you look again at the African map showing the prevalence of sleeping sickness you will note the diagonal black line separating the East and West African diseases. It turns out that this line demarcates in a vertical direction the western edge of the African Rift Valley. Their suggestion is that the current distribution of the disease might reflect a series of climatic changes that occurred in this area about five million years ago when much of both West and East Africa was heavily forested.

The effect of climate changes would have been to reduce the forests and increase the dry savannah areas of East Africa. Our ancestors, the apes, and then the early hominids, would then have been brought into close contact with unfamiliar trypanosomes distributed in these savannah regions, that is, the virulent *T.b.rhodesiense* population that had become established in animal reservoirs and then became a major threat to these early humans. Meanwhile, in the still heavily forested regions to the west of the Rift Valley, where *T.b. gambiense* was prevalent, there would have been millions of years for apes and then the early hominids to adapt to this less virulent trypanosome. Consistent with this scenario is the presence of what is known as the SRA gene that can now be detected in *rhodesiense*, but not *gambiense*, trypanosomes. This gene allows the parasite to be resistant to the action of a factor normally present in normal human blood which destroys the circulating parasites. If this resistance gene is present, then clearly it would make the parasite more dangerous to the host. Despite the fact that these two different types of sleeping sickness exist, it should be appreciated that they can't actually be strictly defined by their geographical distribution. The reason I say this is that both types of sleeping sickness can be present in different regions of the same African country, as is the case right now in Uganda.

Fast forwarding a few million years, this is what I learned about human African trypanosomiasis from Max in those first few months after my lecture at the Veterinary School. The problems which needed to be solved seemed to me both difficult and fascinating. We quickly wrote an application for a research grant to what was then known as the European Economic Community (EEC), the forerunner of the modern European Union (EU). It was quite straightforward to write since it was to use well-recognised immunological approaches to an established mouse model of sleeping sickness, to which we will come back later. To our surprise and delight, the application was funded. We soon had a second stroke of good fortune in recruiting a highly talented and enthusiastic young post-doctoral scientist called Chris Hunter who proved to be exceptionally productive over the ensuing three years. Without that flying start that Chris gave us I rather doubt that the work would ever have been so successful. He was recently made a full Professor in the Veterinary School of the prestigious University of Pennsylvania in Philadelphia, an achievement that came as no surprise to us. After Chris left in 1992, the sleeping sickness research group that Max and I established in 1988 was later joined by a series of gifted young scientists and graduate students, many of whom I shall mention as we go on.

Despite all this, our work on sleeping sickness was almost scuppered by political events before it had even begun. In 1989 the Riley committee, chaired by the late Sir Ralph Riley, an eminent scientist who had made seminal discoveries in plant genetics, carried out an investigation of the six veterinary schools in the United Kingdom to see how veterinary education should be best structured and delivered. For reasons that continue to escape me and everyone else I know, they wrote a report which recommended that two of the finest Schools, those at Cambridge and Glasgow Universities, should be closed and amalgamated with the remaining Schools.

As you can imagine, this caused a storm of protests both from the two Schools themselves and many other quarters, some of whom had little or no formal links with these institutions. Glasgow University mounted a formidable and highly effective campaign against the proposed closure of its Veterinary School. As a result, the Conservative government of the day did not accept the Committee's recommendations. So in the end, Glasgow Veterinary School was not closed and it has continued to go from strength to strength.

CHAPTER FOUR

Africa Revisited

DECEMBER 1988. The departure lounge at Heathrow airport for the British Airways flight to Nairobi seemed to contain little of the seasonal spirit of Christmas. Yet it was strangely energised by the hustle and bustle of the steady influx of passengers, many of them clearly excited by the prospect of visiting or returning to East Africa. Some of these travellers, like my Veterinary colleagues Max Murray and Frank Jennings, were old hands at this game, but others, such as myself, were nervous with the novelty of what was to come. What intrigued me most was the prospect of matching my distant memories of Africa as a medical student with a city that promised so much in all kinds of ways. But I was encouraged by one thing in particular, and that was the evident mood of high anticipation that my two friends radiated. Their memories, accumulated over decades of work in the African field, would soon merge with experiences that would begin a new adventure for all of us. The old and the new were about to meet in more ways than one. There were two reasons for this visit. We were to attend an important five-day international symposium on African trypanosomiasis, and we would also establish contact with Kenyan research colleagues who would work with us on the project we had just started. While Max knew all of these people from his long association with Africa, at that time I had only met two of them, and that was only briefly at a social occasion in Glasgow.

The nine hour nocturnal ordeal of the long haul flight passed more quickly and less painfully than I expected, and the following morning we emerged bleary eyed into the bright Kenyan sunshine, a striking and welcome contrast to the damp cold of a typical Glasgow winter. But this time there were no incidents. We were met by Paul

Sayer, a highly respected and accomplished veterinarian and scientist, who grew up in Kenya and was a 1964 Glasgow Veterinary graduate. He was working at the time as a senior scientist at KETRI, an acronym for The Kenya Trypanosomiasis Research Institute, about which we will have a good deal to say later. Paul and his wife Elma had known the Murray family for many years and I have got to know Paul so well that somehow my frequent visits to Kenya never seem quite right unless he is in town. A trim and distinguished looking man, he has been very helpful with our research and a fine friend whenever I have run into any kind of difficulty during my visits. He radiates charm and common sense, and almost seems to provide a zone of safety for all those in his vicinity. He is a good friend indeed to have in Africa.

The car journey from the international airport to the centre of town takes about 20 minutes. The road is rather dusty and busy, and after dark, 'car-jackings' by robbers are a potential hazard, although less so in recent times after road lighting along this route was improved by the new government. I then beheld for the first time the Tudor style façade of the famous Norfolk Hotel. Much has been written about this hotel as it has a history that is intimately connected with the history of Nairobi and Kenya itself. Opened in 1904, it was a dynamic meeting place in the early 20th century for a whole host of 'movers and shakers' of the time that included individuals such as Lord Delamere, the famous pioneer and politician of Kenya after whom the evocative front terrace and bar was named; President Theodore Roosevelt; Neville Chamberlain and Winston Churchill, to name but a few. During both World War I and II, the hotel was an important meeting place for leading military and political personnel, and it has remained to the present day a key focus of social activity for both local people and visitors to Nairobi.

What really impressed me was not so much any outward semblance of luxury, but the powerful ambience that radiated from every corner of its evocative buildings and gardens, as if Kenya's colonial past was speaking to me and saying 'This is where important world events occurred'. And indeed they did. The owners had also placed all kinds of startling memorabilia within the hotel including a rather primitive radio set in one of the dining rooms, and a rickshaw, ox-wagon and an A-model Ford Roadster in the garden. Although I have always felt extremely safe within the borders of the hotel, especially when one considers the lack of personal safety outside the hotel in the city of Nairobi itself, one should remember that as recently as 1980 the hotel's West Wing, including some of the Delamere terrace, was destroyed by a powerful terrorist bomb with tragic loss of life. Also, in the 1990s, during disturbances in the city, the spectre of tear gas reached the Delamere terrace, so it has never been a stranger to potential danger. Yet it is difficult to feel any sense of that danger now. It is so easy for visitors and well-heeled locals to pass the time with drinks, a leisurely meal, and congenial company. Meanwhile, the world carries on in the busy road in front of the hotel where a seemingly endless cycle of mini buses and Land Rovers pick up or offload armies of eager tourists from all round the globe.

Although the Norfolk is now rightly regarded as a very luxurious hotel, indeed one of the 'leading hotels in the world', I always preferred it as it used to be when I first visited. That was before the extensive refurbishments and new developments had taken place in the 1990s. While in those relatively early days the air conditioning and the TV in our small rooms tended not to work too well, somehow I always liked it more that way. But this is in no way to diminish the hotel's unique place in the past and current history of Nairobi. Over the years I have spent progressively less time there as I have become more involved in work further afield. But I use it as a Nairobi base whenever I can, and when I do stay there I always ask to be placed in the older part of the hotel. One of the photographs in that wing is that of Denys Finch-Hatton who was portrayed so effectively by the actor Robert Redford in the highly successful film *Out of Africa*. I have to say that I never saw any physical resemblance between the two but I suppose that doesn't really matter.

The origins of Nairobi are interesting. It came into existence when the East African railway system was built in 1899. Prior to then it was virtually uninhabited. Various accounts suggest the area was a favourite grazing and watering area for cattle and other animals. The swamp land where the early engineers set up camp as a rail depot was named by the local Maasai *'Ewaso Nai beri'*, meaning 'place of cold water'. To those working on the new rail system the spot was known as 'mile 327', a point midway between Mombassa and Kampala. The line from Nairobi to Lake Victoria was part of this 600-mile railway across East Africa that earned the nickname 'Lord Curzon's Lunatic Express'! With the building of the railway, Nairobi became increasingly prosperous, and over time several new administrative buildings and hotels emerged. It became the capital of British East Africa in 1907, and as British colonials explored the area, many set up home in the suburban areas. Nairobi then expanded to become one of Africa's largest cities.

Whenever I first arrive in Nairobi I always feel rather light headed and slightly breathless on exertion for a few days, due to its high elevation at 5,450 feet above sea level. This brought back my memories of altitude symptoms in Chililabombwe in Zambia, although that was 1,000 feet lower than this. Close to the magisterial Rift Valley, Nairobi is surrounded by magnificent mountains with the Ngong Hills to the West, Mount Kenya to the North and Mount Kilimanjaro to the South East.

The evolution of Kenya has not been without conflict, and towards the end of World War II there was growing tension between white settlers and the Kikuyu people (the largest group in Kenya). Some extremists within the Kikuyu turned against others suspected of being on the government's side. The Mau Mau rebellion caused a huge death toll among the Kikuyu, and Jomo Kenyatta was sent to prison because of it. Two years after his release he was made President when independence occurred in 1963.

Nairobi's current population is around 3.2 million with about a third living in Kibera, one of the city's most deprived areas. The site of Kibera was originally given to a group of Sudanese people in recognition of past military service but over time several other tribes moved in. I have seen at first hand several of these deprived areas and always feel very uneasy for all kinds of reasons when driving through the shanty towns. Unfortunately the crime rate continues to rise in this beautiful city.

Opposite the Norfolk Hotel, an area around which I feel perfectly safe while walking, is an administrative building of the University of Nairobi, an elegant and imposing group of connected buildings and gardens including my favourite red and scarlet bougainvillea on the outside part lining the Harry Thuku Road. (The latter is named after a political prisoner in whose cause violent riots took place outside the Norfolk in 1922.) I always like strolling through that building whenever I can.

It should be appreciated that there has been a long and close association between Glasgow University and the Nairobi Veterinary and Medical institutions, one that has had a lasting influence on the way in which scientists and teachers from the two cities have worked with each other over the years. In 1963, a high powered group from the Glasgow Veterinary School under the leadership of the charismatic Ian McIntyre, the School's powerful and influential Dean, established a new Veterinary degree course in what was then the fledgling Veterinary School in Kabete, a suburb of Nairobi. The Veterinary course was highly imaginative and innovative for its time and was known as the 'Conversion Course', and owed much to Ian McIntyre's drive and leadership qualities. This course was so named because it involved the 'conversion' of animal health assistants to the status of vets. There were 30 students from the East African federation (Kenya, Uganda and Tanzania), and when recently asked about it, McIntyre recalled that it was the 12 students from Uganda who were the best. The course lasted four terms over one year and there was an extra term of tuition for those who failed the final examination the first time. The course was paid for by the Rockefeller Foundation.

Max, Paul and Frank had worked at that School in the early 1960s. Until then, the Veterinary course was carried out in Makerere University in Kampala, Uganda. This led in 1964, one year following Kenya's independence, to the production of the first ever graduates (40 veterinary surgeons) of the University of East Africa. Until that time there had only been two such graduates. The University of Nairobi, which was the first national university in Kenya, was then established in 1970. Throughout the last 40 years, scientists from Scotland, especially those working in Glasgow, have continued to establish and maintain academic links with colleagues in Nairobi, both in government research institutions and in University departments. This association has been particularly strong in the field of parasitic diseases in man and animals, including African trypanosomiasis and East Coast fever.

The training of medical students in Kenya also owes a great deal to visiting specialists from Glasgow institutions. In 1966, a team of clinicians from Glasgow helped to establish medical training programmes in Nairobi which would lead on to the establishment of its Faculty of Medicine, formed in 1967 when it admitted its first students. A vivid account of this adventure was given by Noel Blockey, one of these visiting medical doctors. The original idea came from Sir Charles Fleming, the then Dean of the Glasgow Faculty of Medicine, who proposed that a team of clinicians should train Kenyan students in Nairobi.

The initial reconnaissance to East Africa was undertaken by four senior distinguished academics (Charles Fleming, Thomas Symington, Roland Barnes and Edward Wayne) who met with the then Kenyan Minister of Health to agree on the best location for this endeavour. Nairobi was chosen, and volunteers from Glasgow were given permission to leave their current appointments without having their contracts terminated. They were given a 25 per cent 'inducement allowance', additional to salary, a tropical suit, assistance with basic teaching equipment and appropriate housing in Nairobi. An arrangement for personal transport with a local garage was also set up for the duration.

About 30 physicians and surgeons in total from Glasgow University and hospitals came over a period of six years to work and train Kenyan students and doctors. But most of this group stayed for six to 12 months, although a few remained for longer periods to maintain continuity. These doctors practised Glasgow teaching hospital methods to students and registrars (qualified doctors in training), and many travelled widely in the country visiting both provincial and missionary hospitals. The main government hospital where they practised and taught had been named Kenyatta National Hospital after Jomo Kenyatta, and indeed at the present time the University of Nairobi Medical Faculty's clinical work is carried out at this same hospital at the College of Health Sciences, which was created in 1985. So you can see why Glasgow University is still held in such high regard in Kenya. In fact these Glasgow initiatives in the 1960s established what Max calls the 'Glasgow Mafia' in East Africa. Unquestionably, the 'Veterinary Conversion Course' led by McIntyre, and the subsequent medical initiative led by Charles Fleming, represent one of the major higher educational and research developments that have occurred in Africa in the 20th century.

A notable graduate of the Veterinary Medicine Faculty of the University of Nairobi, whom I came to know extremely well over the years, was a very talented and industrious young man called Joseph Mathu Ndung'u. You will recall his name from the beginning when I was involved in a car accident during a later visit to Western Kenya. Born and raised in Nyeri, about 170 km north of Nairobi, Joseph was the protégé of Dr Adriel Njogu, the first Director of KETRI, where the conference we were attending was being held. I had met both Joseph and Adriel at Max's house in Glasgow a few months before. Adriel has been described by Max as 'one of the world's great gentlemen', a view that I can confirm is true. He was a very relaxed, gentle and courteous man of the highest integrity who had been a superb founding director. He had an enchanting, lilting manner of speaking, which always rather intrigued me, and he did everything he could to make us welcome. Joseph Ndung'u had been seconded to Glasgow University for three years from 1987 during which he studied for his PhD degree. For his research he studied heart damage in an experimental model of African try-panosomiasis. Elegant in appearance and manner, rather slightly built, and exceptionally bright and able, it was immediately obvious to me when I first met him that his qualities as a person and a scientist would rapidly propel Joseph to the top of his profession. As it turned out, that happened even faster than I had anticipated.

After we had rested and recovered from the rigours of the long flight, Max, Frank and I drove in our rented car to KETRI for the start of the conference. Throughout the day, especially in the mornings, the roads leaving Nairobi are usually clogged up with ferocious traffic jams, particularly near the city roundabouts where it is 'every man for himself'. Road traffic accidents are frequent in these parts, and the situation was certainly not helped by the numerous adults and youngsters of all ages who tried to sell newspapers or their windscreen wiping services to passing drivers. Eventually we escaped from the city's chaotic fever and passed through several townships, some pleasant green countryside which my two friends recognised from their previous work in Kenya, and then finally to Muguga, about 30 km to the west of Nairobi.

There was a signpost pointing towards KETRI on the left side of the main road which we followed as it led us down through a narrow thoroughfare with a motley array of modest shops and small multi-coloured dwellings. We continued slowly and carefully for a couple of miles and soon descended into a wider road with a striking view of the surrounding countryside that contrasted sharply with what had gone before. At one point on our right was a sign pointing to the Kenya Agricultural Research Institute (KARI), which I would get to know in the future. Our path then led to a horseshoe shaped road through a small picturesque valley which eventually led, via more winding paths, to a series of bumps that our car cautiously negotiated. At last we ascended a hill that led to the security gate guarding the entrance to KETRI. The drive seemed more like an exploration than a journey. We were duly saluted by the guards and then politely waved through to enter the campus.

As we drove up the hill to the main administrative buildings I was enchanted by the attractiveness of the colourful flowers and bushes that adorned the extensive network of internal roads and paths that separated the modern stone buildings. A vista of rolling green hills and farmlands surrounded the institute, and I had not appreciated just how wide an area it encompassed.

So what was this striking place all about? Let me give you some facts and figures that will help put our experiences into context. KETRI was formed in 1977, and two years later became one of the six semi-autonomous research institutes established to promote research and technology development in Kenya. The mandate of KETRI is very clear and is 'to carry out research into all aspects that would eventually lead to the effective control of human and animal trypanosomiasis and to effective reclamation of tsetse-infested lands'. (I should mention at this point that KETRI was reconfigured in 2004 as the Trypanosomiasis Research Centre, or TRC, when it also became part of KARI, but that does not impact on what I have to say about KETRI as I knew it during the period covered in this book.)

The headquarters was based, as we have seen, in Muguga, and comprised the Administration, Primate, Epidemiology, Entomology, Pharmacology and Biochemistry divisions. It was very well staffed with over 700 people when I first visited in 1988, and this total grew to about 900 in the mid-1990s, following which the total staff numbers were substantially rationalised and reduced to around 450 to 500 when Joseph Ndung'u took over as Acting Director in 1995, and then Director from 1998 to 2004. The physical facilities were modern and spacious, especially the Primate unit, where during this first visit Paul Sayer, who was in charge of the unit, showed us the primate model of sleeping sickness which has been used very effectively for extensive drug screening and testing. The whole suite was very modern with a separate quarantine building, and was staffed by highly trained and experienced individuals.

The institute carried out a very wide range of activities in man and animals. These covered the epidemiology of African try-panosomiasis, the investigation of trypanotolerance (an important and innate genetic trait of some animals to resist the development of anaemia and persistent parasite levels in the blood), the manage-ment of the disease and the development of new drug treatment in man and livestock, carrying out research on various aspects of try-panosomiasis, and then the dissemination of research findings and materials to relevant people all over Africa and the world. Training of researchers and technical staff as well as the organisation of seminars and workshops was an important activity for which there were excellent conference facilities at Muguga. That's quite a remit!

KETRI also had extensive national and international links with other institutions. The former included ILRAD (International Labo-ratory for Research in Animal Diseases), where it will be recalled that Max worked for many years, and this included collaborations with scientists from all over the world. As well as these facilities, there were two fly-proof barns on the site at Muguga, capable of holding up to 24 and 64 cows in individual stalls respectively. There was also a dairy herd which produced milk for the staff. The large laboratory and state of the art animal radioisotope facility was inaugurated during that first visit of ours in 1988. I vividly remember the protracted ceremony with its customary polite and gracious formalities by senior institute and management staff, as well as visiting government and foreign dignitaries, including a representative from the International Atomic Energy Agency – the IAEA (try saying that quickly!) – which had funded the facility. Slow to get started and punctuated by long speeches, I wondered when it was going to end. Unfortunately I was seated under the full glare of the mid-morning sun which steadily and ruthlessly burned my unprotected neck. I was too polite and anxious to get up and leave, something that would have gone down very badly, so I suffered and burned in silence. My neck is starting to hurt even as I write this.

KETRI also had a human sleeping sickness treatment centre with clinical and laboratory facilities at Alupe in the Western Kenya district of Busia, about which we will have a great deal to say in the next chapter. There were also two animal field stations that were part of the institute. I was to visit one of these, at Nguruman to the South, a decade later, where I would lose a few pounds but gain a few insights into animal reservoirs and tsetse fly control. The other station was located at the Galana Ranch in the eastern coastal region of the country, a place I have yet to visit.

The Muguga site, which is very extensive with a township, schools and houses, had a distinguished scientific history even before KETRI was established. I am referring here to EAVRO, the East African Veterinary Research Organisation which was established in the early 1950s with the main remit of developing vaccines for animal diseases. One of its most notable achievements was the development of a vaccine for an extremely important disease affecting cattle called rinderpest. A key researcher involved in this work was Walter Plowright who later became a Fellow of the Royal Society for his scientific achievements. I was interested recently to come across a copy of the EAVRO annual report for 1956/7 where the staff list included both Walter Plowright and George Urquhart, who became a good friend as I recall below.

Back to our African trypanosomiasis conference in the stylish and spacious conference centre at KETRI, where we were warmly greeted by Adriel, Joseph who was taking time off from his doctoral work in Glasgow, and a large number of local and visiting veterinary scientists. While I didn't know anyone at all, Max seemed to know just about everyone at the conference and Frank knew quite a few. As well as the scientific delegates from Kenyan and overseas universities, research institutes and other organisations, there were representatives from the pharmaceutical industry, and from cognate government departments. Perhaps it was the fine December weather with bright morning sunshine and tropical warmth that helped make that first contact with sleeping sickness researchers so memorable. Or maybe it was the excitement of Africa revisited itself after so many years and the cultural diversity of the delegates that I found so invigorating. Probably all had their effect. But whatever generated the fascination that week, it sealed my commitment and lasting obsession with this enigmatic disease that decimates the lives of the rural poor in Africa.

All three of us were assiduous attendees of the conference, and we did not miss a single session. I came to appreciate just how much of the research in this area is geared towards control of the disease in domestic livestock; the efficient monitoring of at-risk cattle herds for disease and their treatment; the development of new drug treatments; and the control of the tsetse flies using traps, baits and insecticide spraying in order to reduce man/fly and animal/fly contact. I hadn't appreciated just how important the study of health economics in relation to this disease was in this area of veterinary medicine. However much I might have thought that trypanosomiasis affects domestic productivity, human health and prosperity, and adversely influences the country's economy, the true dimensions of the problem were far worse than I could have ever imagined. I learned how different animal species varied in their susceptibility to trypanosomiasis, the variability of the presentation of the disease depending on the different trypanosome species and animal hosts, and how the different species of tsetse fly infest different ecological areas. For the first few days, as I came to grips with this new scientific language, I felt very much like an outsider. But slowly my mind and mood adapted to the new concepts. Eventually over the ensuing years I would become able to talk to veterinary scientists about both human and animal diseases without feeling as if I was encroaching on their own intellectual and scientific territory.

Between talks there were the customary coffee and lunch breaks which were ideal for getting to know other delegates, some of whom had lifestyles that seemed very glamorous to me at that time. Some owned and managed farms in the picturesque Kenyan countryside, and others made their living as veterinarians or scientists in different rural areas either privately or working for government institutions. Some worked in wetlands while others worked in the savannahs. It was all new to me and I was intrigued by everyone I met. I was less impressed by what I conceived as 'coffee shock'. I had never encountered this before but it is similar in quite a few of the institutions in Kenya I have come to know. I must explain that the one thing I cannot tolerate anywhere is poor coffee. This is odd as Kenyan coffee is known to be excellent. At the meeting breaks, the coffee was invariably instant with an urn of hot water to make up the cup. That was just about tolerable. But then another urn would deliver hot milk containing sugar, which I last used in hot drinks at the age of 12. The result was torture for me and I would usually prefer mild dehydration to drinking this stuff. Over the following years things improved somewhat and Joseph used to give me hot milk without sugar, which was a kindness beyond measure.

I realised from these platform talks the remarkable extent to which my travelling companion Frank Jennings was highly regarded by his peers. Jovial, modest and self-effacing, Frank, a charming and gentle Northern Irishman, was described to me by Max as being 'the unsung hero of trypanosomiasis', and I soon realised why that was. His experimental work was quoted over and over again during the conference, mainly because of his seminal contributions to new drug therapies for African trypanosomiasis. His greatest contribution in my view was the development of the mouse model of sleeping sickness which mimics very well the human disease, and can be used in all kinds of ways to test the effects of new modes of delivery of drugs and new drug combinations. Much of our research programme is based on this model and we shall devote an entire chapter to it later.

At no stage either then or now has Frank ever blown his own trumpet over his considerable achievements. When a small leaving party was held at Glasgow University to honour him a few years ago he seemed rather bemused and surprised by all the fuss we were making. Max sometimes referred to him as one of the 'big five'. Of course he is not referring to the 'big five' game park animals that everyone is meant to see in Africa, namely, lion, leopard, elephant, rhino and buffalo. What he was actually referring to is that he is one of five co-authors on a very famous scientific paper published in 1960 along with Drs Jarrett, McIntyre, Mulligan and Urquhart. This paper described the first commercially produced parasitic vaccine against the bovine lung worm *Dictyocaulus viviparus* and laid the foundation for modern parasitology. These other distinguished names are also well known in the field. Bill Jarrett, a Fellow of the Royal Society and now-retired Professor of Veterinary Pathology, was Max's mentor in Glasgow and is recognised as being one of the most eminent veterinary scientists and virologists of his generation. Ian McIntyre we have already mentioned in his role as a Veterinary Dean, mover and shaker. He is the only one of the five whom I never met in person.

William Mulligan is an eminent Veterinary Biochemist. The late George Urquhart, who was mentioned before, was a highly charismatic and distinguished Professor of Veterinary Parasitology in Glasgow who accompanied Max and myself on our subsequent trip to Nairobi in early 1990. Students and younger scientists, including myself at that time, were attracted to him like flies despite his rather stern exterior. Why this was I am not quite certain but I think it was due to a winning mixture of his direct and considerate friendliness, very powerful and incisive personality, and strong leadership qualities that were particularly necessary to sustain the demanding research programme that he led both in Glasgow and at KARI in Kenya. Shortly before the end of his life he was the temporary Director of the International Trypanotolerance Centre in The Gambia, an institution with which Max had a long association. George died relatively young a few years ago and continues to be greatly missed by all who knew him.

One thing that I found great difficulty in getting my head

round was the very large number of acronyms that everyone except me seemed to know. I am still trying to learn precisely what they all mean and the situation is not helped by the fact that they have a tendency to change over time. To give you a sense of what I mean, we have already mentioned KETRI, KARI, ILRAD and IAEA. Well, you can add to that KEMRI, KEFRI, ICIPE, ILCA, IPR, LIRI, CGIAR, SIT, SAT, OAU and ODA for a start. We will explain most of these when we come to them but you can see why I was a bit confused. To give you an idea in advance of the acronym evolution, in 1995 ILCA in Ethiopia and ILRAD in Kenya merged to form ILRI; in 2004 KETRI became part of KARI and was renamed TRC; and in 1997 the ODA became DFID. I am sure you get the picture!

During that first visit I also came to understand some of the local attitudes and general approach to life of both the local Kenyans (including white Kenyan citizens such as Paul) and expatriates. Every place I have visited is unique in this regard and I was to become aware over the years of the special ambience of Nairobi. The fact that Max knew many of the local people helped a great deal and over the years I also came to know these people pretty well. While I have avoided any kind of involvement in Kenyan politics I obviously became quite familiar with the local and national tensions that periodically affect this region of Africa. Perhaps the most dramatic example of this was during periods of urban unrest in the 1990s when I became caught up by accident in violent student riots in the city not that far from the Norfolk Hotel where I was staying. There were fires in the city, and it was certainly very scary and added a new and unwelcome dimension to my experience of Africa. On another occasion of minor civil unrest, a few minutes after Paul had dropped me off at my hotel one evening after dinner at his house, his car windscreen on the passenger's side was completely shattered by a stone missile. Had that happened while I was in the car a short while before then I might well have been blinded. But such episodes are rare.

During that visit and over the next few years I would come to know several regions of Nairobi, some poor, and some upmarket such as the smart suburban neighbourhoods of Kabete, Karen and Muthaiga. It was always rather depressing to see the inevitable, but clearly necessary, security guards patrolling the entrances to these homes. But the high crime rate in the city leaves homeowners with no other choice. We have already mentioned Kabete as the site of the Veterinary School, and it was also where Max lived for much of his time in Kenya. Two close friends of his, Ron and Ailsa Wood, also live in Kabete where they run the Kabete Kindergarten, an excellent school that adjoins their large and friendly home. The friendship and hospitality of the Woods have also become part of the Nairobi experience for me. Karen is named after Karen von Blixen who wrote many books under her maiden name, Isak Dinesen, and who became familiar to millions worldwide when brilliantly portrayed by Meryl Streep in the film *Out of Africa*, which was based on the book that made her famous. Karen was married to Baron von Blixen-Finecke ('Bror'), who was famous as a white hunter. In her memoir of her mother Nellie Grant (*Nellie: Letters from Africa)*, the writer Elspeth Huxley made the following observation of 'Blix', as the Baron was also known:

> Blix was known also for his charms as a philanderer, and for his shaky finances. On safari, he chased lions and sometimes ladies, but in between his creditors chased him.

The Karen Blixen museum in Karen is certainly worth visiting. Her elegant home with its finely kept and colourful garden is maintained just as it once was, and the wooden structures of the house and its evocative furniture help induce a sense of closeness to the events that would have occurred there so many years ago. I was particularly struck by the rather primitive looking tin bath that would have had to be filled manually. Another place I have visited from time to time for both lunch and dinner is the Muthaiga Club which was opened in 1914. It has a long colourful history and it was there in 1918 that Karen Blixen first met Denys Finch – Hatton who lived for several years in a cottage at the Muthaiga Club until he moved into her house after her divorce from her husband von Blixen. Even now the place exudes a romantic ambience that has witnessed so many significant events in Nairobi's past. It does this in the same kind of way as the Norfolk Hotel, but to my mind the colonial spirit of the Club is somehow more compelling, intimate and direct. I feel a certain sense of privilege when I visit there. The food there is also excellent!

At the beginning of the trip we visited an area of the Rift Valley to the north of Nairobi. The grandeur and beauty of the Valley has never failed to move me no matter how many times I pass through it. The Rift is a massive crack in the earth's surface, running for about 6,000 km from Northern Syria to Mozambique passing through the Red Sea, Ethiopia, Kenya, Tanzania and Malawi. The Great Rift Valley was formed around 20 million years ago by the subsidence of strips of the earth's crust between parallel faults, a fault being defined as a break in the continuity of a bed of rock by movement along a fracture. This faulting contributes to the stunning and asymmetrical appearance of the landscape. The end result in Africa was a spectacular separation of the Eastern and Western rifts. There is often accompanying volcanic activity, and, indeed, the entire Rift Valley is punctuated by a series of volcanoes. There are around 30 lakes within the Rift system with variation in shape, size, composition, vegetation and wild life. Within the eastern rift in Kenya are the shallow lakes such as Lakes Nakuru, Baringo and Naivasha.

You will remember from the last chapter that ancient geographical changes on the two sides of the Rift Valley may have had a crucial influence on the evolution of the two types of sleeping sickness. Our bipedal ancestors living on the eastern savannah regions would have been exposed to new, more aggressive *T.b. rhodesiense* trypanosomes than those remaining on the forested western side of the Rift. So indirectly these massive geological processes that formed the current configuration of the Rift Valley may well have been key factors in determining the current pattern of sleeping sickness.

There are few sights that can be described as genuinely awe inspiring. In my own case the Victoria Falls in Africa and the Grand Canyon in Arizona are at the very top of the list. But the sight of the Rift Valley from the special vantage point along the Nairobi to Naivasha road is just about in the same league. The discovery of bones from our human-like ancestors, including that of 'Lucy' by Maurice Taieb, Donald Johanson and colleagues in 1974, underpins the anthropological significance of the entire Rift region. And there is, yet again, a Scottish connection to all this. For the part of the Rift Valley in Kenya and the North of Tanzania was first described by John Walter Gregory (1864–1932). Gregory had been a Professor of Geology at Melbourne University before taking up the chair at Glasgow University in 1904 where he remained for 25 years. Sadly he died at the age of 68 when his boat overturned in the River Urubamba while on an expedition in Peru. Among his many publications are *The Great Rift Valley* (1896) and *Rift Valleys and Geology of East Africa* (1921).

During the trypanosomiasis meeting at KETRI, we also managed to visit the world class research institute known at that time as ILRAD. The history of this facility, located at Kabete on a large attractive site about 20 minutes' drive from KETRI, is interesting and I came to know it well over the next decade. The original vision was to bring together in one large laboratory in Africa many of the world's finest scientific minds working on tropical diseases. After several international strategic and political planning meetings had taken place, ILRAD was finally formed in 1974 under the auspices of the Consultative Group on International Agricultural Research (CGIAR). Prominent amongst the driving forces for ILRAD's establishment were Ian McIntyre of Glasgow University, John McKelvey and John Pino of the Rockefeller Foundation. The CGIAR is a strategic alliance of countries, international and regional organisations, and private foundations currently supporting 15 international agricultural centres.

These centres work with national research and civil organisations including the private sector. CGIAR continues to be a powerful group whose current mission is 'to achieve sustainable food security and reduce poverty in developing countries through scientific research and research-related activities in the fields of agriculture, forestry, fisheries, policy and environment.' Max was the first scientist appointed in ILRAD in 1975 and he remained there for 10 years as Head of the Pathology and Immunology Laboratory.

On entering the ILRAD campus for the first time it was clear that, despite the similarities to KETRI, there were also major differences. In both institutions you can feel the very spirit of Kenya, the enthusiasm of its employees, and also perceive a spacious campus and beautiful backdrop of green fields and countryside. But at ILRAD the atmosphere was far more international and geared strongly towards cutting edge veterinary science which was certainly comparable with many of the world's finest research centres. ILRAD was also more luxuriously furnished, the research laboratories were better equipped, and there were scientists working there from all over the world, especially Europe and America. It has a scientific buzz that is so typical of many top research laboratories. The cafeteria food was also very good which was rather unusual.

On entering the security gate one soon noticed the large and elegant official residence of the Director and nearby the smaller but still attractively appointed houses and flats for the employees and numerous visitors. On a very clear day using binoculars it was possible to see the distinctive shape of Mount Kilimanjaro in Tanzania to the south. Max had only left ILRAD three years previously so he was still friendly and in touch with many of the scientists and administrators. The research portfolio of the scientists was wide and included a strong element of basic laboratory science including parasite immunology, molecular biology, biochemistry and pathology. Many diseases were studied including animal trypanosomiasis and other infections such as *Theileria parva* which causes East Coast fever in several parts of Africa. Other people worked on parasite epidemiology, health economics, drug therapy, tsetse control and very much more.

I spent time with a number of the laboratory scientists, particularly the immunologists, and almost felt an element of inadequacy in the face of such talent. Despite this, I seemed to hold my own, just about, and delivered a seminar on viral infections in sheep without too much trouble. I was especially impressed by a young Maasai scientist called Onesmo ole MoiYoi who had spent five years in teaching and research positions at Harvard University before moving to ILRAD as a senior scientist. It was clear to me that he was a rising star of great potential and indeed Onesmo has continued to make important contributions to human and animal health research especially in relation to problems in the developing world. Since 2001 he has been Deputy Director General and Director of Research and Partnerships at an important institution called ICIPE (International Centre for Insect Physiology and Ecology) in Nairobi.

The organisation and general areas of research interest of ILRAD evolved over the years following my first visit. I visited several times during the 1990s, largely because of my shared research interests with the parasite immunologists there, but, as the research focus became more oriented towards epidemiology and health economics rather than my area of laboratory science, my interactions slowly tailed off and my visits diminished. In 1995 the Ethiopia-based International Livestock Centre for Africa (ILCA) merged with ILRAD to become the newly-named International Livestock Research Institute (ILRI). The current vision of ILRI is 'a world made better for poor people in developing countries by improving systems in which livestock are important'. So clearly we are all still working towards the same ultimate goal. At present ILRI maintains the campuses at both Addis Ababa in Ethiopia and Nairobi, and employs 700 staff from about 40 countries with an extensive network of strategic partnerships that are working towards achieving its mission. Thirty years on from its inauguration, the original vision of ILRAD's founding fathers continues to be fulfilled.

That week in Nairobi passed quickly despite our feeling that we had achieved so much in all kinds of ways. My personal affinity for Africa, especially Kenya, had not diminished at all and was actually strengthened, despite an unfortunate event that occurred at the end of the trip. Because of the slightly unclear way in which our travel itinerary had been written, we mistakenly assumed that our flight was scheduled to leave in the early hours of the following morning. We had misread 00.30! In retrospect this seemed a rather elementary mistake, but it is surprisingly easy to do. In reality the flight had departed 24 hours earlier, something which we suddenly discovered whilst in the middle of a farewell late evening dinner at our hotel. No matter how hungry you are, acute anxiety immediately kills the appetite. After the shock of this rather ridiculous error, we raced to the airport and Max used to the full his formidable powers of persuasion and organisation. These were certainly required as the pre-Christmas flights were already heavily booked. The end result was that we managed to return that very night and made it back for Christmas. It cost an arm and a leg to be sure, and we returned to Glasgow in far more style and comfort than when we had left.

CHAPTER FIVE

Sleeping Sickness in the Human Patient

JANUARY 1999 SAW A long awaited return to the Alupe Sleeping Sickness Treatment Centre, and a brief respite from the damp cold of a Glasgow winter. The Centre was part of KETRI and was located in the Busia district of Western Kenya on the border with Uganda. The facility had originally been set up with the help of the US Walter Reed Army Institute as a general hospital for the local population including the provision of care for people with leprosy.

In 1991, the Sleeping Sickness Centre was inaugurated there with an exuberant and colourful all day ceremony that I witnessed first-hand along with my young colleague Chris Hunter and Joseph Ndung'u. This was four years before Joseph became Acting Director of KETRI and he had been allotted, unfairly in my opinion, the unenviable task of video-recording the whole event, a job that he carried out with his usual thoroughness despite having to wear a dark suit on a scorching hot day. I recall the seemingly endless speeches and songs against a backdrop of the clearest blue sky, green forests and multicoloured dresses, headgear and shawls. Our state of dehydration and hunger increased alarmingly during the day until we were finally given refreshments in the early evening. Despite the physical discomfort, I had managed to tour the wards with the knowledgeable medical officer in charge and saw many cases of leprosy and other medical conditions. So my memories of the Centre were rather mixed.

By the time of this belated return to Alupe eight years later Joseph had been the permanent Director of KETRI for nearly two years and was keen to pay the Centre a periodic visit to check on its progress. So it was a great opportunity for me to join him and see patients with sleeping sickness for the first time. Learning about the disease from papers and textbooks is very different to actually seeing real patients with the condition, and it's surprising just how many current researchers have never seen what sleeping sickness is really like and just what it does to people. As an active clinician I realised I was very privileged in this regard, and learned lessons that would never be forgotten.

Our journey started with a customary visit to KETRI where I met up with old friends and colleagues, and felt the exciting buzz of the campus. After we drove from KETRI in Muguga to the airport in Nairobi, we boarded the rather aged, but presumably reliable (so I hoped!), plane for the one hour flight to Kisumu, the city which always acts as our base for our western visits. Moses meanwhile had set off earlier in the day to drive the 350 km overland to Kisumu where we would meet at the airport on arrival. I have never stopped admiring his reliability and equanimity. He and Joseph grew up together in Nyeri but then took different career paths. But they have clearly remained good friends despite the apparent differences in their job status. It's a partnership that works very well and you can perceive the quiet, trusting nature of their longstanding friendship. The flight, which I have now experienced six times, is pleasant and relaxing, apart from one dramatic occasion in 2002 when the pilot had to suddenly abort his landing due to a flock of birds that had blocked the runway. His quiet, reassuring words of explanation worked their magic on the planeload of terrified passengers. One almost expects this kind of hazard when working in Africa.

Arriving in Kisumu is always a pleasurable experience although exactly why this is I am not quite sure. Perhaps it is the relaxed atmosphere that seems almost palpable throughout the whole town, one that officially became a city in 2001. Or perhaps it is because Kisumu always marks the beginning and the end of our visits to the far western regions, and so seems physically and spiritually to encompass in discrete time packages all that we seek to achieve there. Whatever the reasons, I always feel safe and comfortable in this rather sprawling and often humid city.

Like all areas described in this book, Kisumu, the third largest city in Kenya, has its own interesting features. Situated on the Winam Gulf beside Lake Victoria, its origins date back to the building of the Ugandan railway line in 1901, and at that time it was known as Port Florence after the wife of the head railway engineer. Famous ships were built here including RMV *Victoria*. Until about 1977 it was a major port but it then went into decline. More recently, it is enjoying renewed popularity as a major international shipment area for petroleum products. Kisumu also contains a famous museum and a bird sanctuary. Homa Mountain forms a dominant backdrop to the city and within Homa Bay are two islands called Rusinga and Mfangano. Rusinga is special to the Luo people in the region (the second largest tribe after the Kikuyu), as it is said to be the burial place of Tom Mboya (1930–1969) who had been a powerful proponent of Kenyan independence and a rising political star until his assassination. I still have vague memories of my household in London being shocked at his death at that time.

For the first few visits Joseph and I used to stay at the Sunset Hotel by the shores of Lake Victoria. Despite the high humidity and heat, not to mention the fact that the door handles seemed rather old and the rooms rather basic by Western or Norfolk hotel standards, I felt extremely safe and comfortable staying there. I have found during my various travels that the level of luxury does not necessarily match the level of spiritual comfort, and in Kisumu this is particularly true. I was impressed at the way the hotel staff would obligingly spray our rooms in the evening with insecticide (appropriately called 'DOOM') so that after dinner we would return to the sight of mosquitoes dropping en masse from the air onto the floor like stricken dive bombers. It literally rained dead mosquitoes. While rather alarming at first, at least I was never properly bitten while staying there. I learned the essential trick of never leaving my arms uncovered in the evenings and applying strong insect repellent on my ankles and wrists as early as 5.00pm.

But the most remarkable feature of staying there was to be seen at sunset itself, for the hotel was most aptly named. At this magical time the room's view of Lake Victoria was quite beautiful as the distant sun would quickly but gracefully descend and disappear over just a few minutes as your gaze was transfixed on the horizon. No amount of money could either predict or buy that magnificent vision. More recently we have stayed at the equally relaxed and atmospheric Imperial Hotel which I have come to appreciate. But however impressive that view of the sunset was when I first stayed there, by 1999 my view from the hotel room, and from the plane as it descended over the city, was obscured and spoilt by a most unwelcome sight that I can best describe as an amazing thick green carpet over much of the lake's edge. I remember asking Joseph what had happened to the lake and he explained the whole story.

Let's start with Lake Victoria itself. This is the second largest freshwater lake in the world (the largest is Lake Superior in North America). Draining into the Victoria Nile and the White Nile, it sits between the East and the West Rift Valleys, and borders on three countries – Kenya, Tanzania and Uganda. It covers 68,800 square m, is 1,100 m above sea level, and is 100 m at its deepest point. The total length of its shoreline is about 3,440 m. It is difficult to appreciate these dimensions from just one view by the lakeside. Fishing is a thriving industry around the lake with Nile perch and tilapia being the two most popular fish, both reflected in the local hotels' menus. But the fishing industry here was threatened by the invasion of a spectacular looking weed which formed this green carpet on the lake.

Two years before our first visit to the area in 1991 the invasion of Lake Victoria by the water hyacinth had already begun, although we had no idea of this at the time. Exactly how this invasion came about is not known, but a similar problem has been known in South Africa and parts of America and Australia. The invasion of the lake caused all kinds of problems for local fishing and transportation and something had to be done to deal with it. A biological solution was finally devised, and quite a remarkable one at that. Weevils were imported and used to check the inexorable growth of the water hyacinths. The species of weevil used were *Neochetina eichorniae* and *Neochetina bruchi* with a target weevil to plant ratio of five to one. This strategy certainly slowed down new hyacinth growth. In 1999 the World Bank funded the Aquarius Project, aimed at destroying once and for all the hyacinths with machines called 'swamp devils' which remove large quantities (up to 400 tonnes) at any one time. Although the target was to shred 3,700 acres of water hyacinth in one year, this particular task was accomplished in half that time. There was also some help from nature itself in that the local winds helped to blow away much of the remaining vegetation. But despite this ingenious combination of methods devised to get rid of this major threat to people's lives and livelihoods, the problem has not disappeared. Full eradication was not achieved, and the three countries are still struggling to contain the weed whose intensity keeps going up and down like sleeping sickness.

Our schedule for the Alupe visit was usually the same. After breakfast in the invigorating and cool morning air and sunshine, Moses, Joseph and I would drive by Land Rover the 120 km to the Busia District in the north-west where the hospital was located. Even at this early hour, Kisumu had a vibrant, bustling and friendly ambience as we drove through it, and that always put us in a good state of mind for the journey. Soon afterwards, we passed through miles and miles of low, dusky, green vegetation and periodically had to negotiate roads that had been left in an appalling state of repair. Some of the potholes were so large that Moses had to negotiate them with incomparable caution and skill. Once, as we mentioned at the beginning, I was almost killed by one. Some of the other cars and lorries on the road in both directions were driven pretty recklessly so the whole ride could be very stressful, at least for me. My main reaction though to the sight of such disrepair is invariably one of anger rather than fear.

After over two hours of this skilful manoeuvring we were

relieved to see the signpost for Busia, and a few miles before the Kenya/Uganda border we turned sharply to the right along a wide clay dirt road that led to the Alupe Treatment Centre two miles away. Busia itself covers an area of 743 square km, and is situated on the eastern region of the Kenyan/Ugandan border. It used to be part of Tororo, now just a few miles to the west in Uganda and to which we shall return later. Busia's population was 227,561 in 2001 and around 83 per cent live in the rural areas, a factor that has important implications for the delivery of patient care.

At the end of the bumpy road we came to a narrow entrance on the left and drove into the grounds of the small hospital. Alupe has several wards, diagnostic areas and administrative offices, with a total complement of about 48 beds in both male and female wards, and 30 staff members. It does not have x-Ray diagnostic facilities which I always thought was a problem. The general wards were in the leprosy hospital where there used to be two doctors, some clinical officers and nurses. When the number of sleeping sickness cases was small the Alupe Centre would also admit patients with other diseases, which generated some income and kept the staff busy. During my initial visits the sleeping sickness patients were looked after by Dr Matete, who, interestingly, trained in veterinary medicine in Nairobi but had a profound knowledge of all aspects of the disease. He had assistance when necessary from Dr Kisivuli, a medical doctor from a neighbouring hospital in the area. Dr Matete was then succeeded by Dr Sulo, a medical doctor whom I got to know quite well, especially when we started to cross the border to Uganda in later years. The number of sleeping sickness cases seen at Alupe varied considerably from year to year. In the outbreak of 1989 the Centre treated 90 cases compared with just 24 in the previous year. A far higher number of cases were seen at the Livestock Health Research Institute (LIRI) in Tororo in nearby Uganda.

The medical and nursing staff always treated me with the utmost kindness and courtesy, and on one occasion I was over-whelmed by the official welcome the whole hospital gave me after

I had arranged the donation of several boxes of medical supplies to assist them. They certainly know how to make you feel appreciated and welcome in Kenya and I felt like an authentic *Bwana mkubwa*! On every occasion I have learned something new from talking with and observing the patients being treated there, and so gradually I became able to truly understand the nature of the disease at first hand. This has definitely influenced my approach to researching the disease in man and also in animal models.

I now want to describe in some detail to you the typical features of sleeping sickness both in its early stage and in its later stage when the nervous system is invaded.

If you have read about the 1916–27 worldwide pandemic of *encephalitis lethargica*, you might know that it was another kind of 'sleeping sickness' and that, in some cases, it led after many years to a crippling and chronic disease known as post-encephalitic Parkinson's Disease. I have seen a few patients with this condition and it was eloquently and movingly described by the neurologist Oliver Sacks in his book *Awakenings,* which was also made into a fine film. But of course the sleeping sickness that we are talking about is a very different disease that affects the brain in a totally different way.

You will recall that there are two types of human African trypanosomiasis, which is the term that we tend to use interchangeably with sleeping sickness. The two terms refer of course to the same disease in humans. The cases of sleeping sickness that I have seen personally have all been due to *T.b.rhodesiense* which is the East African form. The disease course, it will be recalled, is acute in *rhodesiense* infection, lasting a few weeks to months before death occurs in untreated patients; whereas the disease course is much slower and longer in *gambiense* infection where the involvement of the CNS occurs much later and goes on for many months or even years before the untreated patient finally succumbs.

About one to two weeks after being bitten by the tsetse fly, a skin lesion called a trypanosomal chancre may appear around the bite area, usually on the legs but also sometimes on the arms and upper body. In *gambiense* disease this often occurs in the buttocks as the person is bending over while working in a river. The chancre has a characteristic appearance and starts off as a small nodule and then develops into a painful round, rubbery, red 'papule' projecting above the skin surface. After two to three weeks the chancre fades away by itself. The chancre occurs in up to about half of European victims.

A few hours or days after the chancre has appeared, or one to three weeks after the initial bite, the trypanosomes invade the blood stream, lymph glands and other internal organs. This haemolymphatic phase is known as early, or stage one, disease and can certainly do a lot of damage. At this time the unfortunate victim may complain of a variety of what are known as 'non-specific' symptoms, meaning that they are the kind of symptoms that may occur in many different diseases and are not specific to this one. For example, the patient may complain of headache, fatigue, dizziness, weakness all over, pains in the joints and weight loss. Most, but not all, patients at this stage have a fever that is very variable in character. It may go up and down with no particular regularity, and be associated with bouts of severe shivering (known as 'rigors'). These episodes may be prolonged before stopping for a while and then starting again. Between the episodes the patient may feel much better. This is one of the main reasons why patients with sleeping sickness may be misdiagnosed as having malaria, which also produces intermittent fever and rigors. You can just imagine how such a patient might be mistakenly given anti-malarial treatment, which is soon followed by a natural reduction of the fever, giving a false sense of security. This only serves to delay the real diagnosis of sleeping sickness even further. The situation may be made even worse when both malaria and sleeping sickness occur together in the same person – something I have seen happen in Alupe.

During this early stage there is often enlargement of the lymph glands. This is particularly likely in West African *gambiense* disease where the lymph nodes, as they are called, in the back of the neck are characteristically visible and palpable – the famous 'Winterbottom's sign', named, as you may remember from Chapter Three, after the early 19th century physician who first observed it. As well as the chancre, patients also get other types of skin problems, usually a generalised pinkish skin rash over the body, arms and legs, which tends to appear and disappear several times over a few weeks. This doesn't appear in every case, but has a particular tendency to occur in European people. In about half the cases there is severe itching, although the cause of this is not known for certain. Another very characteristic feature at this stage is a painful swelling of the face, especially in the eye area, technically called facial oedema, as well as swelling of the joints, hands and feet that occurs in about one in six people with the disease.

The heart is also a target for the invading trypanosome. An early warning sign for any heart problem is a very fast heart rate. A significant number of patients develop some degree of heart damage that can lead to actual heart failure. When it does, the result includes swelling of the legs and abdomen, breathlessness, actual inflammation of the heart muscle (called 'myocarditis'), and the collection of fluid in the membranous sac surrounding the heart, something known as pericardial effusion, which can severely restrict the normal pumping action of the heart. Some patients may develop problems with the electrical conduction system of the heart or even an abnormal supply of oxygen to the cardiac muscle, causing 'cardiac ischaemia'. Cardiac insufficiency is one potential cause of the oedema which we mentioned before.

The spleen and liver are liable to damage from the infection. The spleen may be enlarged and sometimes palpable by the medical attendant, which is something that also occurs in malaria, another potential cause of confusion between the two diseases. The patient may suffer from anaemia – a reduced red blood cell (RBC) count with a low haemoglobin level – which may be the result of a process called haemolysis where the RBC are destroyed while circulating in the blood leading to a shortened life span. The liver may be palpably enlarged in sleeping sickness but the development of liver disease bad enough to cause actual jaundice is unusual.

The endocrine system, which is responsible for hormone secretion and regulation, is susceptible to malfunction during the early phase of infection, and this can lead to numerous problems. In men there can be loss of libido and impotence, and I once saw a young, most unfortunate man who, after an otherwise good recovery from early stage disease, was left with persistent total impotence. The cruelty of this illness knows no bounds. Men can also develop prominent breast tissue, which is known as gynaecomastia, as well as a fat distribution in the skin that has the same pattern as females. There may also be a reduction of testicular size, an inflammation of the testes ('orchitis'), and hair loss.

Women may also have their endocrine systems seriously damaged as a result of sleeping sickness. They may suffer from high abortion rates, may be left infertile, and have menstrual malfunction which may return to normal after treatment. Infected women can also suffer from a variety of problems related to childbirth. They may have premature births, stillbirths or loss of their babies in the immediate period after birth. Similar to men, they may also have shrinkage of sexual organs and hair loss. As if this was not enough to contend with, both types of human African trypanosomiasis can also be transmitted congenitally, especially in *gambiense* disease. The trypanosomes are able to cross the placental barrier which separates the blood circulations of the mother and the baby developing in her uterus. Babies born of infected mothers may suffer from many kinds of problems including a low birth weight, failure of breast feeding, enlargement of the liver and spleen, increased fluid within the brain and in severe cases, death. However, it is also possible for the babies of infected mothers to be born without any obvious problems.

The disease also has a tendency to affect the sight of its victims. As well as affecting vision by interfering with the nervous system, which we shall describe soon, the parasites can also directly damage the structures within the eye. For example, there may be conjunctivitis, an inflammation of the conjunctiva, the membrane exposed to the air at the front of the eye; or iritis, where the iris, which controls the size of the pupil, is inflamed; or keratitis, an inflammation of the cornea. There may also be severe damage to the optic nerve at the back of the eye which transmits nerve impulses from the eye to the brain. Some of these problems may lead to varying degrees of visual impairment that can result in blindness. During one of my visits to Alupe I asked five patients with early stage disease whether they had any problems with their eyesight. To my surprise three of them told me that they had double vision (known as 'diplopia') which is something that I had not previously read in the textbooks. There is no substitute for experience.

If untreated, the early stage disease will inevitably progress to the late or encephalitic stage when the parasites cross the blood-brain barrier. Encephalitis is the medical term for inflammation of the brain and, as a neurologist, this is where my main interest lies. It can be difficult to know whether the disease has definitely progressed to the late stage purely on the basis of the symptoms, as they are so non-specific. The patient with late stage sleeping sickness may suffer from numerous neurological problems. Rather like HIV/AIDS, there are few regions of the nervous system that the disease cannot affect. Lassitude, indifference, headaches, anxiety and irritability are all common soon after the CNS has been affected, and the early stage may slowly and insidiously merge into the late stage. Psychiatric and mental disturbances are common and may sometimes present as violent, suicidal and manic behaviour, uncontrolled sexual impulses, hallucinations and delirium. Psychotic features are said to be especially common in European patients. Or sometimes there will just be subtle changes of personality and behaviour that may be recognised only by those close to them.

The characteristic sleep disturbances that occur in late stage disease give the disease its name. To understand them one has to know a little about the pattern of normal sleep. Normally, there is a characteristic 24-hour sleep-wake cycle that we are all aware of. We sleep at night and are awake during the day, and then the cycle is repeated. In sleeping sickness there is a reversal of normal sleep-wake cycle with excessive sleepiness (somnolence) during the day that alternates with insomnia and wakefulness during the night. There may be uncontrollable urges to sleep at any time or place. But there is also a disruption of the normal *structure* of sleep. Normally there are five recognised stages of sleep. These are stages one to four followed by stage five or REM (Rapid Eye Movement) sleep. As we pass through stages one to four over a period of approximately 90 minutes, our sleep becomes progressively deeper. Then, after a brief period of our sleep becoming lighter, we enter the phase of REM sleep. The whole cycle is then repeated several times during the night.

The important phase for sleeping sickness is REM sleep which normally occurs in several episodes lasting about 10 to 60 minutes. During this phase there are a number of physiological changes that do not occur during the other stages. The most well-known are the rapid eye movements which can be detected using special recording instruments. If a person undergoing REM sleep is woken up then he or she will say that they have been dreaming, so there is a very close association between REM activity and dreams. Although an electroencephalogram (EEG) – in which recording electrodes are placed on the scalp – shows intense electrical activity in the brain during REM sleep, muscle activity and contraction is reduced even though the heart and breathing rate increases. Very recently, Alain Buguet in France, working with his colleagues in Gabon and Angola, has shown that in late stage sleeping sickness there is an alteration of the normal sleep structure with frequent REM periods occurring at the *onset* of sleep rather than at the *end* of stage four sleep – these have been called 'SOREMPS' (sleep onset REM periods). These episodes should prove to be useful in helping to determine both the stage of the disease and the effects of new treatments.

The late stage of the disease can produce several different kinds of motor problems that can affect speech, the arms, legs, head and upper body. There may be tremors of the tongue and fingers, twitching in the muscles of the face and limbs, increasing muscular rigidity, and various types of involuntary movements of the limbs and body. Speech becomes slurred and difficult for those around to understand. The patient may develop a severe lack of coordination (ataxia) and difficulty walking. There may be weakness, or even paralysis, of one or more limbs that may be temporary or permanent. Sometimes there may be a hemiplegia in which one half of the body is paralysed, as may occur in a stroke. The spinal cord can be affected, leading to weakness in the arms, legs, or both. There is also an increased frequency of abnormal reflexes, which probably indicates malfunction of the frontal lobes of the brain.

There may also be problems with normal sensation. The most frequent symptom is an unpleasant and painful alteration of sensation called 'hyperaesthesia', where even a mild touch on the skin is felt as very unpleasant, and this feeling may occur spontaneously. There may also be a feeling of pins and needles or a lack of feeling in the limbs. The severe itching that some people with sleeping sickness experience may be due in part to disruption of normal sensation. In about a quarter of Europeans there is a 'deep' hyperaesthesia, where squeezing the soft tissues, in the leg for instance, results in delayed intense pain – the so-called 'Kerandel's sign'.

Unless the patient is successfully treated he or she will progress inexorably to the final stage of the illness. The patient is likely to develop epileptic seizures (convulsions), urinary and faecal incontinence, progressive mental deterioration and immobility, severe psychotic symptoms, worsening sleep disruption, intolerable itching, inability to take food and water, and then swelling of the brain, coma, severe chest or urinary infections, and finally, death.

The pattern of infection in children tends to be somewhat different from that seen in adults; frequently a very rapid course with early CNS involvement. Children are less likely to develop swelling of the lymph glands, but do suffer from many of the other features such as anaemia, enlarged liver and spleen, lethargy and behavioural problems. The child may well present late during the illness when the development of seizures and coma has already occurred. Unfortunately, although young people have a general tendency to recover from acute illnesses, this is not the case in sleeping sickness, and even children who survive may be left with significant intellectual and mental impairment as well as problems with movement and sensation.

Untreated, all patients with sleeping sickness will die, sooner or later. On the whole, if the patient with sleeping sickness is treated correctly while still in the early stage, then the outlook for the future, that is, the prognosis, is good. But the outlook for late stage survivors, especially if they have had severe CNS involvement, is not so good, and they may be left with severe and permanent neurological impairment. Amongst the most frequent residual problems are permanent weakness of one side of the body (hemiplegia), seizures, unsteadiness while walking, and involuntary movements of the limbs.

Establishing a diagnosis of sleeping sickness can either be straightforward or very difficult. It is essential to make what we call a definite, *positive* diagnosis, because the treatment is so toxic and you can't just treat someone because you think they *may* have the disease. If a person presents to the doctor with a fever and feeling generally unwell after recently being bitten by a tsetse fly, and in a geographical region in which sleeping sickness is known to be prevalent, then you don't have to be Sherlock Holmes to suspect the diagnosis. But it's still vital to prove the diagnosis before starting treatment. It's also essential to make sure the person doesn't also have another infection such as malaria, something I've seen more than once in East Africa. One issue that has yet to be resolved is whether being HIV positive influences someone's chances of developing sleeping sickness, and whether having HIV/AIDS can modify the course of the disease once it has occurred. More epidemiological research needs to be done to answer these questions, but it makes sense to me that a person who is already weakened and immune deficient from HIV infection is going to be less able to withstand the merciless onslaughts of human African trypanosomiasis.

The diagnosis of sleeping sickness is certain when parasites can be directly detected in the blood of a patient, something that is accomplished by examining a blood sample on a glass slide under the microscope. If the blood has many parasites, they are seen swimming around on a freshly collected wet blood smear. More often they are seen using a special chemical stain applied on the glass slide. The colour plate shows what the parasites look like. This is much easier with *rhodesiense* compared with *gambiense* disease because in the former case a large number of parasites are continuously circulating in the blood ('parasitaemia') so there is a good chance of detecting them. In *gambiense* disease, on the other hand, a parasitaemia is only occasionally present so there is much less chance of finding them. If the patient's lymph glands in the neck are also enlarged it is sometimes possible to aspirate fluid from one of them using a fine needle to try to identify parasites that way.

So how do we diagnose the disease in the West African form if the blood sample is negative for parasites? The method most commonly used is the Card Agglutination Trypanosomiasis Test, or CATT for short. The technical details aren't our concern, but essentially it is a 'serological' test where one looks for evidence of an antibody in the patient's blood which is directed against a particular region of the trypanosome, which is strong evidence that the body has mounted an immune response to parasite invasion. So it is an indirect rather than a direct test. The CATT is simple and quick to perform, and can be carried out in the African field. It is also a very useful test, especially if it is strongly positive – and there are ways of assessing how positive it is – but the problems arise when the test is only weakly positive when we call it an 'equivocal' result. Clinicians in the field have suggested various criteria for proceeding with further tests or otherwise with different CATT levels but there is not a definite agreement on this. Also, a positive CATT test is unable to tell you if the patient's nervous system has already been invaded by the parasite.

Increasingly sophisticated methods of diagnosing the infection have been described over the last few years, some of them very clever indeed. For example, a famous molecular biological technique called the Polymerase Chain Reaction (PCR) has been used for this purpose, and with some success. Using this method it is possible to amplify minute amounts of the parasite nucleic acid, DNA, to demonstrate its presence in the blood. However, there have been some problems with getting this method specific enough for the trypanosome and it is very difficult to imagine using this technology routinely in the field. Very recently my friend and colleague Dennis Grab of Johns Hopkins University has developed a simpler modification of this approach (called 'Loop Amplification') that has real promise for use under field conditions, so we await that with interest.

Since there are no reliable criteria for diagnosing only early stage disease, one never knows for sure whether the CNS has been infected. All patients who are CATT positive, and all those who are even slightly suspected of having late stage infection, must undergo a lumbar puncture to obtain a sample of the cerebrospinal fluid (CSF) which circulates in the spaces in the brain and spinal cord. The lumbar region of the spinal column is the lower part (arthritis in this area can lead to 'lumbago'). This sounds worse than it is and in fact is a relatively quick and simple procedure, one that is also almost painless when performed by experienced hands and a sharp needle. (Most rural clinics in this region, however, re-use their needles, which become blunt and painful.) A small volume of fluid, about five millilitres (ml) is removed with a specially designed fine needle and the fluid is then analysed on a special glass slide with a graticule from which it is possible to work out how many white blood cells (WBC) there are in one microlitre (one millionth of a litre, abbreviated to µL) of CSF. A normal person should not have any WBC/µL at all in the CSF, and their presence indicates that there is ongoing inflammation in the CNS. The CSF is also examined carefully for the presence of trypanosomes themselves using special concentration techniques which don't always work.

Here lies a serious problem since there is a difference of opinion as to what does and what does not constitute a definite CNS infection by the parasite. The World Health Organisation (WHO) criteria for diagnosing CNS infection are the presence in the CSF of either trypanosomes *or* a WBC of more than five/µL. That is the value that is widely used, but some clinicians in West Africa don't accept this and use a CSF WBC count that is higher, at 20/µL, before they consider a CNS infection has occurred. Very recently, some experts have suggested a compromise figure of 10 WBC/µL and perhaps that should be adopted. The problem is that any new diagnostic approach needs to be validated in large numbers of patients, so there remains uncertainty here. There is a pressing need for better diagnostic tests for both early and late stage sleeping sickness that are cheap, user friendly, reliable and workable in the African field. As we shall see soon, treatment for CNS sleeping sickness is very toxic so deciding whether or not a patient does indeed have late stage disease is absolutely critical. If you don't treat a patient for CNS disease when in fact they do have it, then the patient will die. But if you treat someone by mistake who doesn't in fact have CNS involvement, then you are exposing then unnecessarily to the very high risk of side effects from the drugs. This is one of the greatest dilemmas doctors must face when treating this disease.

Several sophisticated tests of brain function and structure have been used in patients with sleeping sickness. I have already mentioned the sleep structure findings which are measured by polysomnography in which patients are wired up to surface body electrodes that record eye movements, brain wave patterns (EEG) and muscular activity (EMG) simultaneously over a prolonged period of sleep. Various patterns can also be detected on the EEG which, while nonspecific, correlate with different stages and types of CNS disease. Brain imaging with computerised tomographic (CT) and magnetic resonance imaging (MRI) techniques have also been performed on patients with late stage disease. MRI, in particular, seems to be a sensitive indicator of brain abnormalities, including those in Western patients returning from safaris in East Africa. Although various types of abnormalities have been detected using MRI, some of which may prove to be very useful in diagnosis, the obvious problem with this is that it can hardly be applied in the African field where it is most needed.

Finally, we come to drug treatment. Basically, there are four main drugs that are used to treat sleeping sickness. Alan Fairlamb of Dundee University, one of the world's foremost authorities on the drug treatment of the disease, has pointed out that some of the current drugs would not have passed contemporary safety standards had they been developed recently. The drugs used to treat early stage disease are different from those that are effective against late stage disease, but all of them suffer from the drawback of not being effective when given by mouth, so they all have to be given by injection into a vein or a muscle.

For treating early stage *rhodesiense* disease the drug of choice is suramin, first used in the early 1920s, which is given intravenously as five injections over a period of about three weeks. The possible side effects include anaphylactic shock, kidney failure, skin problems and neurological problems. The drug of choice for early stage *gambiense* disease is pentamidine, first used in 1940, which is given as daily intramuscular injections for seven to 10 days. The possible side effects include low blood pressure and problems in regulating normal blood sugar levels. The treatment of late stage disease requires a drug that has the ability to cross the blood-brain barrier in order to reach the CNS. The only drug with this property that can be used for late stage disease in both *rhodesiense* and *gambiense* disease is the arsenical drug melarsoprol (Mel B) which was first used in humans in 1949. This is the same kind of drug that David Livingstone had given to that poor horse with animal trypanosomiasis in 1847! The drug has usually been given in two to four courses of three intravenous injections, the actual number of courses being determined by the number of WBC in the patient's CSF – the more cells then the more courses. However, Christian Burri of the Swiss Tropical Institute in Basel, one of the world's leading researchers in new drug treatment for the disease, has recently devised with his colleagues a new shorter melarsoprol treatment regime. This course gives daily doses of the drug for a total of just 10 days. This shorter course is just as effective and actually has advantages over the longer one, including a reduction of the overall costs of treatment, and it is now being adopted as standard therapy for late stage *gambiense* disease.

But melarsoprol therapy has major drawbacks. The most important is a severe brain inflammation that is known as the post-treatment reactive encephalopathy ('PTRE'), also known as the 'melarsoprol-related encephalopathic syndrome'. When this occurs, it is usually after the first treatment in the long course or after the eighth injection of the short course. The patient may suddenly develop seizures and brain swelling, go into coma within hours, or have a combination of deep coma and seizures. The PTRE occurs in about 10 per cent of patients who receive the drug and about half of those patients die from it. So that means that five per cent, that is, one in 20 of all patients who are treated with melarsoprol, actually die as a result of it. It is inconceivable that nowadays a drug that had a five per cent overall mortality would ever be allowed on the market. But – and here is the essential point – untreated, the mortality rate of the disease is 100 per cent. This underpins the vital importance of the correct staging of the disease.

Patients with the PTRE are treated with a combination of corticosteroids to reduce the brain swelling and inflammation, anticonvulsants to control seizures, and general medical support. But the evidence to support the use of corticosteroids to *prevent* the PTRE is somewhat conflicting and so that issue is unclear at present. (Personally I would want them if I was to be treated with melarsoprol!) One thing I learned from seeing patients with the PTRE in Alupe is that once the condition has been successfully treated then

PLATE 2A

David Bruce (1855–1931), Scottish microbiologist who, between 1894 and 1899, discovered the trypanosomal cause of 'nagana' in cattle in Zululand and its transmission by the tsetse fly.

PLATE 2B

Aldo Castellani (1878–1971), Italian microbiologist who, in 1903, first reported trypanosomes in the blood and cerebrospinal fluid in humans.

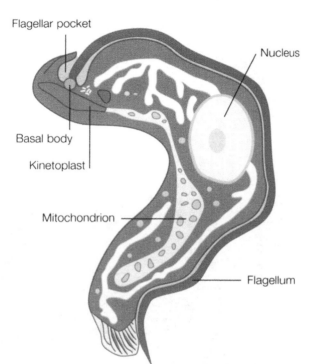

Flagellar pocket

Nucleus

Basal body

Kinetoplast

Mitochondrion

Flagellum

PLATE 3A
Simplified diagram
of a trypanosome.
© *The Wellcome Trust,
with permission*

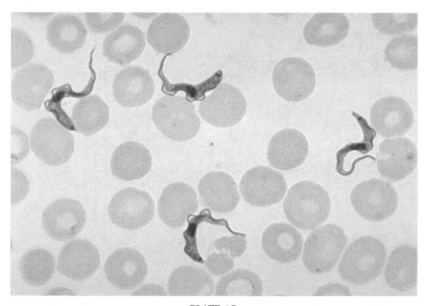

PLATE 3B
Slide of four stained trypanosomes detected in a human blood sample.
Myron G. Schultz, Centers for Disease Control Public Health Image Library

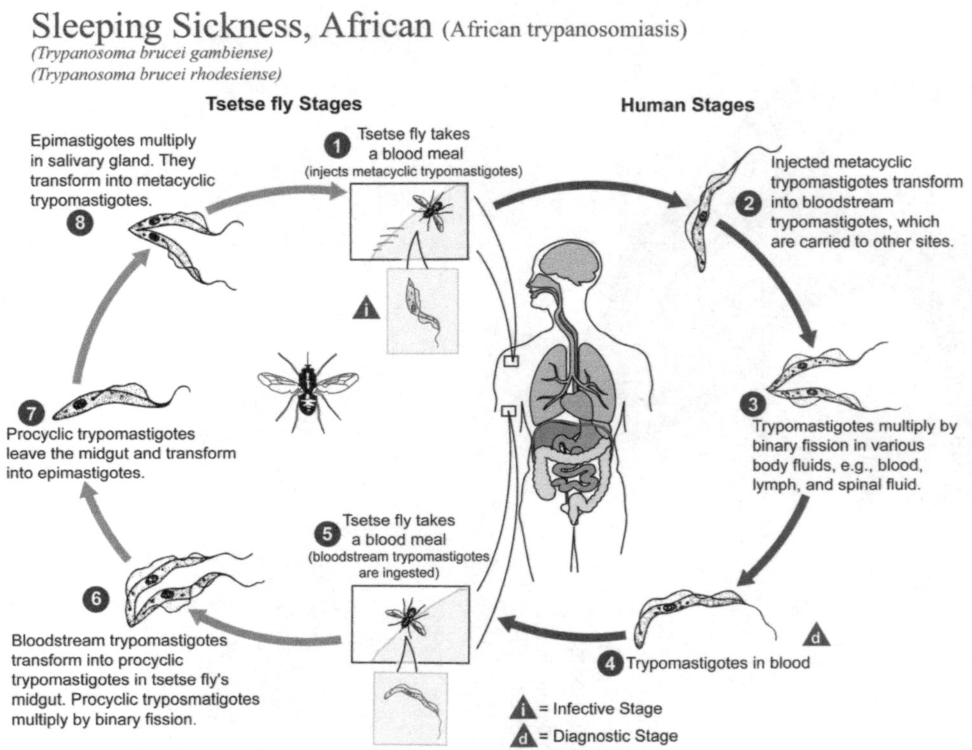

Sleeping Sickness, African (African trypanosomiasis)

(Trypanosoma brucei gambiense)
(Trypanosoma brucei rhodesiense)

Tsetse fly Stages

Human Stages

① Tsetse fly takes a blood meal
(injects metacyclic trypomastigotes)

② Injected metacyclic trypomastigotes transform into bloodstream trypomastigotes, which are carried to other sites.

③ Trypomastigotes multiply by binary fission in various body fluids, e.g., blood, lymph, and spinal fluid.

④ Trypomastigotes in blood

i = Infective Stage
d = Diagnostic Stage

⑤ Tsetse fly takes a blood meal
(bloodstream trypomastigotes are ingested)

⑥ Bloodstream trypomastigotes transform into procyclic trypomastigotes in tsetse fly's midgut. Procyclic trypomastigotes multiply by binary fission.

⑦ Procyclic trypomastigotes leave the midgut and transform into epimastigotes.

⑧ Epimastigotes multiply in salivary gland. They transform into metacyclic trypomastigotes.

PLATE 4

Diagram of the man/fly life-cycle in sleeping sickness (human African trypanosomiasis).
Alexander J.da Silva and Melanie Moser, Centers for Disease Control Public Health Image Library

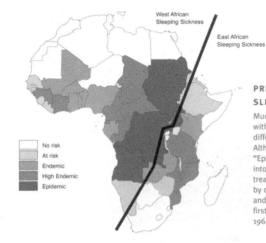

West African
Sleeping Sickness

East African
Sleeping Sickness

No risk
At risk
Endemic
High Endemic
Epidemic

PREVALENCE OF
SLEEPING SICKNESS

Much of sub-Saharan African is afflicted
with human African trypanosomiasis, with
different varieties in East and West Africa.
Although regions vary from "No risk" to
"Epidemic," more countries are now moving
into the epidemic category as surveillance,
treatment, and prevention are disrupted
by civil conflict. Between the late 1920s
and late 1950s, prevalence of the disease
first fell steadily, almost vanishing by
1962, but then rose dramatically.

ANNUAL DEATHS FROM SLEEPING SICKNESS

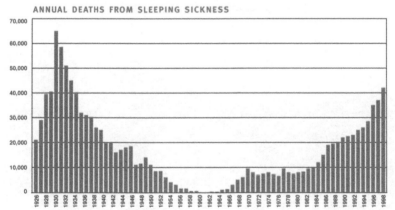

PLATE 5

Diagrams of the prevalence of sleeping sickness in Africa (above) and the
annual deaths from sleeping sickness (below).

Information and diagrams from WHO 2000 modified for Cerebrum, *Dana Press, by
Dawn Rogala, 2003, reprinted with permission*

PLATE 6A
Joseph Ndung'u in Kisumu, Kenya.

PLATE 6B
Max Murray in the Nguruman escarpment, Kenya.
Courtesy of Max Murray

PLATE 7A
The Alupe Treatment Centre in Western Kenya.

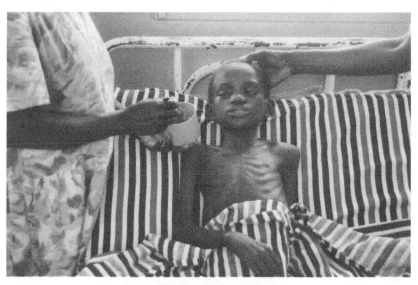

PLATE 7B
A child with combined late-stage sleeping sickness and malaria, Alupe.

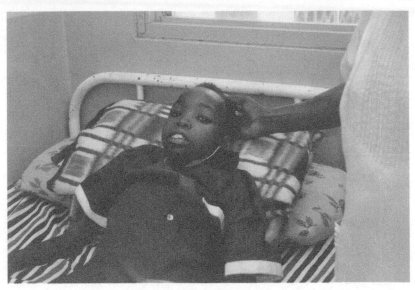

PLATE 8A
A child with early stage sleeping sickness, Alupe.

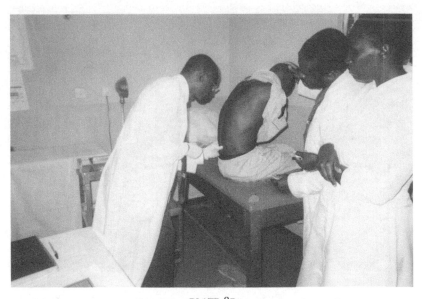

PLATE 8B
Medical staff performing a lumbar puncture on a patient suspected of having late-stage sleeping sickness, Alupe.

PLATE 9A
The village of Akajonit, Busia, Western Kenya.

PLATE 9B
Villagers in Akajonit, many of whom had been affected by sleeping sickness.

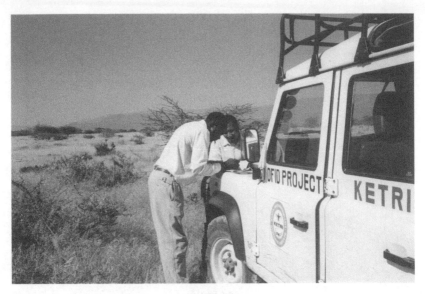

PLATE 10A
Nguruman field station and Maasai ranch showing KETRI Land Rover and senior scientific officer.

PLATE 10B
Nguruman escarpment in the early morning, near the field station.

PLATE IIA
Nguruman. Cattle herding prior to blood sample collection.

PLATE IIB
Nguruman. Wooden enclosure for cattle sampling.

PLATE 12A
Nguruman. Field laboratory for analysis of cattle blood samples.

PLATE 12B
Southern Ethiopia. Cattle being treated with pour-on insecticide.
Courtesy of Peter H. Goll

PLATE 13B
A tsetse fly after ingesting a blood meal.
Courtesy of Geoffrey Attardo and Serap Askoy

PLATE 14A

Ngu tsetse fly trap in use in Southern Ethiopia (the trap is named after Nguruman where it was developed).

Courtesy of Peter H. Goll

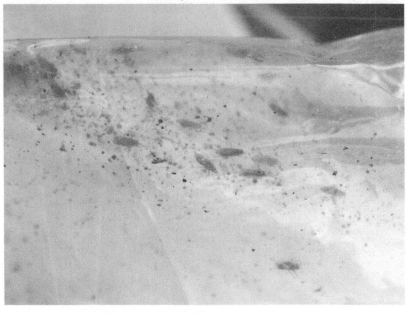

PLATE 14B

Ngu tsetse fly trap. Flies have been collected in the bag at the top.

Courtesy of Max Murray

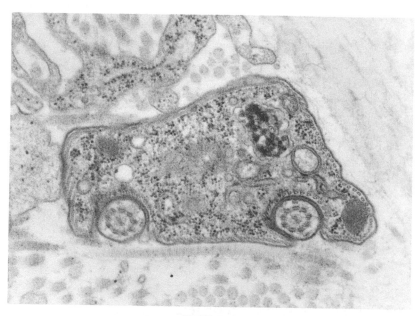

PLATE 15A

Electron micrograph of a trypanosome. Inspection of the figure reveals why Max Murray calls it the vehicle of destruction.

Courtesy of Max Murray

PLATE 15B

A sleeping cow with animal trypanosomiasis.

Courtesy of Max Murray

PLATE 16A
The author and Joseph Sulo at Alupe.

PLATE 16B
One of the buildings of LIRI in Uganda.

it doesn't recur, which is something that has interesting implications for its possible cause that we will come to in the next chapter. Melarsoprol causes other problems too. If the PTRE doesn't get you, then you may still suffer other severe side effects such as heart irregularities, skin rashes, and a serious blood disorder in which the white blood cells are lost. It is very unpleasant and painful for the patient. One person who had received melarsoprol treatment described it to the journalist A.A. Gill as 'like having chilli peppers injected into your heart'. There can also be treatment failures. Although 80 to 90 per cent of patients are cured with melarsoprol, resistance to the drug seems to be on the increase with treatment failure rates of about 30 per cent in Northern Uganda and Angola.

Fortunately, there is another drug that can be used to treat late stage *gambiense* disease, and that is eflornithine (also known as DFMO). The history of this drug is remarkable and we will discuss it in detail in the final chapter. It is a drug that was originally used to treat patients with cancer, and it was later found to be effective against sleeping sickness. In fact, its ability to cure people who had been in a coma led it to be called the 'resurrection drug'. For various reasons it then became unavailable and became an 'orphan drug', but we will come to that story later. All we have to know at present is that it is a drug which prevents the action of a key enzyme called ornithine decarboxylase in the parasite which as a result is rendered unable to make critical substances, called polyamines, that are essential for its survival. Eflornithine is not effective against *rhodesiense* disease, but it is against *gambiense* disease.

Although eflornithine, which was first used in 1981, was originally used only as an alternative, that is, a second line drug, for such patients, it is now being used increasingly as first line therapy for *gambiense* patients. While it still has a number of potential side effects such as bone marrow toxicity and gastro-intestinal problems, is very expensive, and has to be given intravenously several times a day for two weeks, it is a much safer drug than the highly toxic melarsoprol. At present the oral form of eflornithine is not sufficiently effective as for some reason the necessary blood levels of the drug can't be achieved. But that may be eventually possible. While a major drawback of all the drugs that are available for sleeping sickness is that none of them can be given orally, as we shall see, this should soon be possible for early stage disease. The Holy Grail would be to have a safe effective drug for late stage disease, since that would obviate the difficulties of staging with CSF analysis and literally transform the outlook of patients. If we had safe oral drugs for sleeping sickness, then people suspected of having recently caught the disease could start treatment early on, as is the case with malaria. That would be a major advance. In fact, new promising oral drugs for late-stage sleeping sickness have now been developed and these advances are summarised in Chapter 11.

So these are the four drugs that form our main weaponry against sleeping sickness. In my view, a pretty frightening lot. There are other experimental drugs that are being tested at present, as well as new drug combinations, but we will deal with those aspects in due course. Once the patient with sleeping sickness has been cured, either from the early or the late stage, it is essential to follow him or her up with regular clinical and laboratory assessments for two years. Ideally that means performing a repeat lumbar puncture every six months, but as you can imagine not everyone is prepared to undergo that ordeal, so adequate follow-up can be difficult in some cases. Some patients do relapse and get a repeat attack but this is uncommon. If they do get ill again and fulfil the specific criteria for CNS disease, then unfortunately the whole treatment regime has to be repeated. All of this, and much more, I learned from seeing patients and talking to them, their relatives and medical attendants for many years as I repeatedly went back to Alupe. I saw at first hand how this disease can decimate people's lives, and how all too often the treatment can be as harmful as the disease itself. I also began to grow angry at the lack of global investment in new drug development for sleeping sickness.

One of the most memorable visits was one year later in 2000 when

Joseph, Dr Matete and I had finished seeing patients in Alupe, and then went by Land Rover into the surrounding villages in the district of Busia near the main hospital. While being driven in the vehicle by Moses, we were able to see Uganda across the border just a few miles away. We decided to spend an afternoon in a nearby village called Akajonit, in which no less than 17 of its 460 inhabitants had suffered from sleeping sickness in recent months. One reason for this high incidence was likely to have been a common source of infection where people were working and sleeping next to a heavily infested tsetse area. One particular tsetse hotspot was in a group of bushes just next to the river which the villagers used a great deal. Every time they passed by the bushes they risked getting bitten and infected. Had there been a well inside the village then the need to go down to the river would have been obviated and the contact with the infecting tsetse greatly reduced.

Once inside the village we were given a characteristically warm and courteous reception by a large group of people with the usual greetings of *Jambo*, the Swahili hallmark of Kenyan welcomes. It was difficult not to be affected by the cruel way in which the disease had ravaged so many of the inhabitants, some of whom had seen several members of their family stricken, a few with long term complications. The worst example was a child of four years who, as a consequence of a previous trypanosomiasis infection, walked with a marked limp, and looked and behaved like a two year old. She is shown in my photograph of the villagers (PLATE 9).

I also saw a teenage boy who had recovered from a previous episode of sleeping sickness and had recently felt not quite right. Dr Matete examined him and paid particular attention to his palms, something that I had not seen before. He impressed on me just how important it is to have a high index of suspicion of a recurrence of the disease despite previously successful treatment with an apparent cure. A subtle sign which I was shown in this boy was excessive dryness of the palms which, together with other suspicious features, strongly indicated a disease recurrence despite the relative stoicism of the patient. This is something that is not emphasised in the text-books. But this is the real world and these are real people. I was struck by the way these villagers seemed to accept the situation with dignity and equanimity, and this unnerved me slightly. But this accorded with the general way in which the visit was conducted. It was done in a remarkably relaxed way while we sat under the shade of a large tree with protective branches, on an exceedingly hot day even by Kenyan standards.

Following this illuminating visit we made our way to the nearby town of Busia itself, in which were located the District Veterinary Officer and the main headquarters of the FITCA project. Dr S.O. Orot held this senior post and had known Joseph for many years so they had a very good working relationship. During our visit I had frequently heard people talk about this project, so it was good to learn about things first-hand from the project manager and his associates. FITCA is an acronym for 'Farming in Tsetse Controlled Areas Project' which was run from 2000 to 2004, funded by the European Union as part of a regional programme which also involved projects in nearby districts of Uganda.

FITCA was a community-based rural development project using a 'whole-farm' approach. Its primary purpose was to increase live-stock productivity, and this involved tsetse fly and trypanosomiasis control in animals and man, improving livestock practices, and promoting integrated livestock/crop systems. In practical terms, this meant entering into specific agreements with the local community groups in order to initiate specific activities, 16 of which had been identified at that time. Examples of this might be the clearing of vegetation, improving animal health delivery systems, the use of shallow wells for various purposes (as would have been ideal in the village we had just visited), improving the productivity of indige-nous cattle, and growing certain types of tree which could be fed to livestock. The whole concept and approach was entirely new to me as a human doctor. The management of the local project involved three institutions which closely interacted with each other. The

Veterinary Office had a key administrative role, KETRI was primarily concerned with research and diagnostics, while Alupe had the remit of patient management both in the main treatment centre and the surrounding villages.

I recently asked Joseph whether he thought this project had been successful. The answer was that FITCA had its successes and disappointments. While it was set up as a regional programme with activities planned to be undertaken in a coordinated manner, and at the same time on both sides of the Kenya/Uganda border, that became difficult to achieve in practice as each country undertook their activities independently. On the Kenyan side, however, these control activities resulted in a significant fall in trypanosomiasis in both livestock and people from 2003 to 2005 so this was clearly a successful outcome. But a word of warning: in January 2006 the first new case of human sleeping sickness for some time was reported on the Kenyan side so there is a fear that it could be returning, although hopefully not with a vengeance. The great reduction of human cases in Alupe since I was last there is a triumph, but the same is certainly not the case in nearby Uganda, which is the major reason why I and my colleagues recently switched our attention to the disease across the border just a few miles away. But more of that later.

CHAPTER SIX

The Mouse Model of
Sleeping Sickness

IN THE LAST CHAPTER we saw exactly *what* sleeping sickness can do to people. Now we consider *how* the trypanosome wreaks this havoc. To find out about the possible ways in which this brain damage occurs we need to turn our attention to experimental models of African trypanosomiasis. This will also involve some discussion of the immunological mechanisms involved, but any technical terms will be explained as we go along, so if you are unfamiliar with this sort of thing, please don't be concerned.

The most important question we have to get to grips with is how the parasite invasion leads to CNS inflammation, as that is what seems to do most, if not all, of the damage we see in patients with sleeping sickness. The word 'inflammation' means different things to different people, but here we mean a very specific immune-mediated process that comes about as a result of many different factors. The classical description of inflammation is the quartet of *rubor, tumor, calore* and *dolore,* standing for redness, swelling, heat and pain. The typical situation where this process occurs is after a localised injury to the skin or a reaction to an infection or bite, and most people have had some experience of this. It is basically the body's immune system mounting a protective response to injury or invasion by foreign material such as a micro-organism.

The local tissue response at the site of the insult is increased leakiness and size of the very small blood vessels known as capillaries, the attraction of circulating white blood cells to the site, and the transfer of fluid and protein molecules through the leaky capillary wall into the tissues, leading to swelling. The foreign material that invades the tissue may act as an antigen which is a substance, for example a protein or other component of a parasite, which elicits a host immune response. This can lead to the production of another type of protein called an antibody that circulates in the blood and tissue fluids, which combines with the antigen and, in some cases, neutralises it so it can't do any further damage. There are five basic classes of antibodies, or immunoglobulins (Ig), called IgG, IgM, IgA, IgD and IgE. In trypanosomiasis the IgM antibody seems to be particularly important, at least in diagnosis of the infection. Antigens also interact directly with other cell types which are able to 'present' them in a suitable form so as to be recognised by the immune system and destroyed.

The immune system is incredibly complex, and to my mind seems to get more complex by the day, so here we can only skim the surface of the immune-mediated processes that will help us to understand the pathology of sleeping sickness. I continue to be amazed at the sheer cleverness and ingenuity of immunologists in discovering ever more intricate and complex mechanisms in their fascinating field.

It is important to appreciate that in sleeping sickness there is a great deal of inflammation going on inside the brain (and to a lesser extent the spinal cord) which is contained within an enclosed space, bounded by the skull and vertebral column. But there is another physical barrier to invading micro-organisms that under normal circumstances prevents all but very small molecules passing from the blood into the CNS. This barrier is called the blood-brain barrier (BBB) that we have mentioned briefly before. The BBB consists of two layers, an inner 'endothelial cell' layer, or membrane, which is surrounded by an outer layer called the basement membrane. Between these layers there is a space, and the 'foot processes' of another brain cell type called an astrocyte abut onto the basement membrane. There are specialised anatomical regions along the endothelial cell layer called 'tight junctions' that seal the barrier. Under some circumstances the BBB can become more permeable, such as when a person suffers an acute infection and inflammation of the CNS, as occurs in meningitis.

Although it was once thought that the brain is an 'immunologically privileged' site, shielded from the rest of the immune system, it is now known that certain types of immune cells (called activated T cells) can cross the BBB and cause nervous tissue damage. The CNS is also capable by itself of forming Ig molecules under certain circumstances, and taking part in a number of immunological processes. So the CNS is immunologically active rather than sheltered. While some drugs such as melarsoprol can cross the BBB without too much difficulty, other drugs are unable to do so and are therefore unsuitable for treating late stage sleeping sickness. The BBB is currently a major focus of research in the development of new drugs for the disease. Trypanosomes are certainly able to cross the BBB a few weeks after the initial infection. Scientists are currently investigating the factors that allow them to do that in the hope that this will help them develop therapies that can block the passage of trypanosomes into the CNS.

The immune response is classically divided into humoral, or antibody-mediated immunity, and cell-mediated immunity, although the actual mechanisms are very much more complex than this implies. Two basic immune cell types are B lymphocytes and T lymphocytes. By convention it is common practice just to refer to these two types of lymphocytes as B cells and T cells. B cells are formed in the bone marrow and mature in the circulating (peripheral) blood. With 'help' from a special type of T cell (called a Th2 helper cell) the B cell matures into a plasma cell that goes on to make antibody (Ig).

T cells, by contrast, are formed in the bone marrow but then undergo 'education', so to speak, in a gland called the thymus which is located in the chest. They then mature in the peripheral blood and after exposure to antigens they multiply and develop further into two main types of T cell. Some become cytotoxic cells (CD8 cells) which can directly kill invading 'target' cells such as those infected by micro-organisms. In order to do this the foreign antigen has to be 'presented' to the cytotoxic T cell by antigen presenting cells (usually macrophages) in association with the matching up of what are known as MHC class I molecules, but the details of this process are way beyond the scope of our brief survey. A second type of T cell (CD4 cells) becomes either a Th1 cell which is an inflammatory cell that 'activates' another type of very important cell called a macrophage, or a Th2 cell which, as we just learned, helps B cells make antibodies. You can already see how the whole process is interconnected.

The macrophage is extremely important in trypanosome infection. It is part of what is referred to as 'innate immunity' that provides a sort of immediate host defence mechanism against invasion. Macrophages are activated, as we saw above, by Th1 cells, and once that has happened, the macrophage undergoes changes that allow it to produce molecules called cytokines. Cytokines are very important indeed in sleeping sickness and a great deal of our current work is concerned with their role in producing brain inflammation. Cytokines are small molecules that can affect both the proliferation and properties of other cells involved in inflammation, and come in two basic varieties. Some cytokines, such as the ones produced by activated macrophages, are called 'pro-inflammatory' since they enhance the inflammatory reaction in the body. Important examples of this type are tumour necrosis factor-alpha (TNF-α), Interleukin-1 (IL-1), and Interferon-gamma (IFN-γ). Other cytokines do the opposite and damp down inflammation and are called 'counter-inflammatory' cytokines. Examples of these are Interleukin-10 (IL-10) and Interleukin-4(IL-4).

Macrophages can also be activated by some components of the trypanosome structure itself, the most important of which is called the variant surface glycoprotein (VSG), which, as we shall see, is very important for the parasite's evasion from the host immune response. It should be appreciated that activated, 'angry' macrophages can directly engulf and destroy foreign material that it comes across – a process called 'phagocytosis'. We should also mention the major brain cell types that are recognised. Most people are probably aware of the neurons, or nerve cells, which transmit electrical nervous impulses and are a basic structural and functional component of the peripheral and central nervous systems. Normally we have about a hundred billion neurons in our brain (expressed mathematically as 10^{11}). These cells are lost and malfunction in diseases such as dementia. Then there are oligodendrocytes with elaborate processes that form a substance called myelin, which is the insulating fatty sheath surrounding neurons. It is this myelin sheath that is destroyed in the disease called Multiple Sclerosis (MS). There are also cells called microglia that are very important in immunity in the CNS, as they are the 'resident macrophages', so to speak. There are several forms of microglia and they respond to protect injured neurons. Microglia may become phagocytic and engulf foreign material. These cells may also secrete various cytokines including IL-1 and are likely to be involved in the responses to trypanosomes.

But from our point of view the most important is probably the star-shaped astrocyte. This is one of the most important neural cell types in the CNS and has many different functions. Among these are maintaining the structure and nutrition of nervous tissue, a role in forming the BBB as we saw before, proliferation and scar formation following CNS injury, the secretion of different growth factors for other cells such as the precursor cell that forms oligodendrocytes, and, critically for us, the secretion of pro-inflammatory cytokines such as TNF-α and IL-1 after the astrocyte has been activated following an appropriate stimulus. The astrocyte, just like the macrophage, can also present antigens to T cells to initiate an immune reaction. Clearly the astrocyte is a multi-talented cell.

So we are just about ready to discuss the mouse model of sleeping sickness as we are now armed with all the necessary basic immunology and neurobiology involved. To summarise, we have seen the nature and some components of the basic inflammatory response, the structure and importance of the BBB, the essential functions of B and T lymphocytes and plasma cells, the importance of activated macrophages, the two types of pro- and counter-inflammatory cytokines, and the major neural cell types in the CNS, including the important multi-purpose astrocyte which, along with microglia, appear to be key players in the CNS immune response to invasion.

Before we proceed, it is important to make some important general points. First, we have been talking about inflammation as if it were just a protective response of the host to a foreign invader. While it certainly has this role, it is important to realise that the various consequences of the host's inflammatory response can also be harmful. We tend to think of it as a case of 'good' and 'bad' inflammation. We believe that in African trypanosomiasis much of the neurological damage results from the host's reaction to the parasite and treatment. The problem has been to know when the inflammatory response has been beneficial and when it has been harmful. Sometimes we may infer wrongly. This distinction is important as the harmful scenario has implications for treatment.

It is also worth emphasising that the invading trypanosome is extracellular, that is, it resides in the blood but outside the body's cells themselves. It is, therefore, not possible to explain the damage to organs just by invasion of the parasite *per se*. It seems that the damage is done both by toxic substances released by live (or dead) trypanosomes, and the harmful consequences of the body's immune reaction to the parasite. It is a sobering thought that much of the time we don't actually know for sure where many of the host-derived harmful molecules come from. We can make educated guesses and reasonable assumptions based on good experiments, but some of the pro-inflammatory cytokines, for example, could have come from several different kinds of cells such as activated astrocytes, T lymphocytes, macrophages or microglia. Furthermore, some of the cells producing these molecules might have originated outside the CNS and migrated across the BBB to enter it, while others may have been derived from immune cells already residing within the CNS. The whole system is very complex and much of the time we can only make suggestions as to what is important and where.

This last point leads onto another big issue in this field, which is that most of our observations in this disease are what we call 'descriptive' rather than 'mechanistic'. What this means is that we can measure the levels of different potentially toxic substances in the blood and CSF of patients with late stage sleeping sickness but we can only make correlations with the disease, not deductions. You can't perform actual experiments on humans. We can, however, infer how such data may be important, and can certainly use them for diagnostic purposes. We will mention some of these studies as we proceed. The closest we can get to observe the disease at the microscopical level is when we are able to examine the brains of patients who have died from the disease. There have been several such studies and we know pretty well what the typical pathological features look like.

It is important to know about the human CNS inflammatory disease in cellular terms because that is what we hope to reproduce in an experimental animal model where you can manipulate the infection and be 'mechanistic'. The main picture one sees in patients is a 'generalised meningoencephalitis' which means an inflammation of both the meninges – the covering membranes surrounding the brain and spinal cord – and the brain. In these affected areas there is a great increase in the number of cells compared with normal, and this 'inflammatory infiltrate', as we call it, consists of various types of immune cells. Predominant among these are T lymphocytes, plasma cells and macrophages, all key components of the immune response, as we have seen. These cells are mainly found in the white matter of the brain as opposed to the grey matter which is found in the cerebral cortex and deeply placed regions.

A particular type of cell that is absolutely typical of sleeping sickness is the morular or Mott cell which is thought to be a modified plasma cell containing inclusions of IgM. You will recall that plasma cells make antibodies so this Ig inclusion is not unexpected. Another typical finding, one that is often found in other types of brain inflammation, is the presence of perivascular cuffs which are thick collections of lymphocytes, and markedly activated astrocytes and macrophages surrounding blood vessels. Inflammatory cells are also increased in the choroid plexus – a collection of blood vessels lining the brain ventricles – cavities within the brain through which CSF flows. That is another point through which trypanosomes can pass into the CNS – from the CSF to the brain rather than from the blood to the brain.

Although there can be some loss of brain white matter, a process known as demyelination, this usually isn't significant. The inflammatory process can also affect the 'subcortical' regions of the brain, just below the cerebral cortex, and these include areas called the thalamus, hypothalamus and supraoptic nuclei. We shall see that involvement of these latter regions may account for the sleep disorders. You will recall from the last chapter that 10 per cent of patients receiving melarsoprol develop a severe post-treatment brain inflammation called the PTRE. When you look at the brains of the unfortunate patients who have succumbed to this complication, the microscopical changes are similar to ordinary CNS infection, only much more severe. What you don't normally see is large numbers of parasites themselves in these brains.

So at last we come to the mouse model of CNS trypanosomiasis. It is important to appreciate that while we would very much prefer not to do experiments on animals of any kind, unfortunately it is absolutely essential to use animal models to have a chance of studying and understanding the complexities of sleeping sickness. There is no conceivable way that experiments confined to the tissue culture dish could ever mimic the myriad of interconnecting inflammatory processes that occur in humans, or indeed in animals, with the disease. There is a vast difference between the simplicity of a cell culture dish and the incredible complexity of the living animal brain. Moreover, and this is an important point, the mouse model gives valuable information that is highly relevant to both human and animal trypanosomiasis. So the welfare of both could be improved by the better understanding of the underlying disease process and the development of more effective drugs that can be achieved using animal models.

Like all good ideas, the principle of the mouse model is actually pretty simple. It was devised by Frank Jennings over 20 years ago and a key aim was to use it to develop more effective drugs for trypanosomiasis. It is remarkably reliable and reproducible, both very good things to have in science. In this model, mice are infected with trypanosomes of the *T.b.brucei* variety which we have met before in animal trypanosomiasis. We don't use the trypanosomes that produce human disease for safety reasons, as we are not too keen on giving ourselves the disease! A total of 40,000 parasites are inoculated into the mouse peritoneum (a membrane lining the abdominal cavity), following which the parasites soon spread into the blood, lymphatic system and major organs. The actual inoculations are rather tricky to perform and we have been very fortunate that Barbara Bradley, a superb animal technician, has been on our team to run the model. This procedure leads to a chronic infection in which the parasites have traversed the BBB and are established in the CNS by the 21st day following infection. At this stage the CNS shows some very mild inflammatory changes that are similar to that seen in humans with the disease.

At this point the mice are inoculated with a drug called berenil (diminazene aceturate, a drug used for animal trypanosomiasis) that clears the parasites from the bloodstream but not the CNS as it can't cross the BBB. The result of this 'subcurative therapy' is that the mouse develops a marked worsening of the inflammatory changes in the brain that closely resemble the PTRE seen in humans following melarsoprol therapy. We see meningitis, an increase in the numbers of lymphocytes, macrophages and astrocytes within the brain, and frequent perivascular cuffs thickly laden with inflammatory cells. This reaction persists even after the parasites are no longer present in the blood. This experimental PTRE can be made even worse by giving the mice a second injection of berenil about six weeks after the original infection. At this point the inflammatory

Figure 2
The Sleeping Sickness Mouse Model

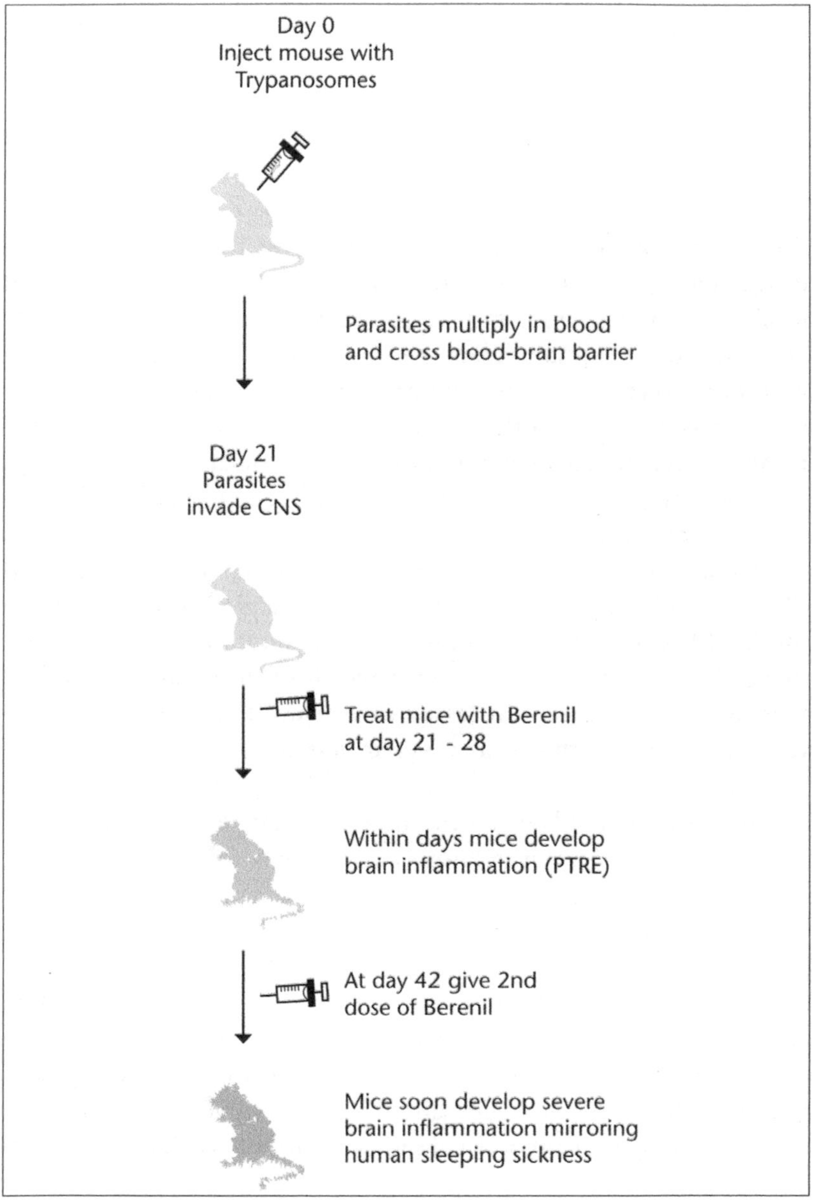

Day 0
Inject mouse with
Trypanosomes

Parasites multiply in blood
and cross blood-brain barrier

Day 21
Parasites
invade CNS

Treat mice with Berenil
at day 21 - 28

Within days mice develop
brain inflammation (PTRE)

At day 42 give 2nd
dose of Berenil

Mice soon develop severe
brain inflammation mirroring
human sleeping sickness

reaction in the CNS is extremely severe, and the mice show marked neurological impairment such as hindlimb paralysis. You don't see many actual parasites within the brain though. The mice will eventually get worse and inevitably die. The whole procedure is summarised in Figure 2.

The reproducibility of the model, and its similarity to its human counterpart, means that it is a reliable and relevant system both to investigate the mechanisms by which the CNS disease is produced (known as 'neuropathogenesis'), and to test the effects of novel drugs. Some people have pointed out that however good an animal model of a disease is, it can never really tell you what is actually going on in the human. That is perfectly true, but we really have no other choice as you can't experiment on humans. And of course we are always aware of the potential pitfall of over-interpreting the results in animal models in relation to human diseases. So we always exercise a degree of caution when we apply the results found in the mouse to the case of man.

We also realised early on that we had to devise some method of measuring the clinical and neuropathological findings in the model. Max Murray often points out the importance of measurement in biology by referring to the words of the great Lord Kelvin who was the Glasgow Professor of Natural Philosophy (Physics) for much of the 19th century. Kelvin stated:

> I often say that when you can measure what you are speaking about, and express it in numbers, you know something about it: but when you cannot measure it, your knowledge is of a meagre and unsatisfactory kind.

We completely agree with that. So we devised a numerical grading scale for measuring both the neurological impairment and the degree of inflammatory CNS reaction. Instrumental in this development was Jean Rodgers, our very gifted post-doctoral researcher who continues to play a pivotal role in our current work. The clinical score runs from 0 (healthy) to 6 (dead or requiring euthanasia). The neuropathology score runs from 0 (no changes) to 4 (severe meningitis and encephalitis), and another talented post-doctoral scientist, Joanne Burke, played an important role in developing this scale. The scores are always noted by two scientists and are done 'blind' whenever possible, where the observers don't know which is which (although they certainly do know what's what!). This scheme has allowed us to use both simple and very complex statistical analyses in the various treatment scenarios, and this has involved close collaboration with the distinguished statistician and scientist, George Gettinby of Strathclyde University.

Our very first post-doctoral scientist on the project, Chris Hunter, was extremely successful in helping us to make several key observations in the mouse model that we think are significant. It was found that the astrocyte plays a pivotal role in inducing the neuroinflammatory responses, as astrocyte activation occurs 14 to 21 days after the initial infection which is before the severe inflammatory areas, or 'lesions', can be detected in the CNS. That implies that the inflammation is a *consequence* of the astrocyte activation rather than its cause. We recognise activated astrocytes because these cells became larger, with longer and more elaborate cell processes, and they stain more strongly than normal with an astrocyte cell marker called GFAP (glial fibrillary acidic protein). We also found that several key pro-inflammatory cytokines appear around the time of astrocyte activation including IL-1 and TNF-α, which strongly supports our interpretation.

Our more recent studies with Jeremy Sternberg, a talented parasite immunologist working in Aberdeen University, have shown that as the brain inflammation gets worse, the pro-inflammatory cytokines such as TNF-α and IFN-γ increase. By contrast, the amounts of the counter-inflammatory cytokines such as IL-10 increase as the brain inflammation lessens. This has led us to suggest that the level of brain inflammation in experimental trypanosomiasis depends on a delicate balance between pro- and counter-inflammatory cytokines, one driving the inflammatory reaction and the other trying to lessen it. What we want most is a scenario where the counter-inflammatory forces ultimately prevail. Recently we have been trying to work out if a similar process occurs in humans and I shall mention that when we come to our studies in the Uganda.

Let me now tell you about the effects in the model of three different drugs, all of which work in entirely different ways. In these experiments we try to do two things: first to prevent the brain disease, and then to improve the severity of an established disease.

The very first drug we tried was called azathiaprine. This is very familiar to physicians as an immunosupressant used to treat various kinds of inflammatory and immune-mediated conditions. Examples of these are the autoimmune neuromuscular disease myasthenia gravis, severe rheumatoid arthritis and transplant recipients to avoid organ rejection. We found that when mice were given this drug, the experimental PTRE could be prevented from occurring. Since the immune system is so important in this condition, we were not surprised at this finding. But there was very little effect on the amount of astrocyte activation in the brain. When we tried to reduce the severity of an already established PTRE, we found that it had no beneficial effects. Azathiaprine is a potentially toxic drug and can cause the bone marrow suppression leading to blood disorders, so it is not a treatment to be given lightly. Many patients suffering from sleeping sickness in Africa are already anaemic and malnourished, and we don't think that trials of azathiaprine in the African field are justified.

The next drug we tried was eflornithine which you will recall is an effective drug for CNS sleeping sickness due to *T.b.gambiense*. So we had high hopes for it in the model even though the species of parasite we use in the mouse was different. Eflornithine prevents the trypanosome's ability to divide rather than actually killing it, and the immune system has to be intact for it to work effectively. This last point is important as it suggests that the drug might act against inflammation, which is exactly what we wanted. In order to test this, Frank Jennings used his characteristic ingenuity to produce a species of mutant trypanosome that was resistant to the direct effects of eflornithine. That meant any beneficial effects of eflornithine in the model would almost certainly be due to its effect on damping down inflammation rather than directly interfering with the trypanosome itself.

The results were even better than we had expected. As with all our work, this was a team effort, and here Jean, Joanne and also Charity Gichuki, an excellent graduate student from KETRI, played important parts. When the mice were given eflornithine in their drinking water, the PTRE could be prevented in that no inflammatory changes were seen in the brains of the infected and treated mice. Even better, when the mice had been made sick with even a severe double dose PTRE, then eflornithine dramatically reduced the brain inflammation. In both prevention and treatment scenarios, the degree of astrocyte activation was reduced along with the neuropathology. In view of these findings it came as no surprise to learn that eflornithine had such promise in the treatment of the human disease. In fact, we still don't understand precisely how this drug exerts its beneficial effects, and we strongly suspect there are several mechanisms at work, which is something that we are investigating at this very moment.

The third drug that we tested in the model was rather more complex although it may turn out to be the most interesting. These experiments came about through a chance meeting that I had in the US in with Susan Leeman of Boston University when we were both working as Fogarty 'Scholars in Residence' at the National Institutes of Health (NIH) in Bethesda, Maryland in 1994. Susan is one of the world's most eminent scientists, and a member of the elite US National Academy of Sciences. Like so many people of that calibre, she is very modest about her formidable achievements. She is also an exceptionally nice person. She is most famous for her discovery in the early 1970s of the chemical structure of two neuropeptides (a group of proteins found in the nervous system), called

Substance P (SP) and Neurokinin. SP has a number of functions, the most important of which is to act as a neurotransmitter in the nervous system, and it has a particularly important role in our perception of pain. But the reason why we were so interested in it was because of its importance in producing inflammatory responses in the body.

Susan's group had just found that antagonists to SP could reduce inflammation in the gut produced by certain bacteria. This suggested that SP itself had a role in producing that inflammation. Using an antagonist to a substance to prove its function is a well tried and tested scientific method. It was also known that SP could induce various immune cells such as T cells to produce different cytokines, and that astrocytes have 'receptors' for SP on their surface (receptors being molecules on a cell to which another substance such as SP can lock onto and combine in a very specific way so as to produce an effect). So the plot was thickening. When Susan asked me one very rainy afternoon in the historic Stonehouse building at NIH whether I knew of a good animal model of CNS inflammation on which her SP antagonists could be tested, I thought to myself: 'Have I got a model for you!'

Things turned out well. When the SP receptor antagonist (called RP-67,580, which sounds more like the name of a robot) was given to infected mice given the PTRE, we found that it could improve both the clinical and the inflammatory changes in the CNS just as we had suspected it would do. We also found that the antagonist reduced the level of astrocyte activation, which we had also predicted. I well remember Jean leaving me in a small microscope room in the Veterinary School for many hours while I counted astrocyte numbers until I felt I was going cross-eyed. I read the slides blind, not knowing which came from which experiment, and can still recall the feeling of elation when the code was finally revealed to me and we knew we had a result. Furthermore, both Jean and I had obtained the same figures independently. These experiments, which lasted over two years as each individual experimental cycle and analysis takes about four months, showed conclusively that SP was playing a key role in generating the neuroinflammatory response in the PTRE model.

I should point out, however, that our recent experiments with Stephen Hunt of University College London, using mice in which the gene coding for SP has been removed ('SP knockout' mice), indicate that the role of SP in this situation is very complex and we still don't completely understand exactly what is going on. But the results are important both for understanding the underlying mechanisms of the PTRE and for potential treatment of human patients with sleeping sickness. The fact that there now exists human forms of the SP antagonists makes this possible, and we shall come to this in the final chapter. Recent findings from other laboratories have suggested that SP may contribute to the pathology of malaria and HIV/AIDS infections – infections that also have global importance.

As we have seen, we know for sure that in the mouse model the PTRE may be produced by subcurative therapy with a drug that clears the parasites from the blood but not the CNS. This is clearly one mechanism that may be important in the human situation and a few years ago we found some evidence for that after analysing the brains of patients who had died from the PTRE. But what else might be going on in patients who develop the PTRE after melarsoprol treatment? There have been various theories put forward and frankly we don't yet know the answer. One suggestion that I personally think might well be correct is that soon after melarsoprol treatment, the parasites are quickly killed in large numbers within the CNS compartment, and this leads to a massive release of parasite components which act as antigens that induce an abnormal immune reaction from the patient. This reaction then leads to the severe inflammatory reaction of the PTRE. If this theory is correct, then you would probably not expect to get a repetition of the PTRE in the same patient when the melarsoprol is restarted after recovery, which is exactly the case as you may remember from our description from Alupe. I feel that this is a very credible mechanism, and it is interesting that in neither the human situation nor the experimental mice do you see many, if any, live parasites in the brains in the PTRE scenario.

Another suggestion is that something called 'immune complexes' are formed between parasite antigens and antibodies produced by the host, and that these complexes can clog up critical regions of the brain, and also induce further harmful immune responses, leading to brain dysfunction. Perhaps this could be important, and such complexes, as well as 'auto-antibodies' to one's own neural cells, have actually been detected in the CSF of some patients. Exactly what all this means in terms of symptoms and disease causation we just don't know. In my view, an argument against an auto-immune reaction is the consistent failure of the PTRE to recur, which you probably wouldn't expect if there were persistent antibodies that were damaging your own brain cells. Finally, a direct form of arsenical toxicity on the brain has been suggested, and, while I suppose this may be possible, it would be very difficult to explain the myriad of immunological abnormalities that one sees if this were the sole cause.

I hope you have been convinced that the brain disease seen in human and experimental sleeping sickness is due mainly to an immune process. But of course that doesn't wholly explain at the *cellular* level just how the CNS damage is done. Actually, that is not uncommon in neuropathogenesis studies where so much of what we observe is mainly descriptive. We can, however, envisage how brain swelling due to inflammation can directly affect the normal functioning of neuronal and other cells by a direct pressure effect, distorting their physical structure and leading to brain malfunction. There is also evidence for a direct toxic effect of particular cytokines on neural cell functioning, possibly by disrupting their structure and electrical activity. It is also very likely that the trypanosome itself releases toxic substances that can interfere with normal neuronal and glial cell function, possibly by disrupting the cell's metabolism. One way in which that may occur is through

Figure 3

Mechanisms of Brain inflammation in Sleeping Sickness

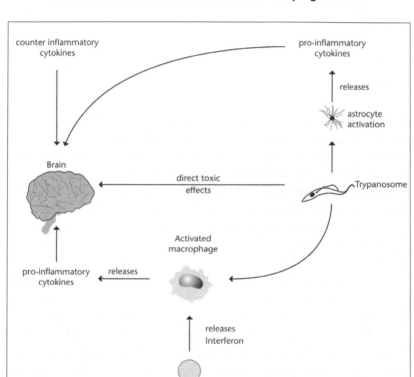

interference with the way in which a neural cell handles calcium which may lead to cell toxicity and death. Figure 3 summarises in a rather simplified fashion the three main ways in which the brain can be affected by the trypanosome infection. The parasite can release toxic substances that can directly damage the brain. The pro-inflammatory cytokines released from activated astrocytes can be toxic to the brain, modified by counter-inflammatory influences. And the same pro-inflammatory cytokines can reach the brain via

other routes such as activated macrophages that have been stimu-
lated by the products of T cells.

The trypanosome is certainly clever. Rather like the viruses
such as HIV and visna, it has evolved a strategy that allows it to
evade the immune response of the host organism. The process by
which it does this is called antigenic variation. The key to this lies
in the VSG genes that account for 10 per cent of the 10,000 genes
the trypanosome possesses. These genes code for the variable surface glycoproteins (proteins that contain sugar components) that
cover the surface of the trypanosome. Ten million versions of a
particular VSG cover the surface at any one time. Now, it is these
proteins that would be expected to induce an immune response from
the host which would then be able to attack the parasite. But what
the parasite does is use its molecular machinery to rapidly switch the
type of VSG that is coating its surface at any time. In this way the trypanosome is always one step ahead of the host's immune system.
By the time the host has made antibodies against a particular VSG, it
is already too late as the target VSG has changed. Only one VSG gene
is active at any one time, but it is enough to allow the parasite to
continuously evade the host's immune response. This was demonstrated very elegantly in the early 1970s by Keith Vickerman of
Glasgow University who was elected a Fellow of the Royal Society
for this discovery. Another consequence of this process of antigenic
variation is that it has not been possible, so far at least, to develop
a vaccine against African trypanosomiasis. To do that scientists
will need to devise a strategy that is even smarter than that of the
parasite. However, some researchers in this area are currently
working on new methods of potential vaccination against sleeping
sickness, so we certainly shouldn't rule out this possibility in the
future.

There have also been some very elegant studies in experimental
trypanosomiasis in rodents which have modelled the symptoms seen
in the human disease. Some of these studies are very significant
because they show infection of particular brain structures whose

function is known to be disrupted in sleeping sickness itself. One of the most interesting of these models has been described by my colleague Krister Kristensson and his co-workers at the Karolinska Institute in Stockholm. After these researchers inoculated rats with *T.b.brucei*, the same parasites that we use in the mouse, they found that the rats showed characteristic abnormalities in their sleep patterns and endogenous (that is, arising from within) body rhythms that were not seen in uninfected control animals. The rats could be monitored using methods similar to those used in patients. They found that the infected rats had characteristic alterations of sleep structure, which, you will recall, is something that is also seen in humans. The rats had abnormal rapid eye movement (REM) sleep patterns and awoke frequently during the day, unusual because they are nocturnal animals. In addition, their endogenous, or 'circadian' rhythms were also abnormal with a disruption of their 'biological clock'. Normally, during a 24-hour period there is a cycle of sleep-wake activity including a variation in temperature. But in the infected rats this cyclical variation was severely disrupted, just as occurs in patients suffering from sleeping sickness.

So where was the problem in the brains of these animals that caused their biological clock to go haywire? The answer is in an organ called the hypothalamus. This vitally important brain structure has many functions. It is in overall charge of the endocrine system which regulates hormone secretion through its influence over the pituitary gland, and controls the autonomic nervous system which regulates automatic functions such as blood pressure and sweating. It also influences body temperature, sleep patterns and appetite. When they examined the brains of the infected rats they found chemical abnormalities in a group of nerve cells called the suprachiasmatic nuclei (SCN) that are located in the hypothalamus just above the optic chiasm where the optic nerves from both eyes cross each other. The SCN plays a key role in acting as a 'pacemaker' for the normal endogenous rhythms that were so disrupted in the rats.

To add to the story, they found that secretion of the hormone melatonin by the pineal gland, and its binding to cells in the SCN, was abnormal in infected rats. This is highly relevant as melatonin is very important in the regulation of sleep-wake cycles. Some people take melatonin supplements to counteract the symptoms of 'jet lag', where the normal sleep pattern has been disrupted because of time zone differences. (I personally never found these at all effective but maybe that's just me!) Furthermore, you may recall that one of the brain regions that shows inflammatory changes in patients is the hypothalamus. So all of this fits together very nicely.

So there you have it. This parasite is a formidable enemy. When it invades the body it can release all kinds of toxic substances that can damage the CNS, and some species are resistant to the factors in the blood that are designed to destroy it before it gets started. When the body tries to attack it, the parasite plays hide and seek with the host immune response, and invariably wins. When the parasite is killed with toxic drugs it often does even more damage to the brain than when it was alive. And, to cap it all, even when the trypanosome is no longer present in the CNS, it leaves behind a legacy of immune destructiveness that all too often can prove fatal. Clearly, the trypanosome is a king amongst parasites.

CHAPTER SEVEN

A Meeting with the Animal Reservoirs

AFTER STUDYING SLEEPING SICKNESS in people and mice for almost 10 years, I decided it was time to learn a thing or two about the disease in cattle. After all, cattle are major reservoirs of the trypanosomes causing the human disease, so it's not possible to fully appreciate the problem of sleeping sickness without at least some knowledge of the animal reservoirs. The key factor linking man and animal is the tsetse fly. Reduce the man/fly contact and you have a handle on controlling the human disease. So perhaps it's not surprising that I ended up learning more about the fly than the cow.

The history of African trypanosomiasis is also the history of the African continent, and the disease has evolved to its current level of pathological virtuosity over many thousands, indeed millions, of years. An intriguing question is just why it has managed to establish and maintain such a powerful stranglehold on both animals and man in Africa. The answer lies in the nature of the parasite, the vector and the host.

The parasite is mighty because the trypanosome evades the host's immune response through successive waves of antigenic variation, and because there are so many sub-species that can produce severe levels of disease. The vector is mighty because the different species of tsetse fly have managed to adapt superbly to a whole range of habitats, ranging from the savannahs, lakeland shore areas and densely forested regions, and also because it has developed a highly efficient biological machinery that allows it to transmit the disease through its complex interaction with the parasite. Most critically, once the fly is infected, it is then infected for life, which makes it a constant threat. Yet the female fly can only be impregnated once, which is its Achilles heel that, as we shall see, can be exploited by man to control the disease.

But the susceptible host is certainly not mighty. It is highly vulnerable to infection by the trypanosome. The range of potential animal reservoirs for infection is very wide, ranging from man to numerous animal species including cattle, pigs, dogs, sheep, goats, camels, horses, small ruminants and many different types of wild animals. So, as you can see, the odds favour the parasite and its vector rather than the unfortunate host.

The place we chose to observe animal trypanosomiasis was the Nguruman field station which was set up by KETRI in 1987. Nguruman is located in the Kajiado district of south west Kenya, about 150 km from Nairobi. My travelling companions on this trip were, as always, Joseph and Moses, and we were joined this time by David Eckersall, a professor from the Veterinary Biochemistry department in Glasgow. As well as being my neighbour in Glasgow, David has also collaborated with us on the mouse model of African trypanosomiasis. He is an expert on what are known as 'acute phase proteins', important proteins in the blood that increase in various types of acute infections. We had found that two of these particular proteins were markedly increased in mice with the PTRE, so they have clear potential to act as disease markers. They also tell us something about the nature of the infections we study. He was interested in applying these biochemical markers to studies in cattle as well, so it made sense for all of us to see what might be possible in the field with a view to setting up some potentially productive collaborations.

After recovering at the Norfolk Hotel from the night flight and minor jet lag, we first visited KETRI, where we gave our respective lectures to a packed audience of scientists, veterinary experts, graduate students, post-doctoral fellows and technicians. As usual, Charity Gichuki, who had been one of our most gifted graduate students in Glasgow, raised the most challenging issues of our work that I addressed as best I could. Clearly her time in Glasgow had been well spent! After this stimulating ordeal by seminar, we worked out the travel schedule with Joseph in his rather spacious office that had one of the most gentle and serene views of the green rolling hills and plains surrounding Muguga that you could ever imagine. This was in sharp contrast indeed to the dreary, often rain-soaked, outlook from my office at the Southern General Hospital in Glasgow. Joseph by this time was well aware of my aversion to hot sweetened milk, and, with his customary courtesy, had arranged for a separately prepared flask of unsweetened coffee and milk to be prepared for us. So, rehydrated and mentally prepared for the adventure (or so we assumed), we set off in February 1998 by Land Rover to the field station in the south.

'You don't have to worry,' Joseph had assured me in his usual relaxed manner before we left, 'the first 100 km is on a tarmac road.'

By now you will have guessed that this did not entirely reassure me since I knew that the whole journey was 150 km long. Presumably the last 50 km was on a 'non-tarmac road' (assuming, of course, there was a road!). My imagination went into customary overdrive, which is exactly what Moses had to do with his vehicle once we had reached the end of the tarmac stretch.

The first two hours of the journey was a breeze, with rapid progress southwards on a narrow, undulating, well maintained tarmac road, until we reached Lake Magadi. The word 'Magadi' comes from the Maasai word *emakat,* meaning 'soda'. The lake is shallow and alkaline in a low-lying basin on the Rift Valley floor (actually the second lowest in the Rift Valley), and it extends 26 km from north to south, is 8 km wide and 600 m above sea level. Hot springs supply the lake with water which also feeds into a number of shallow lagoons. The covering of soda supports large numbers of flamingos and other birds, but the vegetation is sparse and dry, and the temperature very hot. So Lake Magadi is generally regarded as one of the world's unfriendliest lakes, with one source graphically referring to it as 'a shimmering pink coloured hellscape of over-powering heat and smell and temperatures well above 100°F'. I have to say that I personally wouldn't go quite that far, but my acquaintance with the lake was only brief.

The lake, which is the world's second largest source of sodium bicarbonate, is unique in that its deposits well up from beneath the earth's surface. Mining by the Magadi Soda Company has been a thriving industry for more than 80 years with an annual output of 220,000 tonnes of the mineral. It is then processed into soda ash (used in glass-making) and sodium chloride (table salt). This process takes place in the town of Magadi itself, and the factory where this work is carried out is also run by the Magadi Soda Company. The lake marked the end of the tarmac road and the beginning of a novel driving experience, at least for me.

The Magadi Salt Factory is just across the lake as you arrive, and to get to the other side you have to drive across a narrow causeway made of soil and interspersed with rickety wooden bridges. The good news was that Moses was driving, but even he seemed to be just a little tense as he expertly negotiated the causeway at a snail's pace. Once safely across, and after our heart rates had reduced to slightly lower levels, we started the final part of the journey. This was a real bone shaking experience as the 'road' was very rough and made of dirt and loose stone. For over an hour, which actually seemed much longer, Moses kept the vehicle on the straight and narrow while it violently shook and vibrated, and I was amazed that we didn't encounter a puncture or a major structural problem. The amount of legroom was highly limited at the back – which was slightly uncomfortable for me being rather short at just five feet eight inches, so it must have been agony for David who is over six feet tall. But he was remarkably stoical, which was even more impressive since he was suffering from a mild gastro-intestinal upset at the time. The absence of rear seat belts continued to worry me, and I think today that all of my internal organs must be pretty well fixed inside as that drive was enough to dislodge all but the most firmly attached structures.

We thought the shaking would never end, but of course it did. The road became smoother and flatter, and we soon passed through the attractive outskirts of the ranch and field station at Nguruman.

Large cattle barns, a few Maasai villagers wielding farming tools, and assorted animals including cows, goats, sheep and donkeys were to be seen here and there, all blending with the picturesque scenery that contrasted sharply and pleasantly from what had gone before. The pace of life seemed slow and relaxed here, in stark contrast to the chaotic clamour of Nairobi.

The Nguruman escarpment lies to the east of the Maasai Mara game park and makes up the western wall of the Rift Valley in the extreme south of Kenya. By definition, an escarpment is located along a steep slope at the edge of a plateau, or separating areas of land of different heights, and this is what we have here. It appears as a series of steps of rocky faults originating from the southern Ewaso Ngiro River on the valley floor at between 900 and 2,000 m on the top of the escarpment. This contrasts with the more even plains of Lolita and the Maasai Mara. The predominant colour of vegetation that I perceived at that time, which was just before the onset of the long rains that start in March every year, was green, but a green tinged with yellow, and with a multitude of different yellow-green shades, each one of which seemed to change gracefully into another as the amount of bathing sunlight varied during the day. The vegetation consisted of open or dense acacia woodland, and open plains with grassland and bushes, all varying with location.

I saw a few rocky streams as well, and these were clear and fast running, flowing down gracefully from the escarpment itself. Some of these areas were heavily infested with tsetse flies, and livestock productivity was consequently constrained by the scourge of trypanosomiasis. The area is also home to a variety of wildlife including birds, and, indeed, some regions of the escarpment are recognised as a suitable location for tourism, something that has, not surprisingly, been picked up by tourist companies. We never encountered any tourists during our visit, nor lions for that matter, which I half expected to see in view of our proximity to the famous Masaai Mara game park.

Once inside the field station proper, we were greeted with the now familiar warmth and courtesy of genuinely friendly *jambos* coming at us from all sides. The station covers about two acres of land, and at that time there were about six members of staff, although this was very variable depending on the workload. There were four senior staff houses, where we were to stay, a block for junior staff, a field laboratory and a kitchen. The station was located about 17 km from the border with Tanzania and about 40 km from the famous Lake Natron, which I have yet to see. A wide range of research activities have taken place over the years in the scenic group ranch, owned and managed by the local Maasai residents, and covering a large area of about 300 square km. There was a very friendly, productive and co-operative relationship between the local Maasai farmers and the research staff at the station. Each gained a great deal from the activities of the other, with valuable research data on tsetse flies and livestock obtained by the scientists, which could then be used to increase the productivity of the farms in various ways.

In general terms, the research undertaken by KETRI scientists there was in the fields of entomology, epidemiology, and socio-economics. In the first category were studies of tsetse fly ecology and the effectiveness of various tsetse control measures, including adaptation to the local conditions. In the second were longitudinal studies (that is, carried out over time rather than at just one moment) on the prevalence of disease in livestock, the susceptibility of different breeds of livestock to trypanosomiasis, and the impact of multiple diseases on livestock productivity. In the third were studies on the adoption and sustainability of tsetse and trypanosomiasis control methods by local communities. Since the station was established, a great deal of high quality scientific research has been successfully carried out by both Kenyan and a number of visiting scientists.

Our visit started off at a fast pace as if there was not a moment to lose. Within a few minutes of our arrival we had dropped off our travel bags in the one-room 'house' that had been allotted to us, and set off to explore the area in a muddy but robust Land Rover driven by the senior KETRI scientist in charge. Clearly his official duties here had to be flexible. Although it was still February, the rains had been very heavy over the previous week, which made the passage through the roads of the villages and escarpment extremely difficult. Large areas which we drove through were heavily flooded, and at some points it was virtually impossible to work out the true demarcation of natural rivers and flooded woodlands. When the Land Rover's wheels negotiated the floods we cold hear the same kind of whooshing sound that you expect from a ship or boat sailing through water. 'We are swimming again,' Joseph would say to me as we came across yet another flood. And all the time our guide and driver worked the steering wheel, clutch and brakes in the nonchalant and relaxed manner of a person who has not a care in the world. Here again was the equanimity of Kenya, one that always makes me feel a kind of admiring envy. Not once did the vehicle stall, even during our frequent courtesy stops to gently chat with the Maasai villagers whom we came across driving in the opposite direction. Not to have stopped to talk with them for a minute or two would have been regarded as a gross breach of etiquette, and I admired that too. Every conversation was conducted in the most relaxed and friendly manner you could imagine, and the contrast between that and the way I talk to even familiar colleagues at home seemed almost stark.

Every now and then we would come upon tsetse fly traps, carefully placed in strategic areas at a density of four traps per square kilometre. These consisted of outer blue and inner black pieces of cloth occupying about one square metre altogether. This was the moment when I began to see how tsetse control can be achieved in the real world of bush and field, and when what had been learned from lectures and papers was transformed into reality. So let's have a quick overview of the various methods currently in use for tsetse fly control.

The essential goal of tsetse control is to stop the fly's transmission of the trypanosome to the susceptible host, and in principle that can be achieved in several different ways. Eradication of the tsetse fly is the ultimate way of accomplishing this, but that is easier said than done. Over the last 25 years, the overall area of Africa affected by the tsetse fly has not actually diminished despite all the tsetse and trypanosomiasis control services and programmes that have been put in place. While there has been some progress in particular regions, there has been actual expansion of the tsetse belts in others. It has been estimated that less than 10 per cent of Africa has been cleared of tsetse in the last 100 years.

Vector, that is, tsetse, biology has probably made the greatest progress in the last 25 years in terms of practical measure to control the disease. We owe a great deal to the pioneering work of Glyn Vale and his colleagues working in Zimbabwe, who identified the key visual and olfactory (odour) stimuli that attract tsetse flies to the cows. Based on this knowledge, increasingly sophisticated fly traps have been developed and used effectively in the field. It was found that the flies were particularly attracted to a blue colour as well as black. These workers also found that the breath of an ox was highly attractive to the flies, the important components being carbon dioxide, acetone and a chemical called octenol. These key attractants can be manufactured artificially and the traps impregnated with them in order to attract the flies. So a typical trap would have blue cloth outside to attract the flies, which would then alight onto the black cloth surface. Good as these artificial odours are, they are still not as effective as real ox's breath in attracting flies so, clearly, there must be some additional factor that is important. The blue and black trap shown in [PLATE 14] is known as an Ngu trap as it was developed in Nguruman by Robert Brightwell and Robert Dransfield in the 1980s.

But traps have their drawbacks. For instance, the flies can sometimes fly out through the same route by which they entered the trap, and they require frequent inspection, which is labour intensive. The flies also die from heat exhaustion. So fly targets were then developed in which the odiferous blue and black cloths act as bait but are also impregnated with insecticide. When the fly alights onto the cloth it picks up enough insecticide on its belly such that even if it flies away, it dies later. Over the last few years there have been various developments in both target design and the type of odiferous attractant and insecticide used. In some regions of Africa these techniques have proved highly effective in reducing the tsetse fly population, by as much as 90 per cent in some regions.

A more recent development has been the use of 'pour-on' techniques in which the susceptible cattle are effectively live baits as they are treated with insecticide. When the flies land on them, they are contaminated with insecticide, which later kills them. This technique is proving increasingly popular and under some situations can be very cost-effective. The insecticide is applied to the back (10 to 20 ml depending on the size of the animal) and then spreads through the covering layers across the entire animal. Any insect that lands on the treated animal picks up a dose of insecticide, becomes immobile and dies and/or is eaten by insect predators on the ground. The commercial formulations of 'pour-on' can be effective for up to three months. Most importantly, if all or most of the cattle in an area are treated, they not only reduce the number of tsetse flies but also reduce the numbers of other biting flies including mosquitoes so the incidence of malaria also falls. As an added bonus, the tick burden on the cattle is greatly reduced and it is this aspect that is most readily apparent to the farmer and a key element in motivating them to use insecticide 'pour-ons'. The cost can be US$1 per treatment, but in many schemes the price is subsidised to encourage widespread usage, which is essential if the technique is to be effective.

An essential feature of all of these local techniques is that they are highly suitable for local rural community participation. They are low cost, often very effective, and their ease of maintenance means that they can be used by community-based control schemes, which are largely independent of external funding and management. This is very much what we observed in Nguruman. A key problem, though, with this approach has been sustainability, as all kinds of local political or financial problems can impact strongly on the efficient implementation of these local programmes. Community support for these measures can't always be taken for granted. I should add that after this trip I never again wore my usual blue shirts or jacket in the field. And I still haven't been bitten by a tsetse fly, so I was clearly not attractive to them even when I was wearing blue. I guess I didn't smell right.

Another approach to eradicate the tsetse has been the use of insecticides as sprays on the tsetse fly habitats. This has been more controversial because of the obvious implications for contaminating the local environment. Ground based insecticide spraying with a 'residual application' method has been used for many years and involves the application of high doses of insecticide such as DDT which persist for long periods. This can be cost-effective because repeated applications are not required. But such indiscriminate use of insecticides has been met with a lot of opposition because of harmful effects on wildlife and vegetation. More recently, 'discriminative' ground-spraying techniques have been used in some areas and are less harmful to the environment.

For many years 'non-residual' methods of spraying insecticides have also been available, usually by aerial spraying from aircraft. This involves the use of lower insecticide doses, which have to be repeated at regular intervals. This has been refined into a form of large-scale tsetse control method called the sequential aerosol drift technique (SAT) in which a low concentration and volume of insecticide is distributed at low altitude over a wide area from a fixed-wing aircraft. This technique, which has provided greater accuracy and minimal applications of insecticide, has proved to be effective in tsetse control in several regions of Africa, particularly in Botswana where SAT has eliminated tsetse flies. Despite such successes, not everyone is in favour of insecticide-based programmes and it remains a hot political issue.

Another method of large-scale area-wide elimination of the tsetse population is the sterile insect technique (SIT). This has become possible because of recent improvements in tsetse fly-rearing technology. The flies are reared in massive numbers and the males sterilised using irradiation. The sterilised flies are then released in very large numbers to the particular area where tsetse eradication is planned. The aim is to out-compete the fertile wild male tsetse fly in breeding, and, to achieve this, it is necessary to release about 10 sterile male flies for every normal wild male. Once a wild female fly is mated by a sterile male, she does not mate again, and therefore does not reproduce throughout her life. Over the course of several fly generations, and after the release of vast numbers of sterile male flies, the breeding rate in the local population is undermined and eventually collapses. The SIT approach was successful in eliminating the tsetse fly populations from the island of Zanzibar. When I recently picked the brains of a distinguished colleague about the future role of SIT, she told me that her feeling was that there is a potential place for SIT in tsetse control, especially for the elimination of small pockets of well-isolated flies. Also, she thought that if information on population genetic structuring of flies is incorporated in the application of SIT, then its effectiveness could be improved. But whether SIT could in the future produce permanent eradication of tsetse flies on a large scale is much less certain.

The enormous recent advances in molecular biology have also been extremely helpful in developing potentially very exciting new methods to block trypanosome transmission by the tsetse. The details of these, even if I understood them all, are well beyond the scope of this discussion. But essentially what many of them try to do is use molecular genetics and biological techniques to interfere with the switch from the non-infective to the infective parasite that occurs in the fly's gut. For example, one technique is to alter the normal bacteria in the fly's gut in order to make it a hostile environment for the developing trypanosomes to become infective so parasite transmission to the host is blocked.

It has also been possible to alter the actual genetic make-up of the flies themselves so that they are less viable and/or able to transmit infection. In order for this imaginative approach to be successful in the field, it will be necessary to release the 'mutant' flies in to the target area and hope that the existing infective fly population can eventually be replaced by the genetically engineered flies. That day I think is still a long way in the future. It should be appreciated that along with these molecular innovations, there have been huge advances in satellite imaging technology using satellite based Global Positioning Systems (GPS), and the related Geographic Information Systems (GIS). This advanced technology has allowed the construction of detailed satellite maps of climate, vegetation and altitude that have been of great value in predicting and mapping areas of regional tsetse fly distributions. This in turn could be very helpful in evaluating the success of regional and area-wide tsetse control programmes.

So these are the main types of techniques that have been, and continue to be, used in the African field to combat the tsetse fly. But it isn't possible to separate completely the science from the politics, and so I need to say a little about the institutions that have been set up to take these initiatives forward. With financial restructuring and cutbacks in government services, tsetse and trypanosomiasis control has largely depended on substantial externally funded schemes such as the Regional Tsetse and Trypanosomiasis Control Programme for Southern Africa (RTTCP) or the FITCA programme in East Africa that we came across in Chapter Five. The external funding from the European Union (EU) came with stringent environmental conditions and generally limited the widespread use of insecticides by, for example, aerial spraying. In more recent programmes, there has been a strong emphasis on community participation to ensure sustainability of the control measures with mixed results. The past few decades have also seen vigorous debates concerning the relative pros and cons of various control methods including those of tsetse suppression versus eradication.

The emergence of the Programme Against African Trypanosomiasis (PAAT) in 1997 provided a much-needed consensus on many of the issues that we have covered. PAAT is an interagency forum of the Food and Agriculture Organisation (FAO), World Health Organisation (WHO), International Atomic Energy Agency (IAEA) and the African Union-International Bureau for Animal Resources (AU-IBAR) which embraces the international expertise in the control of tsetse and trypanosomiasis. My colleague and friend Peter Holmes, a distinguished Professor of Veterinary Physiology and Vice-Principal for Research at Glasgow University, was the founding Chairman of PAAT. Since 1997 PAAT has played a leading role in publishing high level scientific advice and position papers on various aspects of tsetse and trypanosomiasis, and has developed internationally recognised criteria for identifying areas for disease control in Africa. PAAT continues to be based in the FAO office in Rome and holds annual meetings.

More recently, the Pan-African Tsetse and Trypanosomiasis Eradication Campaign (PATTEC) was launched in 2000 by the Heads of State of the African Union (AU). This powerful political force has led to a much greater awareness of the problem of trypanosomiasis in Africa and its close relationship with rural poverty. PATTEC, which is largely a field-based campaign, has already been successful in persuading the African Development Bank (ADB) to provide loans of US$70 million to increase their tsetse eradication campaigns. Further loans involving a larger number of countries are anticipated in the second phase. PAAT also provides a body of technical expertise to PATTEC as well as general support.

So much for the control of the tsetse fly. Back now to our intrepid Land Rover swimming through the flooded woodlands of Nguruman. It was early evening and already getting dark, but that was not a problem for our guide and driver who knew the entire area like the back of his hand. For some of the time, I felt as if I was dreaming, maybe because of tiredness, but also because of the hypnotic motion of the Land Rover. Despite the intimate presence of water in every direction, we remained perfectly dry, cocooned like submariners but in an open vessel that managed to protect us from the dangers outside. This is a recurring theme while driving in Africa. However flimsy and bare your vehicle is, so long as you are actually inside, you are not exposed to danger, whether it is from wild animals such as lions, or simply the relentless pressure of harsh rains. But once you are outside the vehicle, the balance of power, and therefore danger, completely changes.

Rivers led to woodlands, and paths in thick forests led to narrow passages through the villages, and so we continued in this vein for hours. Eventually we came to the end of the tour and were dropped off to recover our strength in the 'house' that had been allotted to us. It was actually a kind of tiny one room cottage with a fairly large main room that served as both a bedroom and living room, and a small area partitioned off at the back that served as a sort of makeshift bathroom. I have stayed in every kind of accommodation that can be imagined over the years, but by any standards this was basic (and that is being polite). But as always, once you have entered into the spirit of the land and the purpose of an expedition, then levels of comfort become irrelevant at best and just about bearable at worst.

It was extremely hot, and of course there was no air conditioning. The deep sink in the 'bathroom' was placed below a single rusty tap, or pipe, from which a steady stream of cold water eventually emerged. Fortunately we had brought our own towels. On the floor was a small plastic bowl, which I cautiously lifted to expose its interior. I soon wished I hadn't as it revealed a very large slowly crawling insect which then scuttled across the floor. But, to be frank, none of this worried me. What I was really concerned about were the multiple holes in the mosquito nets above the two single beds where we were to sleep. The problem with that is that the carbon dioxide in our exhaled breath might attract the ubiquitous mosquitoes, which could then enter through the holes to bite us without mercy. I had bought rolls of sticky tape, and, supplemented by a box of plasters, we tried, with some success, to seal up the larger holes. I sighed as I realised this was likely to be one of my less comfortable nights in Africa.

The nicest part of our dwelling was the spacious front porch where we could relax in comfortable armchairs as we all discussed our plans for the next day. Although a few of the houses had their own built-in toilets, this was not the case for us. To relieve ourselves, we had to go outside and walk about 50 yards down a narrow pathway where there was a tiny hut with a pit latrine and no functioning light. When it was dark the user had to make a choice. You could either close the door and avoid the mosquitoes and risk slipping into the pit, or keep the door open throughout the operation and risk getting bitten by a mosquito or other flying insect in the most vulnerable parts of your body. There was no contest. I closed the door.

Dinner was more of a spiritual event than a meal, and its memories still wander in my mind. An extensive outdoor buffet had been organised in the grounds of the station near the houses, where the staff, some villagers and ourselves had gathered. We all sat in comfortable chairs round the assorted victuals that had been so generously prepared for us. Various meats, abundant chapati, rice and vegetables produced enticing aromas that slowly wafted between us. But first, as always in Kenya, were the speeches. These, in my experience, always tend to be very courteous, but here the gracious welcoming of the visitors had been raised to an art form. First, the senior local KETRI officer thanked Joseph, who, after all, was the director of the whole institute, for honouring them with his visit. He also welcomed David and myself, and thanked us for taking the time to visit Nguruman. His speech was delivered in a soft, thoughtful way, and every word seemed almost to linger in the gentle stillness that it had produced. Next, Joseph gave an equally generous and gracious speech, and managed to find that critical balance between friendliness and authority that is so essential for those who want to be effective in high positions. He also formally greeted us with genuine warmth. Finally, I got up and said a few words of thanks and told them, with total honesty, how delighted and moved we both were to have received such a wonderful reception. Then we ate. Despite the rigours of the day, for some reason I didn't have much of an appetite. Perhaps it was all the excitement.

It was difficult not to be impressed by the uninhibited clarity of the myriads of stars that were visible in the night sky, a sight half expected perhaps, but no less impressive for that. Although a keen amateur astronomer, I can hardly see anything at night in my native Glasgow because of the clouds, pollution, and artificial light from street lamps that so often obscure the night sky. But here the clarity of the sky was extraordinary, and it was possible to identify numerous stars and constellations, including one or two that I had recognised but never seen before. This unique experience was set against a backdrop of deliciously warm, almost palpable, night air, animated speech, and the intermittent but instantly recognisable sounds of wild animals, some quite near us, or so it seemed. 'This is surreal,' David said quietly to me. And indeed it was. That evening embodied something of the spirit of Africa: surreal and magical.

We survived a predictably uncomfortable night of sleep and awoke to be greeted by a beautiful and bright African morning. The green, yellow and brown foliage around us was majestic in the light from the rising sun, and we felt strong and energised, full of anticipation for what we were soon to see on the Maasai farmlands. So far, virtually everything we had seen had been in the evening and at night, so we didn't quite know what to expect during the day. Breakfast was simple but delicious, with the taste of freshly buttered bread with jam and the aroma of strong coffee lingering pleasantly as we set off in the Land Rover. Our sense of well-being was enhanced by the failure or refusal of the local mosquitoes to bite us despite the inadequate nets. Perhaps it was our smell, or maybe it was the DEET that we had smeared all over us. Or maybe they just had no taste.

It didn't take long for us to reach the ranch where the blood sampling of the cows was just starting. This took place early in the day both to avoid the brutally hot daytime sun and to maximise the chances of identifying trypanosomes in the cattle. I rapidly learned a good deal about animal trypanosomiasis which, as you would expect, has its similarities with, and differences from, its human counterpart. By the end of the day I was more impressed with the similarities. The area was certainly scenic, and here the view was mainly of the open plains, which contrasted starkly with the densely forested woodlands of the previous evening. The whole area was traversed by numerous four-wheel-drive vehicles from KETRI and elsewhere.

We need to be aware of a few details about the animal disease. To recap, there are three main trypanosome species that cause the problems in cattle. The two main culprits are *T.congolense* and *T.vivax*, but our old acquaintance, *T.b. brucei,* can also cause disease. Another parasite strain called *T.evansi* causes severe disease in camels and horses. The animal disease occurs in widespread geographical areas in Kenya, especially in the northern, coastal, and western lake shore regions that are also infested by the tsetse fly. The clinical features of trypanosomiasis in cattle are very variable, but important and common features are weight loss, anaemia, fever and enlarged lymph nodes, very much like the disease in humans. Various factors determine whether the animal gets the disease, in particular the breed of animal, some breeds being more resistant to infection than others, the level of 'tsetse challenge', that is, high or low numbers of the fly to which the animal is exposed, and the innate ability (or 'virulence') of a particular parasite to cause disease.

The impact of the disease is massive in many different ways. It has been estimated that 50 to 70 million animals in Africa are currently at risk from trypanosomiasis. The total cattle population in Africa is approximately 174 million, but only about 30 million of these cattle are found in 7 million square km of tsetse-infested savannah and woodland areas. The Food and Agriculture Organisation (FAO) has estimated that if these 7 million square km of land were cleared of African trypanosomiasis, then the total cattle population in this area could rise by as much as 120 million. But right now this area cannot be utilised effectively for livestock production or other important agricultural activity. This profound and tragic under-exploitation of natural resources has, of course, a massive impact on human health and economic development. So the disease is truly a major obstacle for the achievement of both human and animal health and welfare. Remember that cattle are reservoirs of *T.b.rhodesiense* parasites, the cause of East African sleeping sickness, so the disease in man and animals is intimately connected in other ways as well. We shall consider this aspect further when we discuss the problems in Uganda.

Soon after we arrived, we witnessed the blood sampling of the local cattle herds by the KETRI scientific staff and technicians, assisted by the local Maasai farmers, some of whom we met and talked to during the visit. The working relationship between the Nguruman staff and the local farmers was excellent, and there was a mutual respect and need in combating a shared problem. The cattle were first herded up by the Maasai, and then lined up in close formation from front to back in a long narrow wooden enclosure. The blood samples from the nearest animals were then collected by the station staff in small thin glass capillary tubes, which were carefully labelled so they could be matched up with the particular cows later on. A small makeshift field laboratory had already been set up near our Land Rover where five or six technicians and scientists were sitting round a working bench checking their equipment which had been carefully placed on top of it.

In most field stations, the diagnosis of trypanosomiasis relies on examination of fresh wet blood films, although the chances of detecting the parasites are increased if the blood is first spun down in a small centrifuge. This also enables the volume of packed red blood cells known as the haematocrit, to be obtained. If the haematocrit is lower than normal, then anaemia can be diagnosed. Our laboratory had a 'microhaematocrit' field centrifuge which was powered by a small generator located in our vehicle nearby, as well as glass slides, staining chemicals and a light microscope for analysing the blood on the slides. So we were all set.

After the first technician had spun down the tubes, he handed it to his colleague next to him who prepared a 'buffy coat' sample which was then applied to a glass slide. The greatest chance of detecting the parasites is in the buffy coat layer. When a fresh blood sample is centrifuged, there is an obvious demarcation between the packed red blood cells and the clear plasma. But between these two layers is a thin layer of visible white blood cells; the buffy coat layer. Max Murray and his colleagues had pioneered this particular field technique. It is also possible to gain further information on the type of parasite by special staining methods. One of the scientists beckoned me to the microscope and asked me what I saw. The effect was stunning. I saw, for the first time in my life, live trypanosomes moving incredibly fast across my field of vision. I learned that these were of the *T.vivax* species as they are the only trypanosomes that are capable of such a high level of motility. So they were the cause of the disease in the particular cow that had been sampled.

Once the diagnosis is proven or strongly suspected, there is obviously no option but to treat the animal. But there are grey areas, and the diagnosis of trypanosomiasis in animals can be problematic, just as in humans. In many cases, treatment may be offered if the animal is anaemic and from a tsetse-infested area since trypanosomes are the most common cause of anaemia in adult cattle in these areas. Many farmers treat cattle without any definitive diagnosis of parasitaemia (parasites in the blood), and rely purely on the suggestive clinical signs. They may also underdose in such situations because they rarely have the facilities to weigh the animal first. In some surveys, blood films fixed with special stains are used and allow easier identification of the trypanosome species involved.

As with sleeping sickness in humans, there are several other tests available that have been used to diagnose the disease in animals. For example, it is possible to look for antibodies to the parasite components, and this has been valuable in large-scale epidemiological surveys. But this approach is of little use in an individual animal since it can't distinguish between an existing and a recently treated infection. The advanced molecular technique of PCR that we have encountered before has been examined in a few studies. It appears to be more sensitive than the buffy coat method, and it can also give information on parasite species differentiation. The sensitivity of a technique refers to the percentage of actual cases that it detects in practice, that is, the number of true cases that it doesn't miss. The PCR technique can also detect more mixed infections than other methods, and this is important where *T.b.brucei* is involved and when cattle are also serving as reservoirs for *T.b.rhodesiense* which causes human disease. But PCR is very expensive, and it also picks up parasite DNA in animals that have already been treated, so it will be a long time before it is in routine use in Africa. Just as in humans, the diagnosis of animal trypanosomiasis urgently requires a technique that is cheap, easy to use, field-adaptable, quick and reliable. The problem is that we are still using insensitive techniques that were developed decades ago.

We come to treatment, and again, I have been struck by the depressing parallels that are seen in man and animals where so little seems to change over the years. In most African countries the principal method of disease control continues to be the use of trypanocidal drugs (killing the parasites) to treat and prevent the disease in cattle. It is estimated that 35 million doses of such drugs are administered in Africa every year which is a considerable burden on its already hard-pressed regional economies. You will recall that in humans, there are four drugs that are used to treat trypanosomiasis. In animals there are only three trypanocidal drugs that are available and they have all been on the market for many decades, in fact over 40 years. That sounds familiar, doesn't it? The three drugs are isometamidium, homidium and diminazene aceturate (berenil). You will remember from Chapter Six that subcurative doses of this last drug, berenil, is used in our mouse model of sleeping sickness to induce a PTRE, which is rather worrying in itself. There are no new drugs for cattle trypanosomiasis in the pipeline, so it is essential that the few drugs that we have available continue to be used as effectively as possible.

A major problem with animal treatment is the emergence of

drug resistance. There are many factors that have led to this problem and it is the focus of a great deal of current research interest. Unfortunately, resistance has been documented for all three drugs on the market. One contributing factor has been the increasing availability of these drugs through local channels, with the result that farmers who have purchased these drugs at very low prices are prone to treat their cattle on just the suspicion of disease without the benefit of a proper diagnosis of trypanosomiasis. Such indiscriminate drug usage is a recipe for inducing drug resistance, and it is very likely that a large percentage of cattle treated for trypanosomiasis don't actually have the disease at all. Moreover, it is possible for a particular trypanosome to be resistant to more than one drug. Drug resistance is also more likely to develop when the 'tsetse challenge' is high and this phenomenon can be modelled mathematically. A further, emerging problem is the actual quality of the drugs themselves. Somehow, the market has been shown to contain some poor-quality drugs that have little effectiveness against the trypanosomes. When this factor is combined with the sometimes indiscriminate use of drugs then you have the perfect scenario for serious drug resistance to occur. Having said all this, it should be recognised that in several instances in Africa, drug therapy has been both effective and sustained in controlling the disease.

Peter Holmes and his colleagues in both Africa and Scotland have been studying this thorny problem for some time, and want to help maximise the effectiveness of the three drugs. In a series of studies, they were able to elucidate many of the factors that determine the efficacy of isometamidium and other trypanocides. It was shown that the prophylactic, that is, preventative, cover of isometamidium against drug-resistant trypanosomes could be as long as six months. Using specialised detection techniques, they worked out the protective levels of this drug in the blood. Once challenged by drug-resistant trypanosomes, the drug levels in the blood of infected animals are different compared to those seen with susceptible trypanosomes. Such knowledge in turn allowed them to devise a method of determining the prevalence of drug-resistance in the field. They have developed a single-dose mouse test that can tell them the degree of drug resistance of the trypanosomes in different regions in countries across Africa. So once again the laboratory mouse has assisted us in our battle with this disease. Relevant to this, Mike Barrett and his colleagues in the University of Glasgow have recently devised a simple, but rather ingenious, method of testing for resistance of *T.brucei* parasites to the drug melarsoprol. Resistant parasites have a defect in their surface membrane that can easily be detected using fluorescent markers.

Holmes and his co-workers have also made real progress in identifying some of the factors that lead to the development of drug resistance in trypanosomes. In the long run it will be critical to have a detailed understanding of the pharmacological and molecular mechanisms involved in the process. But to do this there needs to be a great deal more financial backing of laboratory and field programmes designed to tackle the problem. So far that has not happened, despite the enormous significance of drug resistance.

There is another phenomenon that I learned about at Nguruman that is of great significance, both in terms of understanding the nature of the disease and its possible control. Max had often mentioned to me that it had been known for many years that certain West African breeds of cattle such as the N'Dama and the West African Shorthorn, as well as some small ruminants, had the ability to survive in tsetse-infested areas whereas other breeds such as the Zebu readily succumbed to trypanosomiasis. This ability to resist infection is called trypanotolerance, and is characterised by an innate ability to resist the anaemia and to control the parasitaemia, both of which, as we have seen, are typical of the animal disease. These breeds are also resistant to other infections such as those transmitted by ticks. The great importance of this resistant trait is underpinned by the setting up of the International Trypanotolerance Centre (ITC) in The Gambia over 20 years ago. This is a particular area of interest to Max who himself has been closely involved with ITC and West

Africa since the early 1970s. He has invoked trypanotolerance as an indicator of 'the power of genetic resistance'.

A great deal of research has been carried out on trypanotolerance. For example, the mechanisms of genetic resistance in these particular breeds, including the molecular processes underlying it, have been studied. The importance of environmental factors in maintaining the trypanotolerant state has been a further area of interest. As one might expect, the host immune response against the parasite has been shown to be important, with resistant breeds possessing a superior immune system with a more effective antibody response than the susceptible animals. There are enormous potential benefits to be gained from these resistant breeds of cattle. Careful selection and crossbreeding techniques in Africa are now allowing these disease-resistant traits in cattle to be utilised in selective breeding programmes to enhance the productivity of local breeds. With the current availability of clinical markers of trypanotolerance, it should be possible to increase the proportion of such resistant animals in the local cattle populations, which could increase the output of both meat and dairy products.

All this I saw and learned in this remarkable facility, one that was educational for us visitors, and truly inspiring in what it set out to achieve. Pioneering studies had been carried out here by many different veterinary scientists, and the station itself bore lasting hallmarks of many notable accomplishments. I knew at once that the memories of this place that had been burned into my mind would be permanent.

CHAPTER EIGHT

Fear and Wonder in Africa

THROUGHOUT OUR JOURNEY so far into the world of the trypanosome and the tsetse fly, we have seen the cruel nature of sleeping sickness. We have also learned about the extreme dangers of its treatment once the parasite has entered the nervous system. In encountering these grim human realities in East Africa, I have been acutely aware at times of the physical dangers of working in the field as well as a heightened spiritual closeness to the fabric of Africa, one that sometimes seems almost tangible. In this chapter I want to explore some of these feelings and threats.

Let me start on a positive note. I have alluded before to the beauty of African light. It brings everything it touches into a heightened focus, and seems to make flowers and countryside more immediate and vivid than is the case in Europe. There are few more breathtaking sights than sunrise in the early morning on the Maasai Mara game reserve in southern Kenya, an experience perhaps even more spiritual than witnessing the sunset on the shores of Lake Victoria. In both cases, the sun's progress upwards to the sky or downwards to the earth is swift, but tends to be seen under a kind of time-lapse sequence as the mind decides to prolong the vision, perhaps in an unconscious desire to savour what it sees for as long as possible. Whether it is the light on the vast savannahs of the countryside, or the flickering beauty of filtered sunlight in the dense green woodlands, African light is alluring and unique.

Few writers have captured in words the special qualities of African light, colours and foliage as well as Karen Blixen. In *Out of Africa* she vividly describes the atmosphere of her farm at the foot of the Ngong hills, which are at an altitude even higher than Nairobi:

... it was Africa distilled up through six thousand feet like the strong and refined essence of the continent. The colours were dry and burnt, like the colours of pottery. The trees had a light delicate foliage, the structure of which was different from that of trees in Europe...The sky was rarely more than pale blue or violet, with a profusion of mighty, weightless, ever-changing clouds towering up and sailing on it, but it has a blue vigour in it, and at a short distance it painted the ranges of hills and the woods a fresh deep blue. In the middle of the day the air was alive over the land, like a flame burning.

Anyone who has spent time in the Kenyan countryside will recognise that evocative description for its insight and inner truth, but words can only do so much. While they can convey the essence of a vision, only actual experience can truly make you aware of the breathtaking beauty and deep spirituality of the landscape. For me, the sight of a herd of gentle Thomson's gazelle grazing in a sunbathed savannah in the late afternoon is the epitome of an Arcadian serenity that has been forever burned into my consciousness. Others may find excitement and more appreciation of nature at the sight of a lion kill on the rolling plains of the Mara reserve, something I have witnessed more than once.

'It's neither cruel nor not cruel, just nature,' an old hand at Africa knowingly explained to me when I once expressed my understanding, but also genuine horror, at what I could only see as nature's cruelty. The savage tearing of flesh by the two lionesses, and then the slow obscene throttling of the prey by the lion as it delivered the prolonged *coup de grace*.

So much for the daylight. What about the African night? My most vivid experiences of this have been in southern Kenya, once, as we have seen, in Nguruman, and at other times by the side of a blazing evening camp fire amidst the vast terrain of the Mara reserve. The sight of the Southern Cross constellation continues to be a revelation for an astronomy enthusiast from Glasgow. Again, Karen Blixen, who referred to the Southern Cross as 'the doorkeeper to the great world', has eloquently pinpointed the essence of the African night's special qualities and power:

> The sky was serene and silently triumphant, resplendent with stars… The stellar heaven of the equator is richer than that of the north, and you see it more because you are out more at night.

She goes in to explore the special quality of dreams at night, and the rich tapestry of experience they can encompass. She also makes the following comparison:

> The thing which in the waking world comes nearest to a dream is night in a big town, where nobody knows one, or the African night. There too is freedom: it is there that things are going on, destinies are made around you, there is activity on all sides, and it is none of your concern.

An unnerving experience for me, and I suspect many other visitors to Africa, is that sometimes I am not sure that everything I witness is actually happening, and at no time is this more apparent than at night in the field. When it's possible to fall asleep quickly, and to stay asleep until morning, there is no problem. But when it is oppressively hot, humid and uncomfortable, then the discomfort can be greatly heightened by the intermittent sounds of wild animals and the rhythmic singing of the insects. It is not so much a question of 'What am I doing in this place?' but more one of 'Am I really here, in this hut, in this night, in this country 5,000 miles from my home?' Most people who have visited Africa have had this kind of frightening experience, like a feeling of unreality, like a sort of 'fear of Africa at night', but the majority soon recover once the morning light removes the nocturnal demons. The surreal African night is soon replaced by the reality of daytime.

The worst experience I have ever had in this regard was a few years ago in the Samburu game reserve, which, in my personal view, is possibly even more magnificent and mystical than the Mara, with its low moonlike volcanic landscapes, exotic foliage and rare wild life such as the reticulated giraffe, grevy's Zebra, gerenuk and oryx. It was around 30°C, and I was just about alright until midnight when the ceiling air conditioning unit was turned off for the night to save electricity. Even worse, my mosquito net had many holes in it, and I had run out of sticking plaster to cover them, so I was a sitting duck, so to speak. I rapidly became dehydrated, and began to suffer from heat exhaustion, and sweated profusely, which is rather unusual for me. No matter how much bottled water I drank, the symptoms wouldn't abate. I was entirely alone, and the cries of nocturnal predators outside just a few yards from me added to my night terror.

After several hours, sleep came at last as a brief, merciful release at about five in the morning. I was convinced that I might die that night, but managed to keep my nerve. But only just. And that was the most frightening part of this episode. It was not so much the physical symptoms that were the problem, but the fear of the African night where there could be no rescue, or mercy. Only loneliness, and possible death. I have known many people to have had such an experience, but fortunately that was the first and last in my case. I wonder what people with sleeping sickness dream about. I suspect they must dream a lot in view of all the REM activity that their brains show.

So we have now changed our focus and have gone from light to dark, so let me tell you now about some of the physical dangers and problems of visiting and working in Africa. While, inevitably, some of this will come across in a negative way, please remember that I have a profound affinity for Africa and its people, despite my personal vendetta against some of its worst diseases.

The obvious danger that all visitors to Africa face is, of course, malaria. Worldwide this kills far more people that sleeping sickness, probably 20 times as many, but not all people with untreated malaria die, whereas untreated sleeping sickness is a death sentence. Nevertheless, you really don't want to catch malaria if you can possibly avoid it because it can be a very nasty, and frequently fatal, disease even when treated. In Nairobi, the general advice is that anti-malarial prophylaxis is not necessary, unless you venture outside to areas where malaria is known to be a risk. The reason for this is that the high altitude of the city is hostile to the malaria parasites so they don't reside there. Allegedly so. Nevertheless, I have always taken prophylaxis when in Nairobi, but on all visits I have always travelled outside the city as well.

It is noticeable how the approach to prevention has changed since I first visited. Initially the regime was weekly chloroquine with daily paludrine which Max, Frank and I would all take like clockwork every morning at breakfast in our hotel. Passion fruit, paw-paw, banana bread, toast and jam, all laced with a sprinkling of paludrine. But then the malaria parasites became increasingly resistant to these standard drugs, especially in the regions of the country where we visited. Falciparum malaria, a nasty form, was especially resistant, and then the standard classic preventative drugs might well have been ineffective in the southern and western areas of the country where I spent so much time later on. So it was necessary to try something else.

Next I took a drug called maloprim which is a mixture of two drugs, called pyrimethamine and dapsone (this latter drug is also used for treating leprosy). But soon after that my infectious diseases consultant colleagues in Glasgow advised me to switch to something else, even though all these drugs agreed with me, as I was spending most of my time in choroquine-resistant areas of Kenya. So I took the drug mefloquine, which is also known as lariam. The first time I took this I found it very convenient, as it only needs to be taken once weekly. I had no side effects, and it was highly effective in the high-risk regions I was visiting. I was delighted. So far, so good. The following year I took lariam again but this time there were problems. Within a day of the first tablet I felt extremely nauseated, but I could cope with that in the secure knowledge that I was so well protected from malaria. But within a few days I felt very on edge and jittery, extremely anxious, and at times almost paranoid about the security risks in the city. I knew instinctively that something was wrong, and soon had the insight to attribute these frightening symptoms to this drug, which I promptly stopped taking. I switched to another drug and very slowly recovered my normal psychological equilibrium. Of course I can't be 100 per cent sure that it was the lariam that made me feel so jittery, but this is a published and well known side effect of the drug which the manufacturers have always made perfectly clear. I know at least one person who experienced more severe psychological side effects than I did. No permanent harm was done to me, and I always regretted that I couldn't take this very convenient and effective drug again.

The next prophylactic I used was an antibiotic called doxycycline which was not only effective in protecting against malaria, but also, as a welcome bonus, provided significant protection from traveller's diarrhoea, which I shall mention later. The drug is also used for the treatment of acne and can make the skin photosensitive, so overexposure to sunlight is not recommended. This was also fine, but the problem with all of the anti-malarials that I've mentioned so far is that they need to be started about a week prior to leaving for the destination, and must be continued for four to five weeks after returning home. It takes willpower to persist with the tablets for so long. As we noted in the very first chapter, failure to complete the course can lead to a person developing malaria, with the possibility of fatal consequences. It's a great pain, but the course has to be completed. The fact that some people travel to very high risk areas without taking any prophylactic drugs at all, but still don't catch malaria, proves nothing in my view apart from the fact that they have been very lucky.

I finally became more fortunate a few years ago when I was recommended to take malarone, a newer, but not inexpensive drug. Not only has this drug, so far at least, not caused me any side effects, but it only needs to be taken for one week after returning home.

Needless to say, the very best way of avoiding malaria is to not get bitten by the mosquitoes in the first place: we must cover up our arms and legs in the evenings and at night, and also apply liberal amounts of a highly effective insect repellent such as diethyltoluamide (DEET). This substance smells disgusting, but it really does work. The smell quite knocks me out, so God knows what it must do to the mosquitoes of western Kenya who have never forgiven me for using the stuff.

Another potential hazard of African travel, or in fact any tropical visit, is, of course traveller's diarrhoea, which is something I dread every time I go to Africa. I have been stricken with this about four or five times, the last in 2003, and believe me it's no fun. As well as myself, most of my friends and colleagues, and my wife, have suffered the ravages of this ghastly affliction during their first visit to Africa. All of us have many bacteria residing harmlessly in our intestines, but what happens here is that foreign pathogenic organisms gain access to our virgin guts where they wreak varying levels of havoc.

The most common culprit is enterotoxigenic *Escherichia coli* (ETEC for short) which is a bacterium that produces toxins that greatly increase intestinal secretion, producing the nasty symptoms that we all know so well. A number of other micro-organisms, including protozoan parasites, viruses and other exotic bacteria, can also produce the same clinical symptoms. There are many factors that influence our chances of acquiring such an infection, and you can certainly reduce the chances of this happening by such simple measures as only drinking bottled water, avoiding uncooked food, salads, ice cream and ice, practising high standards of personal hygiene, taking care where you swim and so on. That is all true and good practice of course, but prior to at least two of my own episodes I had been meticulously careful and had no idea at all why I had succumbed. Even worse, one of these started just as I was boarding a long haul flight back to the UK.

Is there a case for antibiotic prophylaxis to avoid this irksome and highly distressing problem? Prompt treatment with an antibiotic such as ciprofloxacin can be highly effective in curtailing the symptoms, sometimes limiting the diarrhoea to just a few hours. I suspect I might go for the option of taking prophylactic antibiotics to avoid this when I next visit Africa. Interestingly, I have found that the longer the interval between visits, the greater is the chance of going down with this condition. That presumably has something to do with the protective immune system in the intestines. Immunity again. So here's an interesting thought. I recently agreed with a well-travelled and knowledgeable American colleague that given the choice between losing our supply of ciprofloxacin and malarone, or our hold luggage, we would rather lose the luggage every time.

We come to personal security, both on the roads and in the cities and countryside. The poor state of some of the roads in Kenya and Uganda that I have been compelled to travel on is a constant source of irritation. I have already talked about this a lot as you know, and it is up to governments to sort out. But the problem is made worse by the bad driving and the poor condition of many of the cars and lorries, some of which belch out vast plumes of choking black smoke behind them. The age of the matatus may be on the wane, but recently Joseph, Moses and I were stuck for miles behind a van crammed with passengers that had its back doors wide open and flapping as two boys hung onto them. Every time we tried to overtake it, the van swung out to block our path. It was exceedingly dangerous. Add to this the frequent absence of seat belts, and the lack of strict and enforced drink-driving legislation, and you can see why the roads can be so dangerous.

While the roads make me angry, the traffic causes real fear. I am often asked whether I take a pint of my own blood when I travel to Africa in case I am involved in an accident. The idea is to avoid catching AIDS from a local blood transfusion. I have always regarded such a plan as being totally impractical, if not plain daft, as under such circumstances there is unlikely to be anyone around to set up an intravenous infusion, and just one pint of blood is hardly likely to be sufficient. I did, however, go through a phase for a few years of taking up temporary membership of the flying doctor service in Kenya. If anyone can save your life in the countryside and bush, they can, and it was good to support such a magnificent humanitarian organisation. And they could probably land their small aircraft just about anywhere. Although I sometimes worry about falling ill in the bush and being admitted to the shabby and poorly equipped hospitals that I visit, this is not the real danger. It is on the roads where the real threat of death and injury lies.

Regarding personal security in the cities, that is another matter. While anyone venturing out after dark, or during the day laden with expensive jewellery, is a clear sitting duck for getting robbed in Nairobi, the same could be said for many cities throughout the world. The trick in any big city is to use your common sense. I personally have never been attacked or robbed while in Africa, although I have heard of several people who have. I have certainly felt nervous in various parts of Kenya, but no more than in certain areas of London where I grew up, and some East Coast cities in the US. That said, I have seen the potential for civil unrest to flare up overnight in Nairobi, and I would certainly regard it far more warily in terms of personal safety than most other cities I have visited. And the phenomenon of 'car-jackings' in Nairobi is also something that we hardly ever see in Europe. My adopted city of Glasgow also has a reputation for violent crime, but, again, I have not been troubled in 20 years. It exists for sure, but only, by and large, in certain high risk areas. Maybe I have just been lucky, so far.

There is a curious element to the security issue in Africa. I am referring to the ambiguity that is inherent in some potentially dangerous situations, and the way in which just a brief hesitation can compromise you. Two examples of this come to mind. The first occurred while I was on a week's holiday with my wife, Catherine, in April 2000. We were in a taxi travelling from the airport to our hotel in town when, soon after we set off, a young man suddenly jumped aboard. Initially, he seemed to be a friend of the driver, but he then lunged towards us and tried to sell us a safari tour. We politely declined, and he then moved his hand near my wife's neck as he complimented her on such a lovely necklace. At this point I was worried, especially as the taxi seemed to be driving away from the main city area that I knew very well. Without much thought, I suddenly started shouting at the young man warning him that we were VIPs (which was totally untrue), and that we would be missed very quickly by important officials if anything happened to us. Immediately he looked sullen and upset and the driver swerved the taxi back along the road to the city while they both maintained a chilling silence. The question is simple – were we in any real danger? To this day I don't know.

A second episode occurred later, on the same trip. Just before we entered the Lake Nakuru reserve, our driver dropped us off for a 'comfort break' and a visit to a local, but rather isolated, curio shop where all kinds of wooden carvings, African pottery, jewellery and souvenirs were on display. The young man in the store welcomed us with the usual *jambo* and asked us all sorts of questions. When he asked us what we did, my wife said she was a PhD student, and he said he couldn't understand how that would allow her to make a living. We weren't interested in what he was selling so politely thanked him and slowly made for the door. Blocking our exit, a tall well-built young man smiled at us and insisted that we keep looking around as he was sure that there must be something there that would catch our interest. At this stage I was worried. He kept on asking us questions, but my remarks about having government connections (again untrue) cut no ice this time. We tried to leave again, but then the other man blocked our exit. Finally, to placate them I bought a set of wooden animal carvings sitting around a table for an exorbitant sum, and we were allowed to leave, but not before one of them tried to exchange some useless UK pound coins that he had been given. Interestingly, when we expressed our anger to the driver who had left us there, he had the guiltiest expression that I have ever seen. Again, how much danger were we really in? Should I have initially hesitated? I just don't know. In a straight physical fight, I would have had no chance whatsoever. I should add that these wooden figures, which we call 'the committee', have a special place in our front living room, and they never fail to remind us of the ambiguity and uncertainty of security in Africa.

Sometimes fear and wonder can occur at the same time. A few years ago I had a day free after a conference in Nairobi, just before my return to the UK. So I went on a day trip to Naivasha, about 70 km north of Nairobi. Lake Naivasha is a peaceful, shallow, freshwater lake, and a great beauty spot much frequented by both tourists and locals. The lakeside area in Naivasha is very beautiful with exquisite multicoloured trees and plants, and all kinds of animal wild life, including numerous species of birds, antelope, giraffe, and several large and potentially dangerous hippopotami swimming around in the lake itself. It is possible to take a five minute trip in a small wooden boat with an outboard motor across the lake to the small Crescent Island. This is a submerged volcanic crater, with an interesting and picturesque wildlife sanctuary. After I had been dropped off, and arranged the rendezvous point for the return journey, I started to explore the small island as quickly as I could since my time was limited.

After a few minutes of walking up a large hill, I encountered a remarkable sight about halfway up, and about 30 yards away from me. Staring straight at me, or so it seemed at the time, was the most beautiful antelope I had ever seen. It was snow white in colour and didn't seem to move an inch as it fixed me with its gentle but stern gaze. After about five minutes, I moved forward a few yards and the animal also moved slowly towards me. Then, as I was looking at it, I suddenly shuddered and felt waves of fear and impending danger going through my body. The antelope seemed to be warning me of some nearby danger.

'Be careful,' I felt it say, 'Watch your back! You are in great danger.'

I began to sweat, my pulse quickened, and my forehead grew clammy. It then turned away and I quickly made my way towards the water's edge as if to cleanse and expiate my fear. But the feeling persisted. Soon afterwards, an island security guard carrying a large shotgun and a belt containing enormous long coloured bullets that rather alarmed me, appeared from the other side of the hill. Appearing quite friendly, he asked me if I wanted to be shown the animal sanctuary. I politely declined, and spent the rest of the visit walking around the unusual and enchanting island which seemed to be almost deserted. I later returned safely to the shore on the other side of the lake. Recently, I learned of the increasing crime rate in the town of Naivasha, and the murder of one of the local European lodge owners. I sometimes wonder, however irrational it must sound, whether that mystical white animal knew something I didn't.

PART THREE

Hope for the Future

CHAPTER NINE

Further Afield and the Ugandan Dimension

FEBRUARY 2002 marked the beginning of a new direction for our work on sleeping sickness. Until then, our research had focused primarily on the mouse model of the disease, although of course we retained an acute awareness of the problem in humans. Over a number of years, accompanied by Joseph, I had personally witnessed the ravages of sleeping sickness in Alupe, but there came a need to spread our net of interest outside Kenya. There were two main reasons for this. The first was that the number of human cases in Alupe had declined considerably soon after the millennium, in part because of the success of the FITCA project and other effective control measures that has been spearheaded by KETRI in collaboration with the Ministries of Health and Agriculture in Kenya. That was obviously great news for patients, but limited our own scope for studying the disease. The other reason was our increasing desire to study the CNS disease in human patients, and to see to what extent our hypotheses in experimental models were relevant to man. The key factor in allowing us to alter course in this way was our increasing collaboration with Jerry Sternberg, whom, you will recall from Chapter Six, collaborated with us in measuring various cytokine levels in the blood and CSF of mice with the PTRE. These studies are still going on apace.

Jerry had already established close links with scientists working in the Livestock Health Research Institute (LIRI) in south-eastern Uganda. He is an expert in measuring various cytokine levels in body fluids, and is very experienced in dealing with the technical and logistical challenges of carrying out such investigations in the

African field. These challenges are certainly not trivial. The key finding of his group had been that in patients in this region of Uganda with late stage *rhodesiense* disease, the counter-inflammatory cytokine IL-10 was significantly increased in patients' blood and CSF, but declined to normal levels after successful treatment. We wanted to extend this observation in a larger number of patients, and to see just how such cytokine changes correlate with a whole variety of markers of neurological disease.

The long term aim was to develop a reliable 'biomarker' in the laboratory that could be used to predict an individual patient's disease prognosis, and to monitor the effectiveness of new therapies. To do this, we needed further funding and to our delight in 2002 the UK's Wellcome Trust charity agreed to award us a research grant to carry out the work. Before this work was allowed to proceed, however, rigorous ethical procedures had to be satisfied, including the written agreement of LIRI's local medical ethics committee, the local UK committee, and also the Ugandan Ministry of Health. This level of ethical regulation is a relatively recent development, but is very important. In order to secure these agreements quickly, it was essential for me to meet with the local team in LIRI and explain exactly what we planned to do there.

Our journey to Uganda started with our usual overnight stopover in Kisumu. But this was 2002, and the green carpet of hyacinth weed that had previously covered large areas of Lake Victoria was noticeably less extensive. The weevils had gone to work. During the relaxed and balmy evening at the Imperial Hotel, festooned with wooden walls and friendly furniture, Joseph and I wiled away the time between courses of vegetable soup, sail fish, and savoury tilapia. As we shot the breeze on just about every subject under the sun, I learned more from Joseph about Kenyan customs, the structure of family life, and social morality and workplace hierarchies than I could ever have done from 20 guidebooks or any other source. I hadn't realised, for instance, just how high the marriage rate was in the country compared with Europe. Those pleasant evenings in Kisumu remain for me some of the most enjoyable and evocative experiences of Kenya. And the air conditioning in the rooms that actually worked seemed like the epitome of comfort. Even the mosquitoes declined to bite me. Perhaps they felt that I had done my time in Africa and so deserved a break from their attentions.

After we had rested in Kisumu, Moses performed his usual superhuman feat of avoiding accident and injury on the pot holed road to Alupe, where we stopped and met briefly with old friends and colleagues. Dr Sulo had only recently been appointed as the resident medical officer in charge of the sleeping sickness centre, and he and Joseph dealt quickly and efficiently with KETRI business matters. I saw again a permanent Alupe employee who had suffered from epilepsy following a severe head injury, and I was able to assure him that he should indeed keep taking his anti-convulsant tablets as I had strongly advised him to do the previous year. It occurred to me that I saw him as often as I did some of my patients in the neurological outpatient clinic in Glasgow! His enormous gratitude was way out of proportion to my advice, but generosity of spirit is common in Kenya, so it no longer surprises me when I come across it.

The onward journey from Alupe to LIRI was very short, about 8 km, and indeed particularly so for us as we crossed the Kenya/ Uganda border via the backdoor route, so to speak. Rather than driving all the way to the main town of Busia, where there was the main border checkpoint, the authorities allowed us to use the quieter and quicker way because of our special status as KETRI representatives who were known to have a close and cordial collaboration with LIRI. At one time there had been considerable tension between the two countries, but that is now a thing of the past, and the atmosphere was very relaxed, at least to my eyes.

Our vehicle turned left out of Alupe instead of the usual right back to Kisumu, and we drove down a muddy dirt road towards the border. There were actually three separate security checkpoints along this route, rather like a series of locks that had to be opened.

At the first, to my surprise, the official asked me to show him the Ugandan letter of invitation that I had been given. He scrutinised it then smiled and waved us through. A few hundred yards later, we reached the second post where the security guard standing by a hut about 20 yards away from us kept his rifle by his side, and gave us a genuinely friendly wave. So we continued. Despite the general air of bonhomie, there was still a slight but tangible element of tension in the journey. After another mile of extremely rough, bone-shaking terrain, we reached the third and final hurdle. This was nothing but a thick log blocking a narrow road that led into Uganda. After waiting a few minutes, the log was eventually removed from our path by an elderly official who pulled on a length of thin rope tied to it at one end. At last we were in Uganda, and it felt rather like the end of a board game in which we had given all the right answers.

Once across the border, we drove a few miles along a bumpy red dirt road until the long buildings of LIRI slowly appeared to the left of us. Although smaller than KETRI, it was in a generally better state of repair, in part because of some construction and decoration work that had just been completed. Overall, it made a strong and positive first impression. At the large iron gates that guarded the entrance, we were duly signed in, and then allowed to enter the facility. This consisted of a number of neat, long white buildings, and farther back were the small flat units for resident staff and visiting scientists where both Jerry and his able research assistant, Lorna MacLean, had often stayed in the past. These units were apparently pretty comfortable and pleasant, although bats in the roof had an anti-social tendency to relieve themselves of their droppings from time to time.

LIRI is located in the south-eastern Ugandan district called Tororo, and it was established in 1993 by an Act of Parliament which created the National Agricultural Research Organisation (NARO) by the merger of the Animal Health Research Institute at Entebbe and the Uganda Trypanosomiasis Research Organisation (UTRO) based at Tororo. Prior to that, UTRO was called the East African Trypanosomiasis Research Organisation (EATRO) until June 1997. Our old colleague Adriel Njogu had been a Director of EATRO before becoming the first Director of KETRI. Since 1956, when EATRO was opened for research on human as well as animal trypanosomiasis, a 14 bed hospital attached to the institute was the sole referral centre for treatment of *T.b.rhodesiense* sleeping sickness in south-eastern Uganda. NARO took over the running of the institute from 1994.

In 2002, the year in which I first visited LIRI, the hospital treated a total of 53 cases of sleeping sickness, which was far more than had been seen in Alupe. The institute had about 60 staff when I visited, and there was one medical officer in charge of the hospital. This officer was Martin Odiit whom I came to know quite well. Martin, a very tall, impressive individual, was a medical doctor who had also obtained a PhD working with Mark Woolhouse, Paul Coleman, Eric Fevre, Ian Maudlin and Susan Welburn at the University of Edinburgh's Centre for Tropical Veterinary Medicine (CTVM), and John McDermott of ILRI. Not only is Martin an excellent and experienced doctor, but also, in association with his Ugandan and British colleagues, he has continued to publish important papers on the problem of sleeping sickness in different regions of Uganda. I shall mention some of the work of these scientists later on. Martin has recently left LIRI to work in the Ugandan Ministry of Health, and, sadly, he has not been replaced. At the present time, my information is that the patients with sleeping sickness in LIRI are managed by two dedicated nurses, and that future work at LIRI will focus primarily on livestock and disease vectors rather than on sleeping sickness.

LIRI is located about 10 km south of the town of Tororo, and has the overall objectives (and here I quote from my colleague's 2006 briefing notes) of 'generating information on major livestock diseases, sleeping sickness and vectors, and to develop and transfer disease and vector control technologies to the beneficiaries so as to improve production and productivity of livestock and poultry and effectively control sleeping sickness'. Its focus is on cattle diseases, small ruminant diseases, poultry diseases and human trypanosomiasis. The goal of LIRI (as stated in 2002) is 'to develop technologies that reduce disease constraints of domestic food animals and hence improve on the quantity and quality of animal protein and incomes from livestock enterprises'. I think a point to make here is that, again, the animal and human diseases are very closely related, and that treatment of one may lead to advances in the other. This is invariably reflected in the lengthy mission statements and objectives of such research institutes.

As soon as we arrived, we were greeted with great courtesy by Dr Charles Otim who was the Acting Director of LIRI. He was a most helpful and charming host, and I rapidly learned a considerable amount about the problems of animal and human trypanosomiasis in the Tororo area. He himself had just been bitten by a tsetse fly but did not appear in the slightest bit worried by it. I was also intrigued by his precision at positioning his mobile phone on a window ledge in his large office on the one tiny spot where it could actually receive a signal! We had a long and helpful general discussion of the proposed project, and it was soon clear to me that our project objectives would certainly be achieved here.

While Joseph and Charles spent some time discussing their own institutional issues, I was introduced to Martin, who immediately took me to the sleeping sickness wards where I saw about ten patients with the disease, all showing varying degrees of disease severity. Some had just started treatment, some were recovering from the disease and/or its treatment, and some were still acutely ill. The year before he had treated about 100 cases with the disease. The diversity of the clinical manifestations of sleeping sickness again struck me, probably because I had not seen so many patients in one ward before. I was greatly impressed with the medical skill and knowledge that Martin had used to help these unfortunate people. I was particularly intrigued at the low mortality rate from the disease and the PTRE in this group of patients. This must have owed a lot to Martin's medical expertise as well as to other factors.

The causes and pattern of sleeping sickness in this region of Uganda are of particular interest, and some British readers may possibly have seen a BBC television programme broadcast in December 2003 called *Bodysnatchers* in which the horrors of sleeping sickness were shown, with Martin Odiit as the main presenter. The research which Martin, his local colleagues, and Eric Fevre, Paul Coleman, Mark Woolhouse, John McDermott, Ian Maudlin and Susan Welburn had carried out in the area had shown that new outbreaks of sleeping sickness could be traced to cattle movements going from endemic to previously non-endemic regions. This work had been funded by the UK's Department for International Development (DFID), which until 1997 had been known as the Overseas Development Administration (ODA).

Scientists at the CTVM and LIRI have recently shown, for instance, that when cattle in the markets of the Tororo, Soroti and Kamuli areas of Uganda are sampled, the animals that are infected with trypanosomiasis are more likely to be brought for sale in livestock markets in endemic areas. A key point to make is that both wild and domestic animals are reservoirs of trypanosome species that cause both animal and human trypanosomiasis. In a given population of cattle, the ratio of *T.b.brucei* (causing animal disease) to *T.b.rhodesiense* (causing human disease) is fairly constant at about 3:1. Systematic sampling of cattle in markets in epidemic (but not endemic) areas can give a good idea as to the prevalence of trypanosomiasis in the surrounding villages. These scientists also discovered that when there was an outbreak of human sleeping sickness in the Tororo region, the human trypanosomes isolated from patients there were identical to those identified in the cattle in Soroti. The logical conclusion from this was that the movement of infected cattle that had been brought in from the Soroti markets was the cause of the new outbreak of human sleeping sickness in Tororo which had previously been largely free of disease. Again, the intimate links between the human and animal disease had been demonstrated. You can see the location of Tororo and Soroti on the map at the beginning of the book.

So far we have been talking about *rhodesiense* disease as if that was the only type occurring in Uganda, but this is not actually the case. There are actually two discrete areas where sleeping sickness occurs in the region, *T.b.rhodesiense* in Eastern Uganda, and *T.b.gambiense* in northwest Uganda and southern Sudan. Moreover, the area of Uganda with the acute *rhodesiense* disease had increased 25-fold since 1985. During this period the disease had spread to several new districts because of the movements of infected livestock as we had noted before. Right now, the two forms of the disease are 150 km apart which is far too close for comfort. These scientists warned of the inevitable convergence of the two forms of disease, which would have all kinds of serious consequences in the region, and strongly advised pre-emptive action in monitoring both cattle and humans in these areas. Since the two diseases are treated differently, as we have seen, their eventual convergence in the same area will inevitably complicate their management in hospitals. I find that a particularly worrying thought.

Our research in this region is going very well. At the present moment, we are very busy analysing and making sense of the results. So what did we actually do in Uganda? After we had obtained all the necessary ethical clearances and documentation, we devised a special neurological assessment sheet that could be used by medical officers and experienced nurses in the field to record as much patient data as possible. As well as the usual clinical measurements, we included the Glasgow Coma Score (GCS), which is the most commonly used coma scale in the world. First devised and validated in the early 1970s by two leading Glasgow neurosurgeons, Brian Jennett and Graham Teasdale (both of whom I know well, being in the same institute), it has been shown to be of great use in both monitoring patients with coma from head injuries and other causes, and in predicting short and long term outcome after head injuries. The beauty of the GCS lies in its remarkable simplicity so that any competent and trained observer can use it reliably. The complete neurological assessment sheet is reproduced here for your interest in Figure 4.

Figure 4

Sleeping Sickness Study - Patient Information Form

Name _____
Address _____
Sex _____Age_____I.D. Code_____Consent_____

Clinical history
Onset of illness_____Chancre   Yes / No   _____
Symptoms   Fever (not/ reported), Headache (none/ mild/ severe), Body aches (none/ mild/ severe)
Other symptoms :_____

Other illnesses _____
/treatments   _____
SS before?   _____Family members?_____
Signs (Tick)   GC: (poor/fair/good), Oedema (none/mild/severe), LNs (palpable/not palpable) PA: Liver:
(normal/enlarged), Spleen (normal/enlarged), Ascites (absent/present), CVS: Pulse(   ),
BP (   ), CNS: Gait (normal/aided/unable to walk), Tremors (absent/present), Urinary
incontinence (absent/present-witnessed by health worker), Cranioneuropathies (absent/present)
if present specify, Somnolence (absent/present-witnessed by health worker)
Other signs: _____

Glasgow coma scale

Eye opening	E
spontaneous	4
to speech	3
to pain	2
no response	1

Best motor response	M
To verbal command:	
obeys	6
To painful stimulus:	
localizes pain	5
flexion-withdrawal	4
flexion abnormal	3
extension	2
no response	1

Best verbal response	V
oriented and converses	5
disoriented and converses	4
inappropriate words	3
incomprehensible sounds	2
no response	1

Blood analysis

	BT	FU1	FU2	FU3	FU4	FU5	AT
Date							
PCV (%)							
Hb (g%)							
ESR (mm/hr)							
Wet film(/field)							
Thick film (/field)							
HCT							
Temp (°C)							
2ml Plasma							
Treatment							

CSF analysis

	BT	AT
Parasitaemia (/field)		
WBC (/µl)		
DC	+/-	+/-

Comments

So far, we have managed to collect no less than 130 blood and CSF samples from patients with sleeping sickness in the Tororo district. That is quite a large number of samples and will be a unique and valuable resource for both ourselves and collaborating colleagues in years to come. This could not have been achieved without the help and logistical know-how of our Ugandan colleagues. Some of the cytokine analyses were carried out in the well-equipped diagnostic laboratory in LIRI itself, and I well remember spending time on the project with Lorna there as she worked away at a furious pace for a five week period in the spring of 2003. We have certainly found a relationship between the levels of IL-10 in patients' CSF and the severity of disease and outcome, but we are still working on the problem in attempting to sort out what is cause and what is in effect an age-old issue in clinical research. We are also doing further experiments with the mouse model to see whether giving infected mice a dose of IL-10 improves their brain disease. If it does, then this would support the idea that this cytokine is protective in the disease.

On that first visit in 2002, Dr Otim extended his kind hospitality by taking us all out for lunch in the nearby town of Tororo. This district of Tororo currently has a total population of 402,621, and about 90 per cent of the total population live in rural areas. The town of Tororo is 1,459 m above sea level and agriculture is a major source of employment. The other main industry is cement, and TCI (Tororo Cement Industry) supplies Uganda with cement for lime construction. After entering the town, which was green, relaxed, and slightly dilapidated in a few areas, we had lunch in a popular local hotel. I was greatly impressed with the dominant sight of Tororo Rock nearby which I learned was a major tourist attraction. It was certainly striking, and I had an overwhelming desire to explore it further. I had no appetite for lunch, as is often the case with me at times of intense activity and professional excitement. I sadly missed the opportunity to sample the local matoke, a national dish made from the ubiquitous bananas of Uganda.

Everyone else, however, seemed to be ravenously hungry. But halfway though the meal, we were startled by an alarming and quite dramatic event. There was suddenly a most deafening roar of low flying jets breaking the sound barrier, and everyone stopped eating and ran outside into the street to see what was happening. First, we saw one fighter jet fly at incredible speed just over Tororo Rock, so low, in fact, that I could hardly believe what my eyes were telling me. How could it fly so near the rock? A few seconds later, a second jet roared above us and was hot on the heels of the first jet, flying just as low. One person then shouted that he thought he saw gunfire from the second jet. At that point I became worried. And so did almost everyone else apart from Dr Otim and Joseph, who smiled with enviable sangfroid, and suggested that we all continue with our meal.

Hakuna matata, Joseph seemed to say, which in Swahili means 'no worries'. How many times have I heard that reassuring phrase in Kenya? I once heard our driver say this to reassure us when our Land Rover had broken down in the middle of the Maasai Mara game reserve. And indeed we were fine on that occasion. What people were most concerned about here, though, was that this might be a 'victory role' following a military coup in the country. The reason for thinking this is that such demonstrations of military virtuosity in the air are very unusual in Uganda. Joseph pointed out that if there was a problem, which he very much doubted, then it was likely to be in Kampala, the capital city, and it would take at least three hours for any rebel forces to reach us here on the south eastern border. He reassured me that we should all carry on eating and take our time before returning to Kenya, although I did not relish the thought of being stranded in Uganda under these tense circumstances. But it was the sight of the local people in such a state of anxiety that really unnerved me. And of course there had been no problem at all. People's collective imagination had played tricks on the common consciousness. It was a routine exercise. There was no coup.

In fact there was one very real danger that always lurked in the background of all my colleagues whose work takes them through necessity to Uganda's more northerly regions. The only such region that I am familiar with is the above-mentioned Soroti which is located on the Kampala-Lira Highway and borders the district of Kamuli, Lake Kyoga and Pallisa in the south. It was formerly part of the larger Teso region and is about 2,500 feet above sea level, significantly higher than Tororo. The region of Soroti has a population of 325,522, and its history goes back to about 1904 when the colonial administration set up various projects involving local labour. These included clearing various grassland areas, and eventually constructing huts and later a dispensary close to where the Soroti hospital now stands. In 1912, under the Governor of Uganda, Sir Frederick Jackson, Soroti was made the headquarters of the Teso region. Agriculture and farming are currently key in terms of food and revenue, and Soroti is a leading supplier of sweet potatoes to neighbouring districts. Soroti is also one of the towns that has suffered from the horrors inflicted by the Lord's Resistance Army (LRA).

The LRA is led by Joseph Kony and has been waging war against the Ugandan government since around 1989. But in practice innocent civilians are the main target for their atrocities. Violent crimes are common. Once abducted, children are often taken to LRA camps in Sudan. Although the two northern districts of Kitgum and Gulu have been worst affected, other districts, including Soroti, have also suffered. The origins of the conflict appear to be linked to a longstanding feud between the Acholi people in the north and various ethnic groups in the south. The latter have historically been richer and have had better resources and amenities than those in the north, who have depended mainly on farming with a tendency to join the military services. Fortunately, I have never encountered the LRA (although I know a colleague who has, and lived to tell the tale), and I can think of virtually nothing that would be more unpleasant or frightening if I did. In the regions affected by the

LRA, Médecins Sans Frontières (MSF) has displayed its usual extreme courage in deploying its staff there to give medical aid to the unfortunate victims of this terrifying organisation. Wisely, the MSF staff are never armed.

We eventually said our farewells to our newly found Ugandan colleagues, and set off on the short return journey to Kenya. On the way back we seemed to pass through the three security barriers more quickly than before. Before too long we were back at Alupe, and then sped off to dance among the potholes on the road to Kisumu.

The following year, 2003, we returned to LIRI, but it was in April during the rainy season. Our vehicle was not really designed to negotiate the soggy and rapidly disintegrating dirt roads that linked the two countries along this route, but yet again, we managed to survive the journey. We always do.

CHAPTER TEN

Future Challenges and Priorities for a Cinderella Disease

I HOPE ALL I'VE SAID in the preceding chapters has convinced you of the enormous importance of sleeping sickness in sub-Saharan Africa, a condition that we sometimes call the 'Cinderella Disease' because of the striking discrepancy between the amount of suffering it causes and the global funds that have been devoted to it so far. The disease has been overlooked for far too long, and attracts much less attention than it merits, especially in contrast to diseases that are less effective killers. In this final chapter, I want to tell you about some of the advances in African trypanosomiasis that can be expected over the next few years, and what I think are the main priorities for improving the existing situation, including the treatment currently available to sufferers.

Let's start off with the prospects for better drug therapy for both early and late stages of sleeping sickness. In my view, this is the most important issue we face. Right now, we don't have any effective oral therapy for either stage of the disease, all of the drugs are old, have to be given by injection in hospital, and have potentially severe toxic effects. Worst of all, melarsoprol, the only drug which can treat CNS disease in both types of sleeping sickness, kills one in 20 of the patients who receive it – not exactly a satisfactory situation for treating a killer disease of this magnitude.

But first, it's important to appreciate just how time-consuming and expensive it is to develop and test a new drug from scratch. Once a pharmaceutical company has identified a possible compound after many years of painstaking laboratory research, the drug then has to be subjected to extensive analysis, including animal screening for potential toxicity, before it can first be tested on human subjects.

Only if such 'pre-clinical' testing is satisfactory can it then go to the next stage, which is clinical development. Trials for new drugs occur in three distinct phases. During Phase I trials, the drug is first given to healthy volunteer subjects to make sure it is safe. An example of a drug dramatically failing at this stage was recently highlighted in the British press when six healthy young volunteers all had a life-threateningly severe reaction to a new monoclonal antibody drug that was designed to boost the immune system to help in particular diseases. Fortunately, such adverse reactions are very rare.

The Phase II trial takes the testing further to show that the drug actually does what it is meant to do in a particular disease, and to confirm further the drug's safety. Various important pieces of information as to the optimum drug usage can be obtained at this stage. In fact, the situation is a little more complex than this as these trials are divided into Phase IIa and Phase IIb, with the former involving testing of a small number of patients in an uncontrolled manner, while the more extensive Phase IIb trials test the drug in larger numbers of patients with the disease in a placebo-controlled randomised way. The drug may be compared with another known drug or used in combination with another known drug, to see whether it is more effective than existing treatment regimes.

If all this is satisfactory, and the drug is shown to be safe and probably effective, then a Phase III trial can be conducted. Such a trial tests the drug in large numbers of patients in a tightly controlled way, and statistical help is sought beforehand to work out just how many patients need to be included in the trial to ensure that an unequivocal and meaningful result will be obtained. The more patients who are tested, then the greater the statistical 'power' of the study. If such a trial proves beyond doubt that the drug works and is safe, then, and only then, can it be officially approved by the appropriate drug regulatory body, such as the US Federal Drug Administration, and go onto the market to treat patients with the condition. If an existing and safe drug is to be tested for a new condition, then it's possible to proceed directly to a Phase II trial without the need for a Phase I trial, and this is relevant to some of our own research ideas.

But even if all this proceeds to a satisfactory conclusion, it's very expensive and takes a long time. We are not talking about a few million US dollars, but hundreds of millions of dollars to develop a single drug, and it can be as much as five to 10 years from the pre-clinical development stage to the drug going on the market for widespread use. Furthermore, the failure rate of promising compounds is extremely high, with the vast majority of these biting the dust at the early stages. Perhaps only one or two compounds out of many thousands of potential candidates will ever make it to the finishing line. And this is the key problem with new drugs for sleeping sickness, for it just isn't profitable for the drug companies to invest so much time and money in a drug that will not actually be used in any country other than Africa. After all, the drug companies, understandably, are primarily interested in making large profits and recouping their costs incurred while developing the drug.

There was one new oral drug for use in sleeping sickness on the horizon. The drug known as DB289 was the only new drug likely to be used for sleeping sickness within the next five years. The funding for its rapid development came from a $15 million grant from the Bill and Melinda Gates Foundation in 2000, and it involves a large consortium of scientists in the US, Europe and Africa, led by Richard Tidwell of the University of North Carolina. Joseph Ndung'u has also been closely involved in this work in Kenya. DB289 has the great advantage of being an oral drug, but unfortunately it does not seem to cross the blood-brain barrier, so it will only be useful against early stage, and not late stage disease. Phase I, Phase IIa and IIb trials have now been successfully completed with this drug, and a pivotal Phase III multi-centre trial with large numbers of patients in Africa was undertaken in the hope that, if proved to be effective for early stage disease, then this would be the first major accomplishment in this field for many years. Unfortunately, near the end of the trial, DB289 was abruptly withdrawn because of the development of unexpected liver and kidney toxicity in some patients receiving it. This was, of course, a great disappointment to everyone working in this area.

It's also important to make full use of existing drugs, especially for the enigmatic late stage disease where the CNS is involved. Here I must tell you about the remarkable eflornithine (DFMO) story. We first came across this drug in Chapter Five, where we saw how it was effective for late stage *gambiense* disease, and a valuable alternative to melarsoprol therapy in such patients. Although it was first used for sleeping sickness in 1981, eflornithine was only officially approved for use in the disease by the FDA in 1990. Soon after that, eflornithine acquired 'orphan drug' status. To be designated as an orphan drug it has to be useful to less than a certain small percentage of the total population of a country. In the case of eflornithine, it was of value to fewer than 200,000 individuals in the US. That, as you can imagine, is a real problem for a drug's marketing and availability to patients as there is not the usual financial incentive for the drug companies to be involved with it. The Nobel Prize winning non-government organisation, MSF, for which I have great admiration, has played a major role in making eflornithine widely available in Africa, and the organisation's public literature explains the detailed story very well.

This is what happened. The drug company Hoechst Marion Roussel stopped producing eflornithine in 1995 as it was expensive and not profitable, and by 2000 the available supply of the drug became worryingly low. Then MSF and WHO searched for a drug company with which they could work to ensure adequate supplies of the drug for use in sleeping sickness in Africa. Around this time the company Bristol-Myers Squibb was heavily marketing a drug called Vaniqa which became very popular as a cream for removing unwanted facial hair in women. The remarkable thing was that Vaniqa contained eflornithine! Even today, my current edition of the *British Medical Journal* has a whole page advert extolling the value of Vaniqa, an 11.5 per cent eflornithine cream for 'changing the face of female hirsutism'. This cosmetic coincidence speeded up the interest in eflornithine, and in 2001 WHO and the company Aventis agreed a deal whereby the latter would manufacture and donate a sustained supply of eflornithine as well as melarsoprol and pentamidine. This generous and inspired donation was set at US$5 million annually, initially for five years, and another company, Bayer, agreed to produce suramin and a newer drug called nifurtimox.

This represented an excellent example of the co-operation between the pharmaceutical industry and organisations such as WHO and MSF, the latter sharing responsibility for actually distributing these drugs to different sleeping sickness programmes in Africa. MSF is also currently involved in actual trials of new drug therapies for sleeping sickness. Altogether, a most inspiring story which shows what can be achieved with determination and good will on all sides. Eflornithine is now being used increasingly as first line therapy in late stage *gambiense* sleeping sickness, although administation of the drug continues to be problematic, with 14 days of drug injections requiring hospital admission. Unfortunately, eflornithine is not effective against *rhodesiense* disease. A future goal of scientists is to develop an oral form of eflornithine that is as effective as the intravenous form.

MSF has continued to play a major role in the development of new drugs for neglected diseases such as sleeping sickness. For this purpose, in 2003 MSF co-founded an independent not-for-profit organisation called the Drugs for Neglected Diseases initiative (DNDi). This recent organisation comprises several components, namely MSF itself, the WHO Special Programme for Research and Training in Tropical Diseases (TDR), the Oswaldo Cruz Foundation/Fiocruz (Brazil), the Indian Council of Medical Research, the Institut Pasteur (France), the Malaysian Ministry of Health and the Kenya Medical Research Institute (KEMRI).

Our own group in Glasgow, and several others, have a keen interest in the possible effectiveness of 'combination drug therapy'. It's possible to think of several different possibilities, but one that is of particular interest is the combined use of eflornithine and nifurtimox. A TDR clinical trial of an eflornithine and nifurtimox combination is currently underway in Uganda. Nifurtimox is an oral drug that is registered for use in treating Chagas disease (South American trypanosomiasis caused by *T.cruzi*), but not registered for human African trypanosomiasis. While it doesn't have a potential role for first line therapy, it could well have a role for use in combination therapy. But the drug is toxic and right now there aren't standard treatment protocols for its routine use in sleeping sickness. Other possibilities that have been explored are melarsoprol with eflornithine, and melarsoprol with nifurtimox.

One of the potential advantages of combination chemotherapy is that it might help to reduce individual drug toxicity, increase treatment efficacy, delay the onset of drug resistance, and perhaps even solve the problems of complexity and high costs of current alternatives to melarsoprol. If only we could develop a safe oral drug for late stage sleeping sickness, then so many of the knotty problems of diagnosis and treatment complications would be solved. Indeed, this would represent a most dramatic advance in the field. Remember also that advances should come from more efficient drug schedules for existing drugs. A very good example of this is the intense shortened course of melarsoprol therapy for patients with *gambiense* disease which Christian Burri of the Swiss Tropical Institute in Basel and his colleagues have pioneered. Perhaps this same kind of approach could be applied to the other drugs currently used for sleeping sickness.

We really hope that at least one of the experimental drug treatments we have used in the animal model of African trypanosomiasis may also work in human sleeping sickness, but for this to become reality it will involve a great deal of hard work, resolve and, very importantly, money. While we can guarantee the first two of these, the last is far more problematic. Indeed, over the last few years, we and many colleagues in Europe and the US have had considerable difficulty in trying to convince the various funding bodies to support our trypanosomiasis research work. It is a continuing problem in this area.

One particular avenue that our group in Glasgow wants to explore is that of combination therapy with melarsoprol and a neuropeptide antagonist. Here I need to briefly remind you of some of our relevant findings in the mouse model that we covered in Chapter Six. We had found that an antagonist drug to the neuropeptide Substance P (SP) significantly improved the brain inflammation in mice that had been experimentally infected with trypanosomes. It turns out that the company Merck has produced a drug called EMEND which is a human SP antagonist that has been shown to be very useful in preventing the severe nausea that many patients experience when undergoing chemotherapy for various types of cancer. So we already know the drug is safe. Our idea, which has so far received a broadly favourable reaction from colleagues at DNDi, is to use EMEND as adjunctive, that is, additional, therapy with melarsoprol in patients about to be treated for late stage trypanosomiasis. We should be able to proceed directly to a Phase II trial, but first we need to show that this drug combination isn't itself toxic in the mouse model, something that we believe is highly unlikely, but nevertheless needs to be checked before it is tried on patients. Our more recent work with oral complexed melarsoprol is summarised in Chapter 11.

Another approach that may prove effective in the longer term is for pharmacologists and other scientists to somehow modify existing drugs for CNS disease to make them more able to cross the Blood-brain barrier (BBB). This, theoretically at least, should make them more effective as their levels in the infected brain would be increased. However, this is likely to be a very difficult task to achieve, and a good therapeutic result is by no means guaranteed even if successful. There would also be the potential for the drug's toxic effects to be made worse, so there is a balance to be struck here.

There are many other novel therapeutic approaches which researchers are currently exploring that we don't have the scope to discuss in detail here. Basically, with most of these, the idea is to identify a new biochemical target in the trypanosome that we can block in some way with new compounds. Once such drug targets have been identified as promising, they can be blocked experimentally with drugs in the tissue culture dish to see whether the parasite itself is affected.

To give a few examples, one could target the parasite's glucose metabolism, or a very important molecule to the trypanosome called glutathione, or potentially block key enzymes required for essential structural components of the parasite. Or else one might try to interfere with the synthesis of key fatty components of the parasite's cell membrane, or the way in which it processes important proteins. Another possibility is to perhaps block the serum resistance factor (SRA) that *T.b.rhodesiense* uses to resist the natural ability of human serum to destroy it. A molecule called ApoL-1 has recently been identified as this factor in human serum which can destroy the parasite. If you could block the SRA activity then the parasite would be robbed of one of its most important defences against the human host. Another very real possibility is that we might find that some drugs currently in use for treating different diseases may also have activity against trypanosomiasis. Scientists and clinicians need to think broadly here. A good example of such an increased spectrum is the drug doxycycline that we mentioned in Chapter Eight. While this drug is a useful antibiotic, it was also found to be an effective prophylactic agent for preventing both malaria and traveller's diarrhoea. Perhaps we might find another, previously unrecognised, multipurpose drug that could be useful for treating sleeping sickness.

As well as these attempts to develop new drugs for the human disease, there is, as we saw in Chapter Seven, a corresponding and pressing need to develop new drugs for animal trypanosomiasis. In the latter case, drug resistance is a significant problem, and there are currently only three, as opposed to four, basic drugs in use. The chances that some of these approaches will lead to successful drug treatment of human and animal sleeping sickness are very difficult to predict. But the fact that DB289 had emerged so promisingly, and the increasing focus on finding new drug targets in many leading laboratories, leads me to be cautiously optimistic. But Christian Burri and his colleagues have emphasised that to achieve this, a large number of potential compounds will need to be tested, and, in addition, there need to be permanent collaborations between research and screening specialists in academic institutions and the drug development departments of the pharmaceutical companies. This will require a great deal of increased funding from various sources. Unfortunately, at least for the foreseeable future, there is no realistic possibility of developing a vaccine for sleeping sickness, unless the knotty problem of trypanosome antigenic variation can be overcome. And, frankly, that is very unlikely indeed.

Another area where advances are urgently required is that of disease diagnosis, especially where it involves reliably distinguishing the early and late stages of sleeping sickness. As we have seen, the key problem is that the different experts in the field don't all agree on this. Not only do they not agree on exactly how to distinguish the two stages, but they can't agree on the criteria that have to be met before starting potentially lethal treatment with melarsoprol. You might think that one decision would naturally depend on the other, but this is not the case. The problem would largely go away if an effective oral drug for both stages was available. An internationally agreed consensus on the staging criteria is one of the most urgent requirements in sleeping sickness. I am encouraged by a recent paper that suggested that a CSF WBC count of 10/μL should be the consensus figure for CNS disease, but this critical issue has still not been sorted out. The fact that there are some clinical differences between the two types of human African trypanosomiasis is an additional potentially complicating factor. Another important aspect to clarify is whether there is really an 'intermediate' stage in sleeping sickness where the parasites have got a foothold into the CNS by breaching the BBB, but can still be dealt a death blow by drug treatment with the less toxic drugs.

The CATT test, which you will recall from Chapter Five, is very useful in the African field for detecting *gambiense* disease using patients' blood. But this test has its limitations, one of which is that you can get 'borderline' results where the test is neither clearly negative nor positive, making it difficult to interpret and to act upon. It also doesn't tell you whether the patient has developed CNS disease, so it is still necessary to perform a lumbar puncture on the patient if the test is positive.

What, then, would be an ideal diagnostic test for sleeping sickness? We need a test that is cheap, quick and easy to carry out, reliable, and that can be used in the African field to diagnose early stage disease in both types of sleeping sickness. It's no good developing a highly sophisticated method that works in the laboratory using advanced equipment but can't be used in the field where it really matters. We also need such a test for diagnosing late stage disease, and preferably one that does *not* automatically require a lumbar puncture. Any new test must also have two essential properties. First, it must be very 'sensitive', which means that it picks up as positive *all* the samples that are, in fact, positive. Technically, we say that such a test has a very low 'false negative' rate. The test must also be very 'specific' which means it picks up *only* those samples that are truly positive for sleeping sickness, and not for some other disease. Technically, we say that such a test has a very low 'false positive' rate as it is specific for sleeping sickness.

There is an unusual conceptual problem with developing this kind of test, because there is no 'gold standard' method for diagnosing sleeping sickness when you can't identify the parasites in the blood or CSF. So it's very difficult to say just how effective a new diagnostic test is since there isn't anything great with which it can be compared. This is a research and development requirement that will require more human resources, and a lot more funding than is currently available. Perhaps some of the recent exciting advances in molecular biology may lead to such an advance. Time will tell. Of course, everything that I have said about the importance of new diagnostics in man also applies to this need in cattle. African farmers and vets are in great need of better diagnostic tests for animal trypanosomiasis that would obviate so many of the current difficulties with diagnosis and treatment.

We also need to know much more about the basic mechanisms that lead to the brain damage in sleeping sickness, especially those that occur at the molecular level. We know that the outcome of infection depends on the interplay between the parasite's ability to do brain damage, and the host's immune response to the parasite. What is unclear, however, is just how the complex cytokine networks of the host influence the CNS damage. But the parasite will always win in the absence of effective treatment.

We can expect a good deal more valuable information to come from rodent models of the disease, and our own group in Glasgow continues to be committed to this approach that has so far been a productive one. To my mind, the greatest potential benefit of understanding the complex neuropathogenesis of sleeping sickness is that it might lead to our being able to identify potential targets that could be exploited for new kinds of treatment. We have already seen that with SP receptor antagonists. But once such targets have been identified, it is a long and difficult journey to arrive at the point where such drug treatment can be tested in patients in the field. Above all, we have to do our utmost to ensure that any new treatment regime does not have the potential to make the patient worse through side effects. Sometimes, as we have seen in other medical scenarios, such side effects may be totally unpredicted, but the least we can do is to carry out rigorous animal toxicity testing to keep such a risk to the absolute minimum.

Another very promising area of research is focusing on the BBB function in experimental trypanosomiasis in rodents. My colleague Krister Kristennson and his co-workers have carried out some seminal work in this area, and have shown beautifully how the passage of trypanosomes across the BBB occurs and how it is dependent on the presence of particular cytokines. They discovered this by using gene knockout mice that were unable to make the cytokine, Interferon-γ. In Glasgow we also have an increasing interest in the BBB, and have started experiments in which experimentally infected mice are placed in a very powerful MRI machine specially designed to scan small rodents. We have been able to identify progressive breakdown of the BBB in infected mice, and we hope to use this novel functional imaging technique to test BBB function under a whole variety of test conditions. This approach might also allow us to see whether particular drugs 'open up' the BBB more than others, and in the future to modify drugs so as to make them more efficient in crossing the BBB. That should, in turn, lead to a better therapeutic effect in mice, and then, we hope, in patients.

There is also the promise of genetics in combating African try-panosomiasis. Progress in African trypanosomiasis research can certainly be expected as a result of the recent sequencing of the entire *T.brucei* genome that was reported in 2005 in a multi-authored paper in the eminent American journal *Science*. You will be familiar with the human genome project that was completed a few years ago. That unravelling and mapping of the entire three billion base DNA code of the human genome promises to revolutionise the understanding of both basic molecular mechanisms in humans and its clinical applications. The underlying causes of diseases, novel therapies and an early 'read-out' of everyone's future susceptibility to particular conditions have been talked about a great deal in the popular media. We hope that similar types of advance will be made possible by this monumental effort in trypanosome research.

Let me give you a few examples of the kind of progress I mean. Knowing the precise make-up of the parasite's genetic material will allow scientists to determine many of the key functions of its particular genes with much greater precision than was previously possible. The *T.brucei* genome has just over 9,000 individual genes – specific regions of DNA – that code for particular proteins and functions, which is rather fewer than the number that we humans have (about 20,000–25,0000 genes). The total size of the parasite's genome is also about a hundred times smaller than the human genome. Of course, those comparative figures don't translate directly to the vast complexity of humans in relation to the trypanosome, clever as it is. Not only do we have thousands of billions of cells making up our bodies, compared with the single cell of the trypanosome, but the much greater size and complexity of our genes allows for a hugely greater number of interactions to occur. This vast complexity of our genome has resulted in the stunning sophistication of our bodies with, perhaps our crowning biological achievement, the evolution of consciousness.

Knowing both the sequence and function(s) of certain important parasite genes could lead to scientists developing better therapies for the disease in both man and animals. This might be achieved through drugs that specifically target and neutralise key parasite molecules to kill the pathogen or limit its growth. Another possibility is that our detailed knowledge of the trypanosome genome may lead to better diagnostic tests using molecular techniques, although a problem with this is that such advanced technology may be impractical under field conditions.

Another area that should benefit from this knowledge is that of drug resistance which, as we saw before, is a major problem with animal trypanosomiasis, and an emerging problem in some regions for the human disease. Scientists at Glasgow University, such as Andy Tait and Mike Turner, who were closely involved in the trypanosomiasis genome project, are particularly interested in this aspect. By carrying out genetic tests in different trypanosome strains, some of which show strong drug resistance, this new knowledge should allow them to 'map' specific regions of the parasite genome that are wholly or partly responsible for producing the drug-resistance trait. Once this has been accomplished, it should pave the way for developing molecular methods to combat parasite drug resistance. The other outcome we must bear in mind for this work is that it could lead to the generation of markers for resistance from which a test for resistance could be developed. While this may not be as exciting as combating drug resistance, it is a more attainable goal. Despite these potential advances, what we don't yet know is how long it will be before the true benefits of this new genetic knowledge are realised in the African field.

Africa itself has its own powerful genetic resources. Here I am referring, as you might have guessed, to the phenomenon of genetic resistance of some breeds of cattle leading to trypanotolerance. We have seen how this innate genetic trait, typical of cattle breeds such as the N'Dama, provides a natural biological weapon in the fight against the tsetse fly. The increasing use of selective breeding programmes should boost the numbers of such animals in Africa, and in the long run the extensive exploitation of Africa's natural genetic defences may prove to be just as, if not more, significant as the unravelling of the parasite's genetic make-up.

To obtain full control of African trypanosomiasis, it will be critical to control the tsetse fly vector, as this is the key to disrupting the all-important man/fly contact that leads to the disease. Tsetse fly traps need to be made yet more efficient as they are certainly not equally efficient for all species of fly. Another promising avenue for better control is tsetse repellents, and scientists at ICIPE in Nairobi have been working on these for some time. There also needs to be a better appreciation of the benefits of aerial spraying with insecticides. This technique, which as we have seen is not universally popular, is now greatly improved in the sense of both accuracy of spraying and leaving minimal insecticide residues. Botswana is a very good example of what can be achieved with this technique while using its own resources.

We have also seen the potential of the sterile insect technique (SIT), which exploits the fact that female tsetse flies can be impregnated only once. If the impregnating male fly can be made sterile, then this can have great potential. The spectacular results obtained with SIT in Zanzibar are a testimony to what can be achieved, but it must be appreciated that this is an island where the flies have nowhere to hide, and where there was only one species of fly to control.

It would be naïve to expect that the same level of success could be achieved with SIT in areas of Africa that offer the various species of tsetse fly a myriad of niches in which to shelter and escape from the ingenuity of man.

To achieve better control of both human and animal try-panosomiasis, it is vital to achieve more extensive and efficient parasite monitoring of infected humans and animals. This is par-ticularly important as animals are the main parasite reservoirs for *rhodesiense* disease of humans, and both animals and humans are the reservoirs of *gambiense* disease. Infected people and animals need to be quickly identified, and then treated efficiently and completely so that they do not go on to spread the disease. But one buzz word keeps coming up whenever experts talk about regional or global programmes to monitor, treat and prevent the disease. That word is *sustainability*.

One of the greatest recurrent problems in Africa has been that so many of the control programmes have been short-lived, and it has not proved possible to keep them going for long periods. So what happens is that the various problems are thought about and con-trolled to a greater or lesser extent, and then, through failure to be sustained over long periods, everything goes back to square one and the problem starts all over again. As we have already seen, this 'sustainability' issue has been important in population screening for infection, tsetse control, insecticide spraying and drug treatment. Short-lived control programmes in Africa just will not do. There needs to be a major effort on the part of both the local communities and national governments to develop and stick to sustainable approaches. Organisations such as PAAT and PATTEC have provided important leadership to show how this can be achieved, and it will require a good deal of determination and will to succeed on the part of gov-ernments.

Another buzz phrase that is often mentioned in relation to sus-tainability is *capacity building*. You see these two words used a lot in calls for grant proposals. Essentially the link is obvious, as there needs to be a robust regional infrastructure to maintain these various control programmes. In order to ensure such infrastructures, it is necessary to build the local capacity for it where it does not already exist, which is often the case in poor rural areas in sub-Saharan Africa. This means that local farmers and workers need to receive training and have the necessary equipment and wherewithal to carry out the work. And this, of course, means they must have the necessary funds to do so. The general idea is that experts from the West and elsewhere provide the necessary training and technical know-how, the donor and funding organisations provide all the necessary equipment to do the work, and once the job is done, they leave the newly established infrastructure to the local populations to sustain.

An interesting view on the issues of trypanosomiais control was recently provided by Susan Welburn and her colleagues. These scientists argue that sleeping sickness continues to be controlled by 'crisis management' using active case detection, treatment of cases and vector control. They argue that such measures occur mainly during the major epidemics, but that during the intervening periods it is best for both farmers and communities to fend for themselves. During such endemic periods, the risk of sleeping sickness should be managed on a local basis. They feel that large-scale tsetse control programmes should only be measures of last resort. The emphasis should therefore be on the infrastructural support for local farmers. I don't see that this view is at all inconsistent with the notions of sustainability and capacity building. It is a question of where the main resources are directed.

Finally, we come to the all-important issue of funding. For it is money that in the end is so badly needed to make all that we have discussed actually happen. I personally find that rather sad, but that is the situation and we must face reality. It is clear that at the level of global financial support, regional support within Africa, and in the financially competitive area of drug development, there has been a chronic and severe lack of investment in sleeping sickness over many years. This has been due, in part, I believe, to a genuine lack of appreciation generally of both the severity and vast scale of the problem in man and animals in Africa. But things have already begun to change, thanks to the efforts of MSF, WHO and several other enlightened funding agencies.

Several government and non-government agencies have shown strong financial support for sleeping sickness, improving the control and treatment of African trypanosomiasis. While I obviously can't mention them all, it is important to recognise the sustained efforts of MSF, WHO with its TDR programme in particular, the EU with its innovative FITCA project, the UK's Wellcome Trust with its extensive network of funding for clinical and basic research including support for the *T.brucei* genome project, the UK government through its DFID grants, the US government through NIH funding and capacity building programmes, the Bill and Melinda Gates Foundation, the UN's Food and Agricultural Organisation (FAO), and the IAEA. The important role of associations such as PAAT and PATTEC in influencing government priorities and policies, and in providing leadership, should also not be underestimated.

To give you an idea of the kind of support that we have seen recently, I can give you a few examples. You will recall the US$15.1 million donated by the Bill and Melinda Gates Foundation in 2000 for the development of new drugs for human African trypanosomiasis and leishmaniasis. This has already led to testing of the first ever oral drug, DB289, for sleeping sickness. How interesting it is that such an achievement was made possible by a grant from a private foundation and not a government agency. The amounts of grant money that the Gates Foundation has given, and continues to give, for research into diseases in poor countries is staggering. Particularly impressive is the 2005 Grand Challenges Programme on global child survival, where over US$450 million in grants was given for 43 separate projects to tackle seven key strategic goals. Other recent notable donations in the sleeping sickness area have been the 2001 Aventis/WHO support of US$5 million per year to ensure the production of eflornithine and other drugs for the disease; the 2005 DFID commitment of £6.5 million to DNDi's research for new medicines for neglected diseases, including human African trypanosomiasis; the Wellcome Trust's 2005 grant of £8.1 million over five years to Dundee University to discover new drugs for sleeping sickness, Chagas' disease and leishmaniasis; and the total of US$14.4 million that the National Institute of Allergy and Infectious Disease (NIAID) of NIH gave out in grants for sleeping sickness in 2005.

While all this is obviously good news, and clear evidence that there is an increased awareness of the problem of sleeping sickness, it is not enough. In fact, it is nowhere near enough. The amounts spent on sleeping sickness are way below that spent on malaria, for example, and while I guess that is understandable in terms of the larger number of malaria cases that occur globally, funding agencies need to understand that sleeping sickness has unique problems associated with it. For a start, sleeping sickness always kills you without treatment, whereas malaria may kill you, but by no means necessarily. And as well as the disease killing you, then the treatment for trypanosomiasis might also do the job earlier if you are one of the unlucky five per cent of patients receiving melarsoprol. The situation was movingly encapsulated by an African farmer at the beginning of a recent meeting of the International Scientific Council for Trypanosomiasis Research and Control (ISCTRC) held in Addis Ababa in Ethiopia. This farmer said, 'My child is dying of malaria, but it is African trypanosomiasis that is killing us.'

The numbers of sleeping sickness cases reported annually also underestimate the true proportions of the global trypanosomiasis problem. Perhaps even more significant are the devastating effects that African trypanosomiasis has in terms of limiting livestock production and farming. Farming productivity is inevitably compromised when cattle and people are infected with the disease, and sleeping sickness has also been shown to have a significant negative impact on people's actual quality of life. In terms of the global burden of parasitic disease, calculated as the disability of adjusted life years lost ('DALY's'), as a result of the infection, human African trypanosomiasis is the world's third most important parasitic disease adversely affecting human health after malaria and schistosomiasis. Because of the power of the parasite and the vector, trypanosomiasis also holds a third of the entire African continent captive.

Sufferers from sleeping sickness and farmers struggling to cope with infected cattle deserve a much better deal than they are getting at present. Funding agencies and donor organisations need to be generous, in fact very generous. This was nicely captured in a simple but meaningful notion by Jean Jannin of WHO when he stated that 'for free is not cheap enough'. That is profoundly true. The urgent needs of sub-Saharan Africa require not just free pieces of equipment or free medicines but help with their entire infrastructure for combating the twin scourges of the trypanosome and the tsetse fly.

But are we winning the race to make a difference? I don't know yet, but I am optimistic. The growing global awareness of the problem, and the increasing commitment of the African Union and the international community to finally eradicate this scourge from sub-Saharan Africa leaves considerable grounds for hope for the future. But the remaining time for action is not unlimited. This disease has already shown its ability to strike back with a vengeance shortly after it had appeared to have been eradicated in the 1960s. If sleeping sickness is truly a Cinderella disease, then we should be aware that midnight is not so far away.

CHAPTER ELEVEN

An Overview of Some Recent Developments in Sleeping Sickness

DURING THE ALMOST nine years that have elapsed since the publication of the previous paperback edition of this book there have been a number of significant advances in sleeping sickness. These include better control of the numbers of people affected by the disease which have decreased markedly across sub-Saharan Africa, improved methods of diagnosis, the emerging concept of 'trypanotolerance' in infected humans, new drug treatment regimes, and some increased understanding of the neuropathogenesis of the disease. In this brief overview chapter I shall highlight some of these recent advances. These have occurred mainly because of concerted and co-ordinated efforts made by a number of organisations, especially WHO and non-governmental organisations, as well as those primarily involved in research and humanitarian causes, as well as African governments, to devote both increased research time and extensive financial resources to combating the major challenges posed by a range of 'neglected tropical diseases' including those posed by human African trypanosomiasis (HAT) which I shall continue to refer as sleeping sickness, its popular name.

The number of cases of Sleeping Sickness in sub-Saharan Africa has fallen dramatically over the last decade

One of the perhaps rather surprising but hugely gratifying developments over the last 10–15 years has been the progressive and rapid reduction of the number of new cases of sleeping sickness in sub-Saharan Africa reported to WHO which continues to be a major source of information about the changing epidemiological trends in this and indeed other tropical diseases. As we have previously seen (Chapter 3), in the mid-1980s to 1998 the number of cases of sleeping sickness at any one time estimated by the WHO was around 300,000. But more recent figures paint a far rosier picture than this. Thus, the number of reported cases by WHO was 50–70,000 cases in 2006, and three years later dropped below 10,000 cases per year in that 9,878 new cases were reported in 2009, and then 7,139 new cases were reported in 2010. The numbers are continuing to fall over the past few years, and in 2016 just 2,184 cases of sleeping sickness were reported to WHO. That is quite remarkable and many of us would not have predicted this even a decade ago, and the cases have been detected in both endemic and non-endemic countries and have occurred for both types of sleeping sickness, *T.b. gambiense* and *T.b.rhodesiense*, with a slightly greater relative reduction in the former disease variant. Interestingly, while *T.b.rhodesiense* causes only about 3–5 per cent of all sleeping sickness cases overall, it is found mainly in Uganda and Malawi, is the cause of about 72 per cent of sleeping sickness cases occurring in European and North American tourists returning from East Africa, and constitutes about 18 per cent of the total risk of sleeping sickness throughout the 36 countries in sub-Saharan Africa.

How was this result achieved? The approach, which has been intensive and well-co-ordinated, has been to detect individuals infected with trypanosomiasis, isolate and then treat them effectively. In the case of *T.b. gambiense*, humans are the main reservoir of trypanosome infection so that identifying and promptly and efficiently treating infected patients is a powerful means of reducing the spread of disease. Alongside this measure, vector control has also been rigorously enforced, that is to say measures to kill the tsetse fly vector (which we discussed in Chapter 7) have also been employed though this may well not be as significant a factor as treating human cases in terms of reducing the overall numbers infected. These same measures were probably the key factors which led to the great reduction of sleeping sickness cases that we have already noted in the mid-1960s. But despite these significant advances, a note of caution must be made. First, there may be significant underestimates and under-diagnoses of sleeping sickness cases. For example, a study in 2007 in the Democratic Republic of Congo (DRC) reported more than twice as many cases of sleeping sickness as had been published by the WHO. It is quite possible, if not somewhat likely, that there continues to be a problem of under-reporting of cases. Also, the reduction in cases of *T.b.rhodesiense* may not as great as that seen in *T.b. gambiense* because, as we saw in Chapter 7, cattle are the primary reservoirs of trypanosome infection in the former variant and it would be difficult to completely eradicate all human trypanosome pathogens from such animals not to mention the complete removal of all tsetse fly vectors which transmit the disease from person to person or cattle to people. Further, history has already taught us that this disease can wax and wane, with periodic resurgences and epidemics, so that continued surveillance of humans and animals, persistent enforcement of stringent vector control measures, and a constant awareness of the problems involved in sleeping sickness and vector control will be required to avoid a recurrence of the disease in endemic areas of sub-Saharan Africa.

Methods of diagnosis of Sleeping Sickness have improved

As we saw in Chapter 5 the best way of diagnosing sleeping sickness is to positively identify the trypanosome parasites in the blood or enlarged lymph nodes. While this is relatively easy to achieve in the case of *T.b.rhodesiense* because the level of parasites in the blood is usually very high, in the case of *T.b. gambiense* this is less easy because of the greater adaptation of the parasite to the host resulting in a cyclical and lower level of parasites in the blood (called a 'parasitaemia'). Diagnosis in the more common *T.b. gambiense* disease must therefore rely more on 'serological' methods which are designed to detect antibodies to the parasite indicative of an infection. We noted previously that this has been accomplished for several years with the Card Agglutination Test for Trypano-somiasis (CATT) which is useful in screening for disease, especially in regions of Africa where there is a high prevalence of sleeping sickness, but this test has problems such as false positives and equivocal results as well as using electricity which may not be readily available in the African field. Therefore over the last few years alternative methods of trypanosomiasis diagnosis in humans have been sought. While some new molecular methods of early diagnosis have been investigated, a major advance in trypanosome diagnostics has been the development and introduction of rapid diagnostic tests (called, not surprisingly, RDTs). Our colleague Prof Joseph Ndung'u, whom we have met on several occasions in this book, who is now head of the Neglected Tropical Diseases Programme at FIND (Foundation for Innovative New Diagnostics) in Geneva, together with his colleagues in different countries, has now managed to develop novel RDTs for sleeping sickness which have great promise for trypanosome diagnostics. They developed a test called SD BIOLINE HAT which is an immunological test which recognised two components of the trypanosome (let's not concern ourselves here with the technical details). This test was shown to be as sensitive as the CATT (that is, its ability not to miss false negative samples) at a 1 in 8 dilution and also has the advantage of being user friendly, being potentially useful, especially for screening in areas of low prevalence of sleeping sickness, and does not require electrical instruments. Further, Ndung'u and his colleagues, including Enock Matovu of Makerere University in Uganda, have shown that RDTs for *T.b. gambiense* disease also have the property of detecting antibodies in cattle, findings which indicate their potential utility for some aspects of animal trypanosomiasis. Further, a new RDT recently developed by Joseph and his colleagues is even better than the previous ones, and is more sensitive than the CATT test and is also as specific (that is, it doesn't pick up diseases other than trypanosomiasis) so it has considerable promise for the future.

What about the knotty problem of disease staging in sleeping sickness in which it is so difficult to distinguish the early haemolymphatic from the late encephalitic stage? The short and somewhat depressing answer is that not very much progress has been made in this area since we last considered it almost 8 years ago. It will be recalled from Chapter 5 that the WHO criteria for defining late-stage diseases is more than 5WBC/uL in the patient's CSF, but there is no universal consensus among experts as to what exactly constitutes CNS disease, with some experts using a more stringent criterion of more than 20 WBC/uL. Not surprisingly, a number of clinicians and scientists have attempted to develop better and more specific CSF and other markers of CNS invasion by the trypanosome. For example, both the CSF antibody IgM and the chemical neopterin levels have been associated with CNS disease, and various molecular methods and combinations of different proteins have also been reported as being of potential use as late-stage biomarkers. However, all of these approaches, while perfectly reasonable and interesting, have an intrinsic weakness which is that they are usually being compared with the WHO WBC criterion which, as we have seen, is not a gold standard and not ideal or generally accepted. This is the 'circular argument' problem which is intrinsic to these studies. My colleague from Cameroon Alfred Njamnshi and I have recently discussed this problem in detail and we suggested a novel approach which is to adopt a reverse mathematical analysis in which we would correlate these various possible CSF CNS markers with different CSF WBC in an attempt to identify unambiguously the optimal number of WBC that would likely indicate a CNS infection. How and whether this intrinsic diagnostic staging problem can be overcome I do not yet know, and the issue is further complicated by recent observations that unequivocal neurological symptoms and signs can be seen in patients with early stage disease as defined by the WHO criteria. Of course the presence, which is, perhaps surprisingly, quite unusual, of trypanosomes in the CSF would by itself automatically define CNS disease and in that case the CSF WBC is not an issue.

Sleeping sickness is not uniformly fatal in all patients because of human 'trypanotolerance'

The universal view of almost all experts in this field has for many years considered untreated or inadequately treated sleeping sickness as uniformly fatal. However, although this is probably true in the majority of cases, it has emerged over the last decade or so that a small number of infected individuals do not die from the disease but seem to be 'tolerant' of the trypanosome in an analogous way to the phenomenon of 'trypanotolerance' in certain breeds of cattle that have been recognised for many years and which we have discussed in Chapter 10. There are two different but related scenarios. First, some patients with *T.b. gambiense* who had declined treatment subsequently became asymptomatic with no evidence of trypanosomes in the blood and no serological evidence of trypanosome infection, ie no antibodies to the parasite. Other patients, however, also became asymptomatic after infection and did not have trypanosomes in the blood though they did remain seropositive. While the first group might be regarded as 'trypanoresistant', the latter cold be regarded as 'trypanotolerant'. A key issue is whether the latter individuals represent a source of potential infection to others and whether they should be treated when detected, probably through mass screening. Such scenarios have yet to be demonstrated in patients with disease due to *T.b. rhodesiense*. There are a few case reports of patients with *T.b. gambiense* infection who have been diagnosed many years after the initial infection. Indeed a recent report describes the case of a 62-year-old man with *T.b. gambiense* infection who lived for at least 29 years before developing late stage disease, the longest duration of sleeping sickness so far that has ever been reported. The authors of this report rightly pointed out that such cases has implications for a programme for disease elimination. A remarkable recent study by Annette Macleod and colleagues from Glasgow University has shed potential light on such individuals with chronic sleeping sickness of many years' duration. The authors found that trypanosomes could be detected in the skin, ie an extravascular site, in human skin biopsies in individuals who were undiagnosed as having sleeping sickness. They also demonstrated that substantial numbers of trypanosomes could persist in the skin following experimental animal infection, and that these could be transmitted by the tsetse fly. These findings are of great significance since this novel skin reservoir of trypanosome infection might help explain why the infection may be chronic in some cases, and it also raises major questions about the likely efficacy of current attempts to detect, treat and control the disease.

New therapies for sleeping sickness have recently become available and are under test

As has been emphasised several times in this book, the treatment of sleeping sickness is very unsatisfactory and has relied for many years on the use of just a small number of drugs many of which are toxic and developed many years ago, with the arsenical drug melarsoprol, the only drug that can treat CNS disease in both disease variants, being highly toxic with a significant death rate in the currently used shortened ten day intravenous course. Over the last decade some new treatments for late stage sleeping sickness have been tested and show considerable promise for the future.

The treatment for early stage disease in both disease forms, *T.b. gambiense* and *T.b.rhodesiense*, is unchanged being intravenous or intramuscular pentamidine and intravenous suramin, respectively. These drugs are far less toxic than those used in late-stage disease. The treatment for late-stage *T.b.rhodesiense* is still intravenous melarsoprol which as we have seen produces a severe post-treatment reactive encephalopathy that may be fatal with an overall drug fatality rate of around 8 per cent. However, the first line therapy for late-stage *T.b. gambiense* is now NECT which is a course of combined intravenous eflornithine (DFMO) and oral nifurtimox, an effective drug regime that is less toxic than intravenous melarsoprol which it has now replaced as first line therapy for this variant. Though intravenous eflornithine alone can and has been given to such patients, it is more toxic than NECT and requires a longer drug exposure so this 'monotherapy' is no longer first line therapy for *T.b. gambiense*. As we have previously noted, eflornithine is not effective against *T.b.rhodesiense*. However, intravenous melarsoprol is effective against *T.b. gambiense* though it is now used as second line therapy for this form.

So this is the current drug situation for sleeping sickness. But what new drugs are currently in the pipeline? A drug called fexinidazole, a member of the 'nitroheterocyclic' group, is the focus of much current interest. It was shown to be orally effective and non-toxic against *T.b.gambiense* in experimental animals and was also non-toxic in uninfected individuals in a phase 1 clinical trial. A recently published phase 2/3 randomised 'non-inferiority' trial of oral fexinidazole versus NECT therapy funded by DNDi reported that oral fexinidazole was effective against late stage *T.b.gambiense* though not as effective as NECT therapy, and the incidence of treatment-related adverse effects was not significantly different in the two groups. Further evaluation of fexinidazole's efficacy in *T.b.gambiense* as well as its possible effectiveness against *T.b.rhodesiense* will reveal just how useful this drug will be in the fight against sleeping sickness. While fexinidazole may certainly have a role in treating the disease, I personally, as well as my colleagues, would currently choose NECT therapy rather than fexinidazole if we had unfortunately developed late-stage sleeping sickness due to *T.b.gambiense*. But things may change as more studies are performed.

Another potentially promising new drug for treating late-stage sleeping sickness is a new oral compound of the oxaborole group, the specific one being called SCYX-7158 which has been shown experimentally to be active against trypanosomes. A phase 1 trial of this drug has now been completed successfully, and phase 2 trials in Africa are currently underway, with the eventual results eagerly awaited.

Then we come to a novel drug formulation developed in our own laboratory at Glasgow University. Our team, with our key collaborator Stephane Gibaud of Lorraine University in France, made a drug called 'complexed melarsoprol' which is formed by inserting experimentally the melarsoprol drug inside what is called a 'cyclodextrin' molecule to form a fusion drug. The cyclodextrin is a sugar molecule which is highly soluble in water and has space for 'guest' molecules such as melarsoprol. The end and fortunate result is that this new drug is not only soluble in water (which intravenous melarsoprol is not) making it orally effective, but also when tested in our mouse model of sleeping sickness it not only cured the late stage infection when given orally but was also non-toxic, the latter probably due to a slower and more controlled absorption of the drug in the gut. If this were also as effective in humans then this would be a very significant advance. So far both the European Medicines Agency (EMA) and the US Food and Drug Administration (FDA) have given this novel drug formulation orphan drug status, and also the EMA protocol assistance committee has approved our clinical trial proposal for a 'first in man' phase 2 clinical trial of patients with *T.b.rhodesiense* in Uganda. We are raring to go, as are our Ugandan colleagues, and we are trying hard to obtain the funds required to do this trial, which are not small. The drug might also have a role in treating animal trypanosomiasis which we are also seriously considering.

But there is a fundamental practical problem with carrying out trials of new and potentially toxic drugs in Africa even for a disease such as sleeping sickness that is almost always fatal if untreated and for which current intravenous melarsoprol is extremely painful to administer and kills about 8 per cent of treated patients. I think there are three main issues that have confronted us. The first one is that institutions, such as UK universities, are very risk averse when it comes to sponsoring and/or approving such studies. Why is this? After many discussions I think the main fear is that of so-called 'reputational damage' both to the Institution and the researcher him or herself. There is not actually so much of a problem with the risks of the trial itself as the people conducting the trial always take out clinical trial insurance in case there are unforeseen drug side effects, and all participants in the trial are required by law to give fully informed consent. The fear seems rather to be one of adverse news headlines in the newspapers, television and social media even if a single person in the trial suffers a serious problem or even dies. While this is understandable, the reality is that in the intravenous treatment arm of such a trial at least some individuals might be expected to die anyway because of intravenous melarsoprol's known death rate of around 8 per cent. The whole point of such a trial is to improve this current totally unacceptable situation. Also it is just not possible to trial this drug in uninfected people who don't require it as that would be entirely unethical even though it would give valuable information about the absorption and blood availability of the drug (something which some reviewers of grants seem not to appreciate!). So the only way to know whether this new drug is effective and less toxic than the intravenous form (both of which we think is likely) is to test it directly in patients with late stage sleeping sickness with careful safeguards put in place to instigate 'rescue therapy' with standard treatment should the patients fail to be cured . If one were always overly concerned about the potential risks of new and potentially toxic treatment in such a fatal disease then one would not do or discover anything at all! Also, I think this over-cautious attitude underestimates the common sense and goodwill of the lay public as well, probably, of the popular media. The solution to this apparently insurmountable problem is likely to be better communication with all the parties concerned with the trial, both directly and indirectly, and possibly even before the trial begins.

The second problem is that UK institutions may feel that they have little or no control of a clinical trial that is taking place outside the country, or, indeed, the European Union (as it currently exists!). The final permission to carry out such a trial in Africa would actually be given by the ethics and related regulatory committees of the host country and not the UK or even the EMA. But this is always going to be the case with such studies and there is very little, if anything, that the clinical trialists can do about this. The third problem is one that mainly concerns the funding bodies. I am referring here to the view held by some clinicians that all our energies and financial resources would be better spent on developing and testing entirely new drugs rather than trying to change the unwanted properties of old and toxic drugs. While that view is perfectly reasonable on one level, it also has to be appreciated that intravenous melarsoprol is a highly effective drug against trypanosomiasis. The problem with it is the pain of administration and its severe toxicity. I suggest that both approaches should be encouraged and funded-the development of new drugs which may or may not be effective and non-toxic, and attempts to modify the chemical structure of old and highly efficacious drugs so as to retain their ability to kill trypanosomes but not their most unfortunate propensity to kill patients.

Advances in our understanding of the neuropathogenesis of sleeping sickness have been made over the last few years but are largely incremental

There have been many studies on the neuropathogenesis of sleeping sickness, mainly in experimental animal models of the disease, where we in Glasgow have focussed, but also in patients in the African field. We have certainly gained a good deal of new knowledge and understanding of how the CNS disease may be caused and progress but in my view there have been no massive breakthroughs in this area over the last few years. But we have gained several new insights.

Considerable interest has been focussed on the blood-brain barrier (BBB) in experimental trypanosome infection in animal models. In order for the early stage of sleeping sickness to transition to the late-stage it is necessary for the trypanosomes in the blood to traverse the BBB and enter the CNS compartment. Not surprisingly, scientists are therefore very interested in finding out what factors determine how trypanosomes cross the BBB because a better understanding of this process should facilitate the search for new drugs that potentially could either prevent this process or else themselves better cross the BBB and thereby become more efficient in killing any trypanosomes that are lurking inside the brain. We are now able to visualise leakage in the BBB using the neuroimaging technique of Magnetic Resonance Imaging (MRI) which as we saw in Chapter 5 is used in human patients with sleeping sickness. Using a very powerful 7T magnet using what we call a 'small bore' MRI machine we have been able to scan individual infected mice serially to assess the degree of BBB leakage during infection and also after drug treatment. Advance techniques using bioluminescence and photon imaging can also detect individual trypanosomes in infected mice and this type of new technology has enhanced our ability to investigate how the trypanosome infection progresses and may also be helpful in assessing the efficacy of new potential drugs. Using techniques of this nature, it has been rather surprising to learn that after peripheral infection the trypanosomes appear to enter the CNS at an earlier stage than had been previously thought. Yet perhaps we shouldn't be too surprised in view of field observations that patients in two regions of Uganda displayed neurological symptoms and signs when still in the early stage of the disease. So clearly the situation regarding trypanosome entry into the CNS and its relation to neurological features is more complex than previously thought.

Studies which measure the concentrations of various immune components and other proteins in the blood and CSF of experimentally infected animals have continued as one might expect. But two key issues with this approach are, firstly that a cause and effect relation between what one measures and what one observes neurologically is not necessarily operating, and, second, direct extrapolations of such findings to conditions in humans in the African field do not automatically follow. So correlation, however close, is not the same as causation. Two ways in which causality can be ascertained is to give a particular immune component or other chemical to infected mice and then assess the clinical and pathological effect. For example, administering the cytokine IL-10 to mice reduces both the level of parasites in the CNS and the degree of neuroinflammation as well as lowering the levels of pro-inflammatory cytokines which is very good evidence that IL-10 indeed acts against neuroinflammation. Studies of this cytokine in patients are also consistent with this view. Another method that is increasingly used in attempts to sort out the causation issue is to infect 'gene knockout mice' in which embryonic mice have a particular gene removed in order to examine what effect this may have on some aspect of the adult mice's immune or other function.

We are also learning more about the determinants of different susceptibilities and also resistance to sleeping sickness. For example Annette MacLeod and colleagues in Glasgow recently reported that different APOL1 variants reduce people's trypanosomiasis susceptibility, resulting in their positive selection in sub-Saharan Africa. It will be recalled from Chapter 10 that APOL1 is a factor in human serum that can normally destroy the trypanosome parasites. In another study these authors also found that a particular gene called *TgsGP* confers human serum resistance in *T.b. gambiense*. There can be little doubt that the complex genetic mechanisms that confer either susceptibility or resistance to particular trypanosomes in humans will be further investigated and unravelled. People often ask me whether there is a link between trypanosomiasis and HIV infection in sub-Saharan Africa. This is certainly an interesting question, the answer to which may eventually be found but at present I don't know whether such a link actually occurs.

Prospects for the eventual interruption of transmission of sleeping sickness

The goals of the WHO are to eliminate sleeping sickness as a public health problem by 2020 and to achieve interruption of its transmission by 2030. While these are ambitious and indeed noble aims, complete interruption of transmission of the disease may yet be a far more difficult ambition than greatly reducing the number of new cases. The latter is certainly a feasible proposition and the marked reduction of new cases of sleeping sickness reported to WHO over the last decade gives credibility to the notion that the disease may eventually be reduced to just a few annual cases in particular areas of Africa. In my view this is a real possibility for cases of *T.b.gambiense* mainly because the disease reservoirs of infection are mainly humans and the annual incidence of this disease variant has already been reduced significantly through identification and prompt treatment of infected individuals combined with more rigorous insect vector control.

However, there still remain significant challenges. For example, there are several isolated pockets of infected individuals in remote areas of Africa which makes effective screening and identification of cases to be treated a difficult task to achieve. The fact that the symptoms of sleeping sickness may be non-specific and non-diagnostic, especially in the early stages, adds to this difficulty. The recent demonstration of a reservoir of trypanosomes in the skin and extra-vascular tissues of asymptomatic individuals, who may or may not be sources of infection to other people, also indicates a further confounding factor in the drive towards eradication of the disease. It is also possible that current drug therapy may not be able to reach and then kill parasites in these sequestered regions of the body. There is also the problem of eradicating the tsetse fly vector transmitting the disease which is going to be exceedingly difficult as we have already seen in Chapter 7. Control of tsetse fly numbers is certainly feasible in many regions but complete eradication of the trypanosome-transmitting flies is another matter completely, especially when one considers how little the 'tsetse fly belt' in sub-Saharan Africa has diminished over past decades.

The problems involved in eliminating sleeping sickness due to *T.b.rhodesiense* are even greater. Not only do the above caveats also apply in this case, but also as we have seen the reservoir of parasites in this disease variant are mainly cattle which, at least, in Uganda, harbour both human and animal trypanosome parasites. To eliminate all the parasites from cattle hardly seems a feasible proposition on practical grounds alone, and this problem is confounded by the relative ineffectiveness of current drugs to treat animal trypanosomiasis which are, as we have already seen, even worse than those used for the human disease.

While the challenges involved in completely eliminating sleeping sickness are formidable, nevertheless I am much more optimistic about future prospects for treating and controlling the disease than I was ten years ago. I guess only time will tell.

Postscript

SLEEPING SICKNESS IS A tragically clear example of a disease that could have been controlled, but, because of little concrete action and investment, continues to kill hundreds of thousands of people in some of the world's poorest countries.

Nearly eliminated in the 1960s, the disease made a comeback of epidemic proportions in the past two decades due to war, population movements, resource-strapped national health systems in Africa and an astounding lack of commitment by international donors and the pharmaceutical industry.

In the past two decades, Mèdecins Sans Frontières (MSF) has tested more than two million and treated more than 40,000 patients with sleeping sickness living in six sub-Saharan African countries. Our field teams know first-hand the frustration of subjecting people to repeated and often painful tests to confirm a positive diagnosis. Once we know a patient is infected, our medical staff must use antiquated drugs with potentially fatal side effects. Often our doctors have to wonder if the patient will die of the disease or the treatment – a completely unacceptable situation. Finally, after months of treatment and follow-up care, our health teams find that people often become infected again due to inadequate prevention efforts.

Despite all of these problems, treatment has changed little since the start of the 20th century. The drugs developed and used to treat Africans suffering from sleeping sickness during colonial times are still being used today despite the fact that they are inefficient and dangerous.

The countries and people most affected by sleeping sickness are poor, making the development of new treatments unprofitable for drug companies. For this reason, sleeping sickness remains one of the world's most neglected diseases and efforts, like this book, aimed at raising awareness about the disease, its victims and the lack of safe, effective treatment options are more crucial today than ever before.

Peter Kennedy's book provides a clear, intelligent and insightful overview of the current challenges related to diagnosing and treating patients with this disease due to the difficult conditions and limited tools available.

The book covers the history of the disease from its discovery by colonial governments to the present. It explains how new drugs are brought to market, and analyses the current lack of research and development (R&D) taking place in this field.

There is some good news. Today there are encouraging initiatives, such as the Drugs for Neglected Diseases initiative (DNDi), that MSF helped establish, which is working to develop new drugs and formulations of existing drugs for patients in the second, more advanced stage of the disease. Yet there is still little in the R&D pipeline that offers hope that an adapted drug will be available soon to treat seriously ill patients in the advanced stage of the disease.

On their own, private initiatives such as DNDi cannot make up for the lack of R&D experienced in past decades. Only significant commitment and investment coming from all the actors involved in efforts to prevent, diagnose and treat those with this illness (the public and private sectors, public-private initiatives, international organisations, etc.) can offer a sustainable solution to this deadly problem. This book will complement the ongoing efforts by many organisations, including MSF, to raise awareness about this neglected disease and promote urgently needed action to reduce the devastation it causes. Professor Kennedy's wish to donate part of the income generated by this book to DNDi is a noteworthy effort to raise not only awareness but needed resources to advance urgently needed treatment for neglected diseases like sleeping sickness. Let's hope that many others follow his admirable lead.

Unni Karunakara, MB BS, MPH, DrPH
Medical Director
Médecins Sans Frontières
Campaign for Access to Essential Medicines

Amsterdam
March 2007

Sources and Notes

CHAPTER ONE

p6   *Malaria is also an important occupational hazard for soldiers*: David Brown, 'Failed Safeguards are Blamed for Marines' Malaria Outbreak', *Washington Post* (10 September 2003)

p6   *A mysterious and terrifying disease*: I have previously discussed some of these points in: P.G.E. Kennedy, 'A Wake-Up call About Sleeping Sickness' in *Cerebrum* 5 (2003) pp.39–54

p7   *A real risk of Western travellers returning to home with sleeping sickness*: see V. Lejon, M. Boelaert, J. Jannin *et al.*, 'The challenge of *Trypanosoma brucei gambiense* sleeping sickness diagnosis outside Africa'in *Lancet, Infectious diseases* 3 (2003) pp.804–808, and P.G.E. Kennedy, 'Human African trypanosomiasis – in and out of Africa' in *Neurology* 66 (2006) pp.962–963

p7   *Sleeping Sickness is often referred to as one of the 'neglected diseases'*: E. Torreele, M. Usdin, P. Chirac, 'A needs-based pharmaceutical R&D agenda for neglected diseases'in *Report of Drugs for Neglected Diseases Initiative (DNDi)* (31 July 2004)

p8   *Despite considerable publicity in the medical press*: J. Jones, 'African Sleeping Sickness returns to UK after four years'in *British Medical Journal* 321 (2000) p.1177

p9   *Some visitors to Greece have said similar things about the light found there*: Robert Payne, *The Splendour of Greece* (Pan Books Ltd, 1960) p.13

p10   *UCH surgeon Robert Liston*: *The Oxford Companion to Medicine*, eds. J. Walton, P.B. Beeson, R. Bodley Scott (OUP, 1985) p.675

CHAPTER TWO

p30   *The situation in neighbouring Rhodesia under Ian Smith*: see website: http://news.bbc.co.uk/1/hi/special_report/1998/12/98/zimbabwe/226542.stm

p31   *Chililabombwe was called Bancroft*: see website http://www.britannica.com/eb/article-9024085

p31   *The history of Zambian copper mining*: This account was constructed using the following sources: Francis L. Coleman, *The Northern Rhodesia Copperbelt 1899–1962* (Manchester University Press, 1971) p.15; William Gray, *Globetrotter Travel Guide Zambia And Victoria Falls* (New Holland, 2003) pp.21, 22,

36; Eugena W. Herbert, *Red Gold of Africa Copper in Precolonial History and Culture* (University of Wisconsin Press, 1984) p.15; Andrew Roberts, *A History of Zambia* (Heinemann, 1976) pp.156, 192, 202; Chukwuma F.Obidegwu and Mudziviri Nziramasanga, *Copper and Zambia* (Lexington Books, 1981) p.10; see also, websites: http://news.bbc.co.uk/1/hi/business/1904972.stm and http://www.bized.ac.uk/virtual/dc/copper/kitwe/issue4.htm

p35 *The Ringhals and certain African species of Naja are the most effective 'spitters':* Norris Robert: Snake Envenomations, Cobra. Website: http://www.emedicine.com/emerg/topic544.htm, and also D.A. Warrell & L.D. 'Ormerod, Snake Venom ophthalmia and blindness caused by the spitting cobra (Naja nigricollis) in Nigeria' in *American Journal of Tropical Medicine and Hygiene* 25 (1976) pp.525–529

p41 *'Fusiform' bacteria and also a kind of spirochaetal bacteria:* B. Adriaans, R. Hay, B. Drasar, D. Robinson, 'The Infectious aetiology of tropical ulcer – a study of the role of anaerobic bacteria' in *British Journal of Dermatology* 116 (1987) pp.31–37

p43 *89,000 deaths recorded in Zambia in 2003:* statistics obtained from HIV *InSite, a project of the* UCSF *Center for* HIV *Information.* Website: http://hivinsite.ucsf.edu/global?page=cr09-za-00

p45 *A single annual round of house spraying with insecticide:* B. Sharp, P. van Wyk, J.B. Sikasote *et al.*, 'Malaria control by residual insecticide spraying in Chingola and Chililabombwe, Copperbelt Province, Zambia' in *Tropical Medicine and International Health* 7 (2002) pp.732–736

p53 *The breakdown of government and public services in England:* see website: http://www.nationalarchives.gov.uk/releases

p53 *The 1973 Yom Kippur war:* see website: http://news.bbc.co.uk/onthisday/hi/dates/stories/october/6/newsid_2514000/2514317

p54 *The dreaded Putzi fly, known also as the African Tumbu fly, and technically called myiasis:* For a more detailed description of this revolting fly see the excellent account in *The Merck Veterinary Manual* (Merck & Co. Inc., 9th edition, 2005)

CHAPTER THREE

p63 *Camels and horses were inexplicably stricken:* George Gerster, 'Tsetse' in *National Geographic* 170 (December 1986) pp.814–833

p63 *Affecting sleep in the inhabitants of Western Sudan,* and also, *Thomas Masterman Winterbottom:* B.I. Williams, 'African Trypanosomiasis'in *The Wellcome Trust Illustrated History of Tropical Diseases,* ed. F.E.A.D. Cox (The Wellcome Trust, 1996) pp.178–191

p64   *The following brief extract from his book*: from Thomas
       Winterbottom, *An Account of the Native Africans in the
       Neighborhood of Sierra Leone* (Hatchard and Mawman, 1803)
       extract quoted in Ralph H. Major, *Classic Descriptions of Disease*,
       (Charles C. Thomas, 3rd edition, 1965) pp.224–225

p65   *Livingstone's subsequent greatness from his early humble origins*:
       account of Livingstone's life was constructed using the following
       sources: Tim Jeal, *Livingstone* (Book Club Associates, 1973)
       pp.15–25, Alexander Duncan, *Memorials of the Faculty of Physicians
       and Surgeons of Glasgow 1599–1850* (Maclehose, 1896) p.293, and
       official website of David Livingstone Museum, Blantyre: **http://atschool.
       eduweb.co.uk/ blantyre/living/living.HTMl.**
       I am also grateful to Karen Carruthers of the David Livingstone
       Museum for providing me with very useful information on the
       subject.

p66   *Severe anaemia from bleeding haemorrhoids*: C.S. Nichols, *Elspeth
       Huxley – A Biography* (Harper Collins, 2003) p.390, this quoting
       from Elspeth Huxley, *Livingstone and his African Journeys*
       (Weidenfeld and Nicolson, 1974)

p66   *His letter published in the* British Medical Journal: D. Livingstone,
       'Arsenic as a remedy for the tsetse bite' in *British Medical Journal*
       (1 May 1858) p.360. Reproduced with permission of the BMJ
       Publishing Group.

p67   *The cause of sleeping sickness in both animals and humans was
       finally discovered during the period 1894 to 1910*: This account
       was constructed with the considerable help of the following sources:
       B.I. Williams, 'African Trypanosomiasis' in *The Wellcome Trust
       Illustrated History of Tropical Diseases*, ed. F.E.A.D. Cox (The Wellcome
       Trust, 1996) pp.178–191, and K.Vickerman 'Landmarks in
       Trypanosome Research' in *Trypanosomiasis and Leishmaniasis*, eds.
       G. Hide, J.C. Mottram, P.H. Holmes (CAB International, 1997) pp.1–36

p68   *From an ancient Florentine family*: B. Bentivoglio, G. Grassi-Zuccini,
       K. Kristensson, 'From trypanosomes to the nervous system, from
       molecules to behaviour: a survey, on the occasion of the 90th
       anniversary of Castellani's discovery of the parasites in sleeping sick-
       ness' in *Italian Journal of Neurological Sciences* 15 (1994) pp.77–89

p70   *Mussolini's doctor for 20 years*: Aldo Castellani, *Microbes, Men and
       Monarchs* (Victor Gollancz Ltd, 1960) pp.126–139

p70   *Sir John Boyd wrote a penetrating and meticulously researched article*:
       J. Boyd, 'The Castellani-Bruce controversy' in *Notes and Records of
       the Royal Society* 28 (1973) pp.93–110

p72   *Scientists at present are very interested indeed in the flagellum*:
      C. Cross, 'Moving forward, the trypanosome flagellum' in *Wellcome
      News*, Issue 42, April 2005 (The Wellcome Trust) pp.20–22

p73   *A fossilised tsetse fly has been discovered in Colorado*: George Gerster,
      'Tsetse' in *National Geographic* 170 (December 1986) pp.814–833

p74   *The parasite's life cycle*: For more details of life cycle and two types
      of sleeping sickness, see J. Atouguia and P.G.E. Kennedy,
      'Neurological aspects of human African trypanosomiasis' in
      Infectious Diseases of the Nervous System, eds. L.E. Davis and P.G.E.
      Kennedy (Butterworth-Heinemann, 2000) pp.321–372

p77   *But many other factors play an important role*: see F.A. Kuzoe,
      'Current situation of African typanosomiasis' in *Acta Tropica* 54
      (1993) pp.153–162

p78   *The World Health Organisation (WHO) has for some time kept a
      watching brief on the disease*: see World Health Organisation (WHO),
      'Epidemiology and control of African trypanosomiasis' in *Report of
      a WHO Expert Committee, Technical Report Series* 739 (1986) p.125.
      Also, S.C. Welburn, M. Odiit, 'Recent developments in human
      African trypanosomiasis' in *Current Opinion in Infectious Diseases*
      15 (2002) pp.477–484

p79   *A possible sequence of evolutionary events*: J.R. Stevens, W. Gibson,
      'The molecular evolution of trypanosomes' in *Parasitology Today* 15
      (1999) pp.432–437

p79   *Our physical proximity to the different parasites as we evolved*:
      S.C. Welburn, E.M. Fevre, P.G. Colman *et al*, 2001, 'Sleeping sick-
      ness: a tale of two diseases' in *Trends in Parasitology* 17 (2001)
      pp.19–24

CHAPTER FOUR

p84   *The famous Norfolk Hotel*: This account was constructed using
      personal observations and the excellent and detailed official hotel
      website: **http://www.lonrhohotels.com/norfolk/history.html**

p86   *The origins of Nairobi are interesting*: This account of Nairobi was
      constructed using the following sources: M. Fitzpatrick, N. Ray,
      T. Parkinson, 2003, *East Africa* (Lonely Planet Publications, 2003,
      6th edition) pp.391–2; John Reader, *Africa: A Biography of the
      Continent* (Penguin, 1998) p.641; D. Richards and V. Richards,
      Globetrotter Travel Guide Kenya (New Holland, 4th edition, 2005)
      p.54; R.W. Walmsley, *Nairobi: The Geography of a New City*, East
      African Studies No.1 (The Eagle Press, East African Literature
      Bureau, 1957) pp.18, 36; H. Herbert Werlin, *Governing an African*

City: A study of Nairobi (Africana Publishing Co., 1974) p.38; and websites: **http://www.nairobicity.org** (shows current population figures), **http://news.bbc.co.uk/1/hi/world/ africa/2297237.stm http://www.overlandafrica.com/overlanding-destinations/ kenya/nairobi.asp**

p86   *Lord Curzon's Lunatic Express:* Charles Miller, *The Lunatic Express* (Westlands Sundries Ltd., 1972) pp.322–323

p87   *Established a new Veterinary degree course:* N.J. Blockey, Bulletin of the Royal College of Physicians and Surgeons of Glasgow 26 (1997) pp.8–10

p87   *And was known as the 'Conversion Course':* This account is based on personal communications from Max Murray, Peter Holmes and Ian McIntyre.

p88   *The training of medical students in Kenya:* This account is strongly based on that of Noel Blockey's article: N.J. Blockey, Bulletin of the Royal College of Physicians and Surgeons of Glasgow 26 (1997) pp.8–10

p91   *The mandate of KETRI: KETRI Strategic Plan 1990–2000*, Revised version

p93   *The East African Veterinary Research Organisation: E.A.V.R.O. Annual Report 1956–1957*, published by Authority, Government Printer, Nairobi

p96   *A very famous scientific paper published in 1960:* W.F.H. Jarrett, F.W. Jennings, W.I.M. McIntyre *et al*, 'Immunological studies on *Dictyocaulus viviparous* infection. Immunity produced by the administration of irradiated larvae' in *Immunology* 3 (1960) pp.145–151

p98   *In her memoir of her mother Nellie Grant:* Elspeth Huxley, *Nellie: Letters from Africa* (Weidenfeld and Nicolson, 1980) p.84

p98   *The Muthaiga Club which was opened in 1914:* Elspeth Huxley, *Nellie: Letters from Africa* (Weidenfeld Nicolson, 1980) p.48

p99   *Karen Blixen first met Denys Finch-Hatton:* see website: **http://www.karenblixen.com/finchhatton.html**

p99   *The grandeur and beauty of the Valley:* This account was constructed using the following sources: J.W. Gregory, *The Rift Valleys and Geology of East Africa* (London Seeley Service & Co. Ltd., 1921) pp.357 and 412; Nigel Pavitt, 2001, *Africa's Great Rift Valley* (Harry N. Abrams Inc., 2001) p.87; 2; M. Fitzpatrick, N. Ray, T. Parkinson, *East Africa* (Lonely Planet Publications, 6th edition, 2003) p.376

p100   *Including that of 'Lucy':* Richard Leakey, *The Origins of Humankind* (The Guernsey Press Co. Ltd., 1994) p.30

p100   *John Walter Gregory:* Australian Dictionary of Biography online edition: website: **http://www.adb.online.anu.edu.au/biogs/ A090104b.htm**
   special.lib.gla.ac.uk/Gregory

p100   *ILRAD was finally formed in 1974:* See M. Murray, 'The parasites, predators, places and people I have known: a great adventure' in *Veterinary Parasitology* 81 (1999) pp.149–158. See also official ILRI website: **http://www.ilri.cgiar.org/**

p100   *The CGIAR is a strategic alliance:* See official CGIAR website at: **http://www.cgiar.org/**

p102   *An important institution called ICIPE:* See *Meeting the needs of a changing world: ICIPE's Vision and Strategy 2003–2012* (The Regal Press, Kenya, Ltd., 2003) and ICIPE's official website **http://www.icipe.org/**

CHAPTER FIVE

p105   *Kisumu:* This account of Kisumu was constructed using the following sources: *Fodor's Kenya, Tanzania, Seychelles* (Fodor's Travel Publications Inc., 3rd edition, 1990) p.192; M. Fitzpatrick, N. Ray, T. Parkinson, *East Africa* (Lonely Planet Publications, 6th edition, 2003) pp.391–2; D. Richards and V. Richards, *Globetrotter Travel Guide Kenya* (New Holland, 4th edition, 2005) p.54

p106   *Lake Victoria:* This account was constructed using the following sources: D. Richards and V. Richards, *Globetrotter Travel Guide Kenya* (New Holland Publishers, 4th edition, 2005) pp.54–5; World Lakes Database, website: **http://www.ilec.or.jp/database/afr/afr-05. html** (size and measurements of lake)

p107   *The invasion of Lake Victoria by the water hyacinth:* See Activities of Aquarius on Lake Victoria, website: **http://library.thinkquest.org/ C0126023/kenya.htm**

p109   *Busia itself covers an area of 743 square km:* See website **http://www.busia.go.ug/background/index.htm**

p110   *Another kind of 'sleeping sickness':* Oliver Sacks, *Awakenings* (Picador, 1982, first published 1973)

p110   *Two types of human African trypanosomiasis:* see J. Atouguia and P.G.E. Kennedy, 'Neurological aspects of human African trypanosomiasis' in *Infectious Diseases of the Nervous System*, eds. L.E. Davis and P.G.E. Kennedy (Butterworth-Heinemann, 2000) pp.321–372

p115   *There is an alteration of the normal sleep structure:* A. Buguet, S. Bisser, T. Josenando *et al.*, 'Sleep structure: a new diagnostic tool for stage determination in sleeping sickness' in *Acta Tropica* 93 (2005) pp.107–117

p116   *The late stage of the disease:* P.G.E. Kennedy, 'Sleeping sickness –
        human African trypanosomiasis' in *Practical Neurology* 5 (2005)
        pp.260–267

p118   *The diagnosis of sleeping sickness:* P.G.E. Kennedy, 'Human African
        trypanosomiasis of the CNS: current issues and challenges' in *Journal
        of Clinical Investigation* 113 (2004) pp.496–504, and World Health
        Organisation (WHO) (1998), 'Control and surveillance of African try-
        panosomiasis' in *Report of a WHO expert committee. Technical
        Report Series*, No. 881 (1998) p.114

p120   *Some experts have suggested a compromise figure:* F. Chappuis,
        L. Loutan, P. Simarro *et al*, 'Options for field diagnosis of Human
        African trypanosomiasis' in *Clinical Microbiology Reviews* 18 (2005)
        pp.133–146

p121   *We come to drug treatment:* See P.G.E. Kennedy, 'Human African
        trypanosomiasis of the CNS: current issues and challenges' in *Journal
        of Clinical Investigation* 113 (2004) pp.496–504

p121   *Would not have passed contemporary safety standards:*
        A.H. Fairlamb, 'Future prospects for the chemotherapy of human
        trypanosomiasis. 1. Novel approaches to the chemotherapy of try-
        panosomiasis' in *Transactions of the Royal Society of Tropical
        Medicine and Hygiene* 84 (1990) pp.613–617

p122   *A new shorter melarsoprol regime:* C. Schmid, M. Richer,
        C.M. Bilenge *et al*, 'Effectiveness of a 10-day melarsoprol schedule
        for the treatment of late-stage human African trypanosomiasis:
        confirmation from a multinational study (IMPAMEL II)' in *Journal of
        Infectious Diseases* 191 (2005) pp.1922–1931

p122   *The post-treatment reactive encephalopathy ('PTRE':* P.G.E. Kennedy,
        'Sleeping sickness-human African trypanosomiasis' in *Practical
        Neurology* 5 (2005) pp.260–267

p123   *'Like having chilli peppers injected into your heart':* A.A. Gill, 'Why
        Africa is losing its fight against disease' in *The Sunday Times
        Magazine* (17 September 2000)

p123   *Eflornithine (also known as DFMO):* P.G.E. Kennedy, M. Murray,
        F. Jennings, J. Rodgers, 'Sleeping sickness: new drugs from old?' in
        Lancet 359 (2002) pp.1695–1696

CHAPTER SIX

p129   *The immune system is incredibly complex:* The summary given here
        is very simplified. For a more detailed and challenging account of the
        different components of the immune system the reader is referred to
        the excellent article by J. Parkin and B. Cohen, 'An overview of the

immune system' in *Lancet* 357 (2001) pp.1777–1789. Also see:
I. Roitt & P.J. Delves, *Roitt's Essential Immunology* (Blackwell,
2001, 10th edition)

p132 *We have about a hundred billion neurons in our brain:* Susan
Greenfield, *The Human Brain: A Guided Tour* (Weidenfeld and
Nicolson, 1997) p.79

p132 *There are several forms of microglia:* W.J. Streit, C.A. Kincaid-
Colton, 'The Brain's Immune System' in *Scientific American*
(November 1995) pp.38–43

p134 *The human CNS inflammatory disease:* For a detailed description of
the pathological features and pathogenesis of human CNS sleeping
sickness see V.W. Pentreath and P.G.E. Kennedy, 'Pathogenesis of
human African trypanosomiasis' in *The Trypanosomiases*, eds.
I. Maudlin, P.H. Holmes, M.A. Miles (CAB International, 2004)
pp.283–301

p135 *The mouse model of CNS trypanosomiasis:* This has been used and
described in many papers, but the principle is explained in P.G.E.
Kennedy, 'The pathogenesis and modulation of the post-treatment
reactive encephalopathy in a mouse model of Human African
trypanosomiasis' in *Journal of Neuroimmunology* 100 (1999)
pp.36–41

p138 *Kelvin stated:* This view of Lord Kelvin was reproduced in the article
entitled: M. Murray, 'The parasites, predators, places and people I
have known:a great adventure' in *Veterinary Parasitology* 81 (1999)
pp.149–158

p139 *The astrocyte plays a pivotal role:* C.A. Hunter, F.W. Jennings,
P.G.E. Kennedy, M. Murray, 'Astrocyte activation correlates with
cytokine production in central nervous system of Trypanosoma
brucei brucei-infected mice' in *Laboratory Investigation* 67 (1992)
pp.635–642

p139 *A delicate balance between pro- and counter-inflammatory cytokines:*
J.M. Sternberg, J. Rodgers, B. Bradley *et al.*, 'Meningoencephalitic
African trypanosomiasis: Brain IL–10 and IL–6 are associated with
protection from neuro-inflammatory pathology' in *Journal of
Neuroimmunology* 167 (2005) p.81–89

p140 *The effects in the model of three different drugs:* These are covered
in the following three articles: C.A. Hunter, F.W. Jennings,
P.G.E. Kennedy *et al.*, 'The use of azathiaprine to ameliorate post-
treatment encephalopathy associated with African trypanosomiasis'
in *Neuropathology and Applied Neurobiology* 18 (1992)
pp.619–625; F.W. Jennings, C.W. Gichuki, P.G.E. Kennedy *et al.*,
'The use of the polyamine inhibitor eflornithine in the

neuropathogenesis of experimental murine African trypanosomiasis' in *Neuropathology and Applied Neurobiology* 23 (1997) pp.225–234; P.G.E. Kennedy, J. Rodgers, F.W. Jennings *et al*., 'A Substance P antagonist: RP–67,580 ameliorates a mouse meningoencephalitic response to Trypanosoma brucei brucei' in *Proceedings of the National Academy of Sciences of the USA* 94 (1997) pp.4167–4170

p146 *Rapidly switch the type of VSG that is coating its surface at any one time:* See J.D. Barry, 'The biology of antigenic variation in African trypanosomes' in *Trypanosomiasis and leishmaniasis*, eds. G. Hide, J.C. Mottram, G.H. Coombs (CAB International, 1997) pp.89–107

p146 *Which have modelled the symptoms seen in the human disease:* Several of these studies from Krister Kristensson's laboratory are summarised in: M. Bentivoglio, G. Grassi-Zucconi, T. Olsson, K. Kristensson, 'Trypanosoma brucei and the nervous system' in *Trends in Neurosciences* 17 (1994) pp.325–329

CHAPTER SEVEN

p151 *Lake Magadi:* This account was constructed using the following sources: *Fodor's Kenya, Tanzania, Seychelles* (Fodor's Travel Publications Inc., 3rd edition, 1990) p.158; N. Pavitt, *Africa's Great Rift Valley* (Harry N. Abrams Inc., 2001) p.124; D. Richards and V. Richards, *Globetrotter Travel Guide Kenya* (New Holland, 4th edition, 2005) p.74; A. Smith, *The Great Rift: Africa's Changing Valley* (BBC Books, 3rd edition, 1988) pp.209–10

p151 *A shimmering pink coloured hellscape:* D. Richards and V. Richards, *Globetrotter Travel Guide Kenya* (New Holland, 4th edition, 2005) p.74

p153 *The Nguruman escarpment:* see website: **http://www.birdlife.org/ datazone/sites/index.html**

p153 *By definition, an escarpment:* see *The Oxford Compact English Dictionary* (Oxford University Press, 2nd edition, 2000) p.372

p154 *A large area of about 300 square km:* E.K. Mwangi, 'Variation in susceptibility to tsetse-borne trypanomiasis among three *Bos Indicus* cattle breeds in different tsetse endemic localities in Kenya' (PhD thesis, University of Glasgow, 1993)

p155 *The essential goal of tsetse control:* I am indebted to Peter Holmes for his generous and valuable input into this discussion of tsetse control and the role of PAAT and PATTEC.

p156 *The pioneering work of Glyn Vale and his colleagues:* G.A. Vale, 'The responses of tsetse flies (Diptera: Glossinidae) to mobile and stationary baits' in *Bulletin of Entomological Research* 64 (1974) pp.545–588. See also: George Gerster, 'Tsetse' in *National Geographic* (December 1986) pp.814–833

p158   *The use of insecticides as sprays on the tsetse fly habitats:* I.F. Grant, 2001, 'Insecticides for tsetse and trypanosomiasis control: is the environmental risk worth it?' in *Trends in Parasitology* 17 (2001) pp.10–13

p158   *The sequential aerosol drift technique (SAT):* R. Allsop, 'Options for vector control against trypanosomiasis in Africa' in *Trends in Parasitology* 17 (2001) pp.15–19; I.F. Grant, 2001, 'Insecticides for tsetse and trypanosomiasis control: is the environmental risk worth it?' in *Trends in Parasitology* 17 (2001) pp.10–13

p158   *The sterile insect technique (SIT):* S. Askoy, I. Maudlin, C. Dale *et al.*, 'Prospects for control of African trypanosomiasis by tsetse vector manipulation' in *Trends in Parasitology* 17 (2001) pp.29–35

p159   *Picked the brains of a distinguished colleague:* I am very grateful to Serap Askoy for helpful insights into SIT and tsetse fly molecular manipulation.

p159   *Alter the actual genetic make-up of the flies:* S. Askoy, 'Control of tsetse flies and trypanosomes using molecular genetics' in *Veterinary Parasitology,* 115 (2003) pp.125–145

p160   *PAAT:* B.S. Hursey, 'The Programme against African Trypanosomiasis: Aims, Objectives and Achievements' in *Trends in Parasitology* 17 (2001) pp.2–3

p161   *PATTEC:* N. Bhalla, 'Pan African group takes lead against the tsetse fly' in *Lancet* 359 (2002) p.686

p165   *The total cattle population in Africa is approximately 174 million:* KETRI *Strategic Plan 1990–2000* (Revised version, Nairobi)

p165   *If these 7 million square km of land were cleared:* KETRI *Strategic Plan 1990–2000* (Revised version, Nairobi)

p166   *The diagnosis of trypanosomiasis:* I am indebted to Peter Holmes for his valuable input into this discussion of the diagnosis.

p167   *Max Murray and his colleagues:* M. Murray, P.K. Murray, W.I.M. McIntyre, 'An improved parasitological technique for the diagnosis of African trypanosomiasis' in *Transactions of the Royal Society of Tropical Medicine and Hygiene* 71 (1977) pp.325–326

p168   *A major problem with animal treatment:* I am indebted to Peter Holmes for his valuable input into this discussion of treatment.

p168   *The emergence of drug resistance:* S. Geerts, P.H. Holmes, O. Diall, M.C. Eisler, 'African bovine trypanosomiasis: the problem of drug resistance' in *Trends in Parasitology* 17 (2001) pp.25–28

p170   *Testing for resistance of T.brucei parasites to the drug melarsoprol:*

M.L. Stewart, S. Krishna, R.J. Burchmore *et al.*, 'Detection of arsenical drug resistance in Trpanosoma brucei with a simple fluorescence test' in *Lancet* 366 (2005) pp.486–487

p170 *This ability to resist infection is called trypanotolerance:* M. Murray, 'The parasites, predators, places and people I have known: a great adventure' in *Veterinary Parasitology* 81 (1999) pp.149–158

CHAPTER EIGHT

p172 *In* Out of Africa: Karen Blixen (Isak Dinesen), *Out of Africa* (Penguin, 2001, first published 1937). This and following extracts reproduced with the permission of Gyldendal Denmark (Karen Blixen's Danish publishing house) and The Rungstedlund Foundation.

p178 *'enterotoxigenic* Escherichia coli': M.J.G. Farthing, 'Traveller's Diarrhoea' in *Medicine* (The Medicine Publishing Company Ltd., 2003) pp.35–40

CHAPTER NINE

p188 *Cytokine IL-10 was significantly increased:* J.M. Sternberg, 'Human African trypanosomiasis: clinical presentation and immune response' in *Parasite Immunology* 26 (2004) pp.469–476

p190 *LIRI is located in the South Eastern Ugandan district called Tororo:* This summary of LIRI was constructed using *LIRI reports* kindly made available to me by Joseph Ndung'u.

p192 *The goal of LIRI:* See LIRI website **http://www.naro.go.ug/research_ institutes/LIRI.htm**

p193 *Fairly constant at about 3:1:* E.M. Fevre, A. Tilley, K. Picozzi *et al.*, 'Central point sampling from cattle in livestock markets in areas of human sleeping sickness' in *Acta Tropica* 97 (2006) pp.229–232

p194 *The two forms of the disease are 150 km apart:* K. Picozzi, E. Fevre, M. Odiit *et al.*, 'Sleeping sickness in Uganda: a thin line between two fatal diseases' in *British Medical Journal* 331 (2005) pp.1238–1241

p194 *The Glasgow Coma Score (GCS):* G. Teasdale, B. Jennett, 'Assessment of coma and impaired consciousness: a practical scale' in *Lancet* 2 (1974) pp.81–84

p196 *This district of Tororo:* See website: **http://www.tororo.go.ug/**

p198 *The region of Soroti:* See website: **http://www.soroti.go.ug/**

p198 *The Lord's Resistance Army:* See Damon Galgut, 'On a hiding to nothing' in *The Sunday Times Magazine* (4 December 2005); M. Fitzpatrick, N. Ray, T. Parkinson, *East Africa* (Lonely Planet Publications, 6th Edition, 2003) p.496; Human Rights Watch/ Africa, Human Rights Childrens Project, 1997, The Scars of Death.

Children abducted by the Lord's Resistance Army in Uganda, copyright Humans Rights Watch, Library of Congress, USA.

CHAPTER TEN

p201   *Trials for new drugs occur in three distinct phases*: J. Keiser, A. Stich, C. Burri, 'New drugs for the treatment of human African trypanosomiasis: research and development' in *Trends in Parasitology* 17 (2001) pp.42–48

p202   *The drug known as DB289*: L.M. Sturk, J.L. Brock, C.R. Bagnell *et al.*, 'Distribution and quantitation of the anti-trypanosomal diamidine 2,5-bis(4-amidinophenyl) furan (DB75) and its N-methoxy prodrug DB289 in murine brain tissue' in *Acta Tropica* 91 (2004) pp.131–143

p203   *Eflornithine acquired 'orphan drug' status*: A. Sjoerdsma, P.J. Schechter, 1999, 'Eflornithine for African sleeping sickness' in *Lancet* 354 (1999) p.254

p203   *The organisation's public literature explains the detailed story*: See MSF *Fact Sheet*, 'Sleeping Sickness or Human African trypanosomiasis' (May 2004) pp.1–4

p206   *More able to cross the Blood-brain barrier*: P.G.E. Kennedy, M. Murray, F. Jennings, J. Rodgers, 'Sleeping Sickness: new drugs from old' in *Lancet* 359 (2002) pp.1695–1696

p206   *The idea is to identify a new biochemical target in the trypanosome*: M.P. Barrett, R.J.S. Burchmore, A. Stich *et al.*, 'The Trypanosomiases' in *Lancet* 362 (2003) pp.1469–1480

p207   *A molecule called ApoL-I has recently been identified as this factor in human serum*: L.Vanhamme, F. Paturiaux-Hanocq, P. Poelvoorde *et al.*, 'Apolipoprotein L-I is the trypanosome lytic factor of human serum' in *Nature* 422 (2003) pp.83–87

p208   *A large number of potential compounds will need to be tested*: J. Keiser, A. Stich, C. Burri, 'New drugs for the treatment of human African trypanosomiasis:research and development' in *Trends in Parasitology* 17 (2001) pp.42–48

p208   *Whether there is really an 'intermediate' stage in sleeping sickness*: P.G.E. Kennedy, 'Human African trypanosomiasis of the CNS: current issues and challenges' in *Journal of Clinical Investigation* 113 (2004) pp.496–504

p210   *How the passage of trypanosomes across the BBB occurs*: W. Masocha, B. Robertson, M.E. Rottenberg *et al.*, 'Cerebral vessel laminins and IFN–γ define Trypanosoma brucei brucei penetration of the blood-brain barrier' in *Journal of Clinical Investigation* 114 (2004) pp.689–694 p211 *Make them more efficient in crossing the* BBB: The UK Medical Research Council (MRC) has very recently agreed to fund this work.

p211 *The recent sequencing of the entire T.brucei genome*: M. Berriman, E. Ghedin, C. Hertz-Fowler *et al.*, 'The Genome of the African Trypanosome *Trypanosoma brucei*' in *Science* 309 (2005) pp.416–422

p212 *By carrying out genetic tests in different trypanosome strains*: G. Newton, 'United front: uncovering the trityp genomes' in *Wellcome News* (The Wellcome Trust, Issue 42, April 2005) pp.17–19

p215 *Continues to be controlled by 'crisis management'*: S.C. Welburn, P.G. Coleman, I. Maudlin *et al.*, 'Crisis, what crisis? Control of Rhodesian sleeping sickness' in *Trends in Parasitology* 22 (2006) pp.123–128

p215 *There has been a chronic and severe lack of investment in sleeping sickness over many years*: See, for example, P. Trouiller, P. Olliano, E. Torreele, 'Drug development for neglected diseases: a deficient market and a public-health policy failure' in *Lancet* 359 (2002) pp.2188–2194

p216 *Particularly impressive is the 2005 Grand Challenges Programme on global child survival*: J.M. Litzow, H. Bauchner, 'The grand challenges of the Gates Foundation: what impact on global child health?' in *Journal of the Royal Society of Medicine* 99 (2006) pp.171–174

p217 *Total of* US$14.4 *million that the National Institute of Allergy and Infectious Diseases (*NIAID) *of NIH gave out*: Personal communication from Anne A. Opinger, News and Public Information Branch, NIAID.

p217 *It is African trypanosomiasis that is killing us*: in 'Workers on African trypanosomiasis unite' in TDR news 76 (March 2006)

p217 *Disability of adjusted life years lost*: D.H. Molyneaux, V. Pentreath, F. Doua, 'African trypanosomiasis in man' in Manson's Tropical Diseases, eds. G.C. Cook (W.D. Saunders Company Ltd, 1996) pp.1171–1196.

CHAPTER ELEVEN

p219 *the progressive and rapid reduction of the number of new cases of sleeping sickness in sub-Saharan Africa reported to* WHO: see website: http://www.who.int/trypanosomiasis_ african/country/country_ situation/en/

p220 The *numbers are continuing to fall over the past few years*:

P. Büscher, G. Cecchi, V. Jamonneau *et al*, 'Human African Trypanosomias', *Lancet* 390 (2017) pp.2397–2409.

p221 *there may be significant underestimates and under-diagnoses of sleeping sickness cases*: P.G.E. Kennedy, 'Clinical features, diagnosis, and treatment of human African trypanosomiasis (sleeping sickness)', *Lancet Neurology* 12 (2013) pp.186–194; D. Mumba, E. Bohorquez, J. Messina et al, 'African trypanosomiasis in the Democratic Republic of the Congo' *PLoS Negl Trop Dis* 5 (2011): e1246

p222 *the development and introduction of rapid diagnostic tests*: S. Bisser S, C Lumbala, E. Nguertoum *et al*. 'Sensitivity and Specificity of a Prototype Rapid Diagnostic Test for the Detection of Trypanosoma brucei gambiense Infection: A Multi-centric Prospective Study' *PLoS Negl Trop Dis* 10 (2016): e0004608; C. Lumbala C, S. Biéler, S. Kayembe *et al*, 'Prospective evaluation of a rapid diagnostic test for Trypanosoma brucei gambiense infection developed using recombinant antigens' *PLoS Negl Trop Dis* 12 (2018): e0006386; E. Matovu, A. Kitibwa, A. Picado *et al*, 'Serological tests for gambiense human African trypanosomiasis detect antibodies in cattle', *Parasites and Vectors* 10 (2017): p546.

p223 *My colleague from Cameroon Alfred Njamnshi and I have recently discussed this problem in detail*: A. Njamnshi, G.G. Gettinby, P.G.E. Kennedy 'The challenge of diagnostic staging in human African trypanosomiasis. 2017', *Transactions of the Royal Society for Tropical Medicine and Hygiene* 111 (2017): pp.199–203.

p224 *A small number of infected individuals do not die from the disease but seem to be 'tolerant' of the trypanosome*: V. Jamonneau, H.H. Ilboudo, J. Kaboré *et al*, 'Untreated human infections by Trypanosoma brucei gambiense are not 100% fatal', *PLoS Negl Trop Dis* 6 (2012):e1691; P.G.E. Kennedy, 'Clinical features, diagnosis, and treatment of human African trypanosomiasis (sleeping sickness)', *Lancet Neurology* 12 (2013) pp.186–194.

p224 *A recent report describes the case of a 62-year-old man with T.b. gambiense infection who lived for at least 29 years*: D. Sudarshi, S. Lawrence, W.O. Pickrell et al', Human African trypanosomiasis presenting at least 29 years after infection – what can this teach us about the pathogenesis and control of this neglected tropical disease? *PLoS Negl Trop Dis*. 2014 8 (2014): e3349.

p225 *The authors found that trypanosomes could be detected in the skin*: P. Capewell , C. Cren-Travaillé, F. Marchesi *et al*, 'The skin is a significant but overlooked anatomical reservoir for vector-borne African trypanosomes', *Elife* 5 (2016) p.ii: e17716.

p225 *The first line therapy for late-stage T.b. gambiense is now NECT*:

G. Priotto, S. Kasparian, W. Mutombo, *et al*, 'Nifurtimox–efl ornithine combination therapy for second-stage African *Trypanosoma brucei gambiense* trypanosomiasis: a multicentre, randomised, phase III, non-inferiority trial', *Lancet* 374 (2009) pp.56–64.

p226 *A recently published phase 2/3 randomised 'non-inferiority' trial of oral fexinidazole versus* NECT *therapy*: VKBK. Mesu, W.M. Kalonji, C. Bardonneau C *et al*. 'Oral fexinidazole for late-stage African Trypanosoma brucei gambiense trypanosomiasis: a pivotal multicentre, randomised, non-inferiority trial', *Lancet* 391(2018): pp.144–154.

p227 *'Complexed melarsoprol' which is formed by inserting experimentally the melarsoprol drug inside what is called a 'cyclodextrin' molecule to form a fusion drug*: J. Rodgers J, A. Jones A, S. Gibaud et al, 'Melarsoprol cyclodextrin inclusion complexes as promising oral candidates for the treatment of human African trypanosomiasis', *PLoS Negl.Trop.Dis* 5 (2011): e1308.

p230 *We are now able to visualise leakage in the* BBB *using the neuroimaging technique of Magnetic Resonance Imaging (*MRI*)*: J. Rodgers, C. McCabe, G. Gettinby *et al*. 'Magnetic Resonance Imaging to assess blood-brain barrier breakdown in murine trypanosomiasis', *American Journal of Tropical Medicine and Hygiene* 84 (2011) pp.344–350.

p230 *Advance techniques using bioluminescence and photon imaging can also detect individual trypanosomes in infected mice*: E. Myburgh, J.A. Coles, R. Ritchie *et al*, 'In vivo imaging of trypanosome-brain interactions and development of a rapid screening test for drugs against* CNS *stage trypanosomiasis', *PLoS Negl.Trop Dis* 2013; 7: e2384.

p230 *Patients in two regions of Uganda displayed neurological symptoms and signs when still in the early stage of the disease*: L.M. MacLean, M. Odiit M, J.E. Chisi *et al*, 'Focus-specific clinical profiles in human African trypanosomiasis caused by *Trypanosoma brucei rhodesiense*', *PLoS Negl Trop Dis* 4(2010): e906.

p231 *Administering the cytokine* IL-10 *to mice reduces both the level of parasites in the* CNS *and the degree of neuroinflammation*: J. Rodgers J, B. Bradley B, P.G.E. Kennedy *et al*, 'Central Nervous System parasitosis and neuroinflammation ameliorated by systemic* IL-10 administration in Trypanosoma brucei-infected mice', *PLoS Negl.Trop Dis* 2015; 9 (2015): e0004201.

p231 *Different* APOL1 *variants reduce people's trypanosomiasis susceptibility*: A. Cooper, H. Ilboudo H, VP Alibu *et al*, 'APOL1 renal risk variants have contrasting resistance and susceptibility associations with African trypanosomiasis', *Elife* 6 (2017). p.ii: e25461.

p231   *A particular gene called TgsGP confers human serum resistance in T.b.gambiense*: 'P. Capewell, C. Clucas, E. DeJesus *et al*, 'The TgsGP gene is essential for resistance to human serum in Trypanosoma brucei gambiense', *PLoS Pathogens* 9(2013): e1003686

Glossary of Medical and Scientific Terms

AIDS

Acquired Immunodeficiency Syndrome. The infectious disease, usually transmitted by sexual contact, blood transfusion or infected hypodermic needles, that is caused by the Human Immuno-deficiency Virus (HIV). There is no known link between AIDS and sleeping sickness.

Anaemia

A condition characterised by reduced red blood cell count and low haemoglobin level resulting in tiredness, pallor, and shortness of breath.

Animal reservoirs

Infected animals, that may or may not have symptoms of the disease they carry, and that act as a constant source of parasites (or other infections) that can infect other animals and/or humans.

Animal trypanosomiasis

The term used for the trypanosome infection in a variety of domestic and wild animals. Although it may be caused by several different subspecies, the three most important trypanosomes in animals are *T.vivax*, *T.congolense* and *T.b.brucei*.

Antibody

A protein that circulates in the blood and tissue fluids, that combines highly specifically with an antigen, thereby leading to a wide range of events aimed at immune protection. Also known as Immunoglobulin (Ig) of which there are five main classes, with IgM being the most important in sleeping sickness.

Antigen
A protein, sugar, or other molecule that is capable of producing an immune response in the host.

Antigenic variation
The ability of trypanosomes and other organisms to evade the host's immune response by constantly changing the proteins coating their surface. This property has contributed to the difficulties encountered in producing a vaccine for sleeping sickness.

ApoL-I
A molecule that has recently been identified as the factor in human serum which can destroy the trypanosome parasite.

Astrocyte
A cell type found in the nervous system with a wide variety of functions, including an important role in regulating immune responses within the brain in sleeping sickness.

Autoantibody
An antibody that is 'misdirected' to bind to a normal part of one's own body, rather than bind to a foreign, external antigen. In some cases, autoantibodies may cause autoimmune disease.

B Lymphocyte
A cell of the immune system formed in the bone marrow that makes antibodies.

Berenil (diminazene aceturate)
One of three drugs used for treating animal trypanosomiasis. Berenil is also used in the mouse model of sleeping sickness where it produces brain inflammation because of subcurative therapy.

Blood-Brain Barrier (BBB).
A physical barrier consisting of two main cellular layers that prevents all but very small molecules passing from the blood into the brain.

Buffy coat layer
The thin layer of visible white blood cells that forms between the layers of red blood cells and clear plasma after an animal blood sample has been centrifuged. The trypanosome parasites are most likely to be detected in the buffy coat.

Burkitt's lymphoma
A rare tumour of the immune system where the B cells, which make antibodies, multiply out of control to produce tumours of the lymph nodes, usually in the neck and jaw.

CATT
Card Agglutination Trypanosomiasis Test. This is a very useful, although indirect, method of diagnosing sleeping sickness where one looks for evidence of an antibody in the patient's blood that is directed against a particular region of the trypanosome.

Cerebrospinal fluid (CSF)
The fluid that circulates in the cavities called ventricles inside the brain and also between the covering layers of the spinal cord.

Chagas disease
Another name for American trypanosomiasis which is caused by a different trypanosome (*Trypanosoma cruzi*) from that causing sleeping sickness. Chagas disease occurs in Central and South America, affects more people than does sleeping sickness but causes fewer deaths per year. It particularly affects the heart.

Chancre
The skin lesion that may first appear around the tsetse fly bite area, usually on the legs but also sometimes on the arms and upper body.

Choroquine
A drug that is used for the treatment and prophylaxis of malaria. Unfortunately many of the malarial parasites in several regions of Africa are now resistant to this drug, thereby limiting its usefulness.

Circadian rhythms
The normal biological clock of sleep-wake activity and variation in temperature during a 24-hour period in man and animals. In patients with sleeping sickness and trypanosome-infected rats this cycle is severely disrupted and accounts for the abnormal sleep patterns seen in such patients.

Clinical drug trials
The three phase process (Phases I, II and III) of testing a new drug that is required by law and good clinical practice prior to the test drug being made available for patients.

CNS
Central Nervous System, which consists of the brain and spinal cord.

Computerised Tomography (CT)
A widely used method of scanning the brain and other organs that was developed before MRI, and which revolutionised non-invasive imaging of the body. It relies on x-rays rather than magnetic fields, and in neurological patients it provides detailed images of the brain and spinal cord. Routine CT gives less detailed information about brain structure and function than does MRI.

Cytokines
Small molecules, of great importance in immune responses, that can influence the properties and proliferation of various cells involved in inflammation. Cytokines can be pro-inflammatory where they enhance immune responses, or counter-inflammatory where they dampen down immune responses.

DB 289
The only new drug that was likely to be used for sleeping sickness within the next five years. It can be given orally, which is a great advantage, but it could only be effective for early stage disease. Unfortunately, near the end of its final evaluation in a multi-centre Phase III clinical trial in Africa, it was abruptly withdrawn due to

the unexpected development of liver and kidney toxicity in some patients receiving it.

Diethyltoluamide (DEET)
A highly effective insect repellent.

Diplopia
Medical term for seeing objects as if they were duplicated (double vision).

DNA
Deoxyribonucleic acid, the cell's nucleic acid that harbours the genetic code. Most of an organism's DNA is usually found in the cell nucleus.

Doxycycline
An antibiotic drug that can be taken daily as malaria prophylaxis. It also provides significant protection from traveller's diarrhoea.

Drug resistance
This is said to occur when the organisms such as trypanosomes are no longer susceptible to a particular drug's actions, making the drug less effective or completely ineffective. This occurs especially in animal trypanosomiasis, but also increasingly against melarsoprol in the human disease in northern regions of Uganda.

East African sleeping sickness
The form of the disease caused by *T.b.rhodesiense* that occurs mainly in eastern regions of Africa.

Eflornithine (DFMO)
A drug that can be used as an alternative to melarsoprol in late stage West African (*gambiense*) sleeping sickness. It is not effective against the East African disease, but is now being increasingly used as first line therapy in *gambiense* disease. While not free from side effects, it is much less toxic than melarsoprol.

Electroencephalogram (EEG)

Neurological test in which recording electrodes are placed on the subject's scalp to provide a recording of the electrical activity in the brain. The EEG is abnormal in late stage sleeping sickness.

EMEND

A drug that can be used in humans which acts as an antagonist to the Substance P receptor. It may have a possible role in the future in dampening down the CNS inflammation seen after melarsoprol therapy.

Encephalitic stage

The other name for the late stage, or stage two, of sleeping sickness when the BBB has been breached, thereby allowing the trypanosomes to cross into the CNS. This leads to brain and/or spinal cord symptoms.

Encephalitis

A very serious condition resulting from inflammation of the brain due to infection with micro-organisms or other causes. It often occurs together with meningitis.

Enterotoxigenic *Escherichia coli*

A bacterium that produces toxins that greatly increase intestinal secretion, producing severe diarrhoea.

Flagellar pocket

This forms the base of the flagellum and allows the trypanosome to interact with nutrients and foreign material that it encounters in its environment.

Flagellum

An elongated rod-like structure that forms part of the trypanosome. The flagellum is important in determining the overall shape of the trypanosome, and propels it as it moves throughout the body. It also has other important functions.

Fusca group of tsetse flies

These infest the forested regions of West and Central Africa.

Genes
Specific regions of DNA that code for particular proteins and functions, and which define the organism's genetic make-up.

Glasgow Coma Score (GCS)
An important and very widely used method of measuring a patient's level of consciousness using a scale from 3 (deep coma) to 15 (normal). The GCS has been of particular value in monitoring patients with coma from head injuries and other causes, and in predicting short and long term outcome after head injuries.

Haemolymphatic phase
Another name for the early stage, or stage one, of sleeping sickness. The blood, lymph glands and internal organs are infected but not the CNS.

Hemiplegia
Paralysis of one side of the body, affecting the arm and the leg.

Human African trypanosomiasis (HAT)
Another name used for sleeping sickness in humans. The two terms tend to be used interchangeably and refer to the same disease.

Hypothalamus
A vitally important brain structure that is in overall charge of the endocrine system, regulating hormone secretion through its influence over the pituitary gland. The hypothalamus also controls the autonomic nervous system which regulates automatic functions such as blood pressure and sweating, and it also influences body temperature, sleep patterns and appetite.

Insecticides
These insect killers such as DDT have been used in various ways to kill tsetse flies in their natural habitats. They can be applied by, for example, ground-based application on infested vegetation or by aerial spraying from aircraft. Their use has raised important environmental issues.

Interferon-gamma (IFN-γ)
A cytokine which has a variety of pro-inflammatory effects in the immune response and plays a role in producing the brain disease seen in sleeping sickness.

Interleukins (IL)
A group of cytokines, some of which, such as Interleukin 1, have pro-inflammatory effects, while others, such as Interleukin 10, have counter-inflammatory effects in the immune response. A number of Interleukins appear to play an important role in the brain disease of sleeping sickness, and the balance of these may be critical.

Keratitis
Inflammation of the cornea, the translucent structure found at the front of the eye.

Kinetoplast
A structure which is attached at one end to the trypanosome's flagellum and is located inside the mitochondrion. The kinetoplast contains a large amount of deoxyribonucleic acid (DNA) which defines the organism's genetic make-up.

Kwashiorkor
A serious condition, usually seen in young children, due to severe protein deficiency. Advanced cases have a high mortality.

Lariam (mefloquine)
A drug that is taken weekly for malaria prophylaxis, i.e. to prevent a person from developing malaria. While very effective, it may have some problematic side effects in some people.

Lumbar puncture
A neurological procedure in which a fine needle is inserted into the fluid filled spaces within the lower part of the spinal column in order to obtain a sample of cerebrospinal fluid (CSF).

Macrophage

Key cell in the immune system that when 'activated' can directly engulf and destroy foreign material – a process called 'phagocytosis'. Macrophages also produce other immunological important molecules such as cytokines.

Magnetic Resonance Imaging (MRI)

A method of scanning the brain and other organs that uses a very powerful magnetic field. It produces detailed images of organ structure, and in neurological patients it can visualise brain structures and abnormalities in great detail, and in ways that are not attainable by plain x-rays or routine CT scanning.

Malaria

An infectious human disease of exceptional global importance caused by protozoan parasites of the genus *Plasmodium*. Transmission is by the bite of the female anopheline mosquito. The cerebral form is particularly serious with a high mortality.

Malarone

A more recently developed drug that is highly effective for malaria prophylaxis. Though expensive, it only needs to be taken for a week after returning home from the at-risk region.

Melarsoprol

An arsenic-based drug which is used for the treatment of late stage sleeping sickness where the CNS is invaded. Although it is the only drug that is effective in both types of sleeping sickness, it is highly toxic, killing five per cent of those receiving it.

Meningitis

A condition resulting from inflammation of the meninges, which are the layers covering the brain and spinal cord.

Microglia

A brain cell type, of which there are several forms, that functions in a similar way to macrophages in the blood. Like macrophages, microglia engulf and destroy foreign material and also secrete cytokines, making them an important part of the brain's immune system and its response to injured neurons.

Micrometre
One millionth of a metre. A trypanosome is about 20 micrometres long.

Mitochondrion
A cellular structure located in the cytoplasm outside the cell nucleus which is crucial for the energy production of the cell. Some of the cell's DNA is found in the mitochondrion.

Morsitans group of tsetse flies
These are distributed in the African savannah regions.

Mott cell
Also known as a morular cell, this is thought to be a modified plasma cell that contains IgM. This finding, which is visualised under a microscope, is said to be diagnostic of sleeping sickness brains.

Nagana
The animal form of trypanosomiasis that was unrecognised for centuries, and whose cause and tsetse fly transmission was discovered by David Bruce at the end of the 19th century.

Neuron
The neural cell type that transmits electrical impulses. It is found throughout the nervous system including the brain, spinal cord and nerves. The primary role of the neuron is in the functioning of the nervous system.

Neuropathogenesis
The mechanisms by which CNS pathology and disease is produced. In the case of sleeping sickness this is known to be complex and involves a number of immunological factors.

Neuropeptide
A small protein that is found mainly within the nervous system, is produced by neurons and also other cells, may function as a neurotransmitter, and can be involved in immune responses. Neuropeptides can also be hormones. Substance P is an example of a neuropeptide.

Ngu fly trap
This tsetse fly trap has a blue cloth outside to attract the flies, which then alight onto a black cloth surface. A frequently used development of the fly trap is known as a fly target in which the odiferous blue and black cloths act as bait that are also impregnated with insecticide which kills the tsetse flies that land on them.

Nifurtimox
A drug that has a possible role as part of combination therapy with eflornithine or melarsoprol in treating patients with West African sleeping sickness. Although it is not currently registered for the treatment of sleeping sickness, it is registered for the treatment of Chagas Disease (American trypanosomiasis).

Octenol
A key component of ox's breath that is highly attractive to tsetse flies. Octenol is therefore a key attractant that is impregnated into fly traps.

Oligodendrocyte
A major cell type in the CNS that forms myelin, the fatty insulating sheath surrounding neurons. Myelin is destroyed in demyelinating diseases such as Multiple Sclerosis.

Orchitis
Inflammation of the testes. Sometimes occurs in early stage sleeping sickness.

Palpalis group of tsetse flies
These occur in the wet 'riverine' areas as well as forested regions throughout Africa.

Parasitaemia
The scenario where parasites are detected in the blood circulation of the patient or animal. This is usually seen in East African sleeping sickness.

Pentamidine
The drug that is used in patients with early stage West African (*gambiense*) sleeping sickness.

Polymerase Chain Reaction (PCR)
A widely used laboratory technique which is capable of greatly amplifying and detecting even minute amounts of DNA in a test sample.

Polysomnography
Procedure in which patients are wired up to surface body electrodes that record eye movements, brain wave patterns (EEG) and muscular activity (EMG) simultaneously over a prolonged period of sleep.

Pour-on technique
This is the method where susceptible cattle are effectively live baits as they are treated with insecticide which kills any tsetse flies that land on them.

Protein
A fundamentally important biological molecule that is made up of one or more amino acid chains. Enzymes, which promote biochemical reactions, are proteins, as are antibodies and hormones.

Protozoa
Single celled organisms, some of which, such as trypanosomes, can cause serious infectious diseases in man and animals.

PTRE

Post-treatment Reactive Encephalopathy. This is a severe brain inflammation which occurs in about ten per cent of all patients who receive the drug melarsoprol. Since about half of these patients die from the PTRE, the overall mortality from melarsoprol therapy is five per cent, that is, one in 20.

REM sleep

The periods during normal sleep when rapid eye movements (REM) occur which correlate with dreaming. In late stage sleeping sickness the normal sleep structure is disrupted with frequent episodes of REM at the onset of sleep (SOREMPs).

SARS

Severe Acute Respiratory Syndrome caused by a virus called a coronovirus. There was a much publicised global outbreak of SARS in 2003 when the disease spread from Asia to America and Europe.

Sequential Aerosol Drift Technique (SAT)

A large-scale tsetse fly control method in which a low concentration and volume of insecticide is distributed at low altitude over a wide area from a fixed-wing aircraft.

Sleeping sickness

The infectious disease in humans, always fatal if untreated, caused by the protozoan parasites of the genus *Trypanosoma*, and transmitted by the bite of the blood-sucking tsetse fly. It is caused by either *Trypanosoma b.gambiense* (West African form) or *Trypanosoma b.rhodesiense* (East African form). The term human African trypanosomiasis refers to exactly the same disease.

SRA gene

A gene that is found in *rhodesiense*, but not *gambiense*, trypanosomes. This gene allows the parasite to be resistant to the action of a factor normally present in human blood that destroys the circulating parasites.

Sterile Insect Technique (SIT)

A large-scale area-wide tsetse fly control method, in which the local tsetse fly population is flooded with very large numbers of sterile male flies. The aim is to out-compete the fertile wild male tsetse flies in breeding leading to a significant drop in the tsetse population.

Substance P (SP)

A neuropeptide that has many functions, including a transmitter role in pain pathways and a role in CNS inflammation, as is the case in the mouse model of sleeping sickness.

Suprachiasmatic nuclei (SCN)

This group of nerve cells is located in the hypothalamus just above the region where the optic nerves running back from both eyes cross each other. The SCN plays a key role in acting as a 'pacemaker' for the normal circadian rhythms that are disrupted in rat models of sleeping sickness.

Suramin

The drug that is used in patients with early stage East African (*rhodesiense*) sleeping sickness.

T Lymphocyte

A cell of the immune system. Following exposure to antigen an immature T cell can develop into two mature T cells that either play a vital role in regulating the immune response (CD4 cell) or directly kill foreign cells (CD8 cell).

Trypanosome

The protozoan organism that causes human and animal try-panosomiasis. First identified as the cause of the disease by David Bruce in the 1890s.

Trypanotolerance

An innate genetically determined ability of some breeds of cattle, such as the N'Dama and the West African Shorthorn, to resist the anaemia and to control the parasitaemia that normally occurs in trypanosomiasis.

Tsetse fly

This is the insect vector of the genus *Glossina* that transmits both sleeping sickness and animal trypanosomiasis. Different species of tsetse fly transmit the two forms of sleeping sickness. There are at least 31 different species of tsetse fly in Africa.

Tumour necrosis factor-alpha (TNF-α)

A cytokine which has pro-inflammatory effects in the immune response and appears to play a role in producing the brain disease seen in sleeping sickness.

Variable Surface Glycoproteins (VSG)

Proteins containing sugar components that cover the surface of the trypanosome. Ten million versions of a particular VSG cover the surface at any one time. The constant genetic switching of the VSGs is responsible for the antigenic variation shown by the trypanosome, thereby allowing it to evade the host's immune response.

Vector

Animal – in the case of sleeping sickness, the tsetse fly – that transmits the disease from one animal to another, usually by biting.

Visceral leishmaniasis

A serious and widespread chronic infectious disease which is caused by a protozoan parasite *Leishmania donovani*. The disease is transmitted by the bite of the sandfly, infects multiple internal organs, and occurs in the Middle East, Asia, South America, the Mediterranean and Africa.

West African sleeping sickness

The form of the disease caused by *T.b.gambiense* that occurs mainly, but not exclusively, in western regions of Africa.

West Nile infection

An infectious disease caused by the West Nile virus that can some-times lead to a severe infection of the nervous system causing West Nile encephalitis or meningitis. The virus is transmitted by an infected mosquito vector, and the infection travelled to the US from the Middle East around 1999.

Winterbottom's Sign

This refers to visible lymph node swelling in the back of the neck occurring in West African (*gambiense*) sleeping sickness. Named after the physician Thomas Masterman Winterbottom (1766–1859) who first described it.

Index

Some other books published by **LUATH** PRESS

Selim Aga: A Slave's Odyssey
James McCarthy
ISBN 1 905222 17 3 HBK £16.99

Selim Aga was just eight years old when he was abducted from the remote Nuba Mountains of Sudan by Arab slavers and auctioned 2,000 miles away in the Cairo slave market.

Selim was bought and sold at least eight times before being released from slavery by Robert Thurburn, the British Consul at Alexandria, who took him to his family home in Aberdeenshire in 1836. Little is known of his time in Scotland but what is certain is that Selim grasped every experience and opportunity to learn, and later became an author, lecturer and explorer, as Sir Richard Burton's manservant in West Africa.

James McCarthy's biography is a fascinating piece of detective work that sets Selim's life in the context of European imperialism and the international trade in human cargo. A rare and highly significant document, Selim's own remarkable narrative of his early life is also presented here in its entirety.

Grounded in the horrors of actual fact... thoroughly researched... but this is not [James McCarthy's] only service to history. As well as telling Selim's life, he reprints also two autobiographical essays by Selim: a narrative of his early enslavement and a memoir of his 1863 trip with Burton.
THE FINANCIAL TIMES

Selim's adventures have all the ingredients of a Hollywood blockbuster.
THE VOICE

The Blue Moon Book
Anne MacLeod
ISBN 1 84282 061 3 PBK £9.99

Love can leave you breathless, lost for words.

Jess Kavanagh knows. Doesn't know. Twenty-four hours after meeting and falling for archaeologist and Pictish expert Michael Hurt she suffers a horrific accident that leaves her with aphasia and amnesia. No words. No memory of love.

Michael travels south, unknowing. It is her estranged partner sports journalist Dan McKie who is at the bedside when Jess finally regains consciousness. Dan, forced to review their shared past, is disconcerted by Jess's fear of him, by her loss of memory, loss of words.

Will their relationship survive this test? Should it survive? Will Michael find Jess again? In this absorbing contemporary novel, Anne MacLeod interweaves themes of language, love and loss in patterns as intricate, as haunting as the Pictish Stones.

High on drama and pathos, woven through with fine detail.
THE HERALD

Luath Press Limited
committed to publishing well written books worth reading

LUATH PRESS takes its name from Robert Burns, whose little collie Luath (*Gael.*, swift or nimble) tripped up Jean Armour at a wedding and gave him the chance to speak to the woman who was to be his wife and the abiding love of his life. Burns called one of 'The Twa Dogs' Luath after Cuchullin's hunting dog in *Ossian's Fingal*. Luath Press was established in 1981 in the heart of Burns country, and is now based a few steps up the road from Burns' first lodgings on Edinburgh's Royal Mile. Luath offers you distinctive writing with a hint of unexpected pleasures.

Most bookshops in the UK, the US, Canada, Australia, New Zealand and parts of Europe either carry our books in stock or can order them for you. To order direct from us, please send a £sterling cheque, postal order, international money order or your credit card details (number, address of cardholder and expiry date) to us at the address below. Please add post and packing as follows: UK – £1.00 per delivery address; overseas surface mail – £2.50 per delivery address; overseas airmail – £3.50 for the first book to each delivery address, plus £1.00 for each additional book by airmail to the same address. If your order is a gift, we will happily enclose your card or message at no extra charge.

Luath Press Limited
543/2 Castlehill
The Royal Mile
Edinburgh EH1 2ND
Scotland
Telephone: 0131 225 4326 (24 hours)
email: sales@luath.co.uk
Website: www.luath.co.uk